Gifts

Mothers Reflect on How Children with Down Syndrome Enrich Their Lives

Edited by Kathryn Lynard Soper

Foreword by Martha Sears, RN

Woodbine House   2007

All rights reserved under International and Pan-American copyright conventions. Published in the United States of America by Woodbine House, Inc., 6510 Bells Mill Rd., Bethesda, MD 20817. 800-843-7323. www.woodbinehouse.com

"Aidan's Gift" by Valle Dwight originally appeared in *Family Fun* magazine.

"Where There's a Will, There's a Way" by Kelly Anderson was published simultaneously in this collection and in *Kidaroundtown* magazine.

Cover photograph: Sebastian Servos (featured in Essay 45), photographed by Sheri Heath.
Editor photograph: Maralise Petersen
Cover Design: Johnna Cornett
Photo Formatting: Rebecca Phong
Book Design: Joel and Carla Reeves, Rebecca Phong

Library of Congress Cataloging-in-Publication Data

Gifts : mothers reflect on how children with Down Syndrome enrich their lives / edited by Kathryn Lynard Soper.
    p. cm.
  ISBN-13: 978-1-890627-85-0
  ISBN-10: 1-890627-85-2
  1. Parents of children with disabilities--Case studies. 2. Children with disabilities--Family relationships--Case studies. 3. Mother and child--Case studies. 4. Down syndrome--Patients--Family relationships--Case studies. I. Soper, Kathryn Lynard.
  HQ759.913.G54 2007
  306.874'30874--dc22

                                                                    2007004950

Manufactured in the United States of America

10   9   8   7   6   5   4

Dedication

In honor of our children,
life's greatest gifts

And in special memory of:
Zachary Luke Damurjian
Cariana J. Gonzales
Nevaeh Grace Onesti
Seth W. Price
Sophia June-Raquel Salomao Schmidt
Ike Kent Wise

Life is so generous a giver,
but we, judging its gifts
by their covering,
cast them away as ugly
or heavy or hard.

Remove the covering
and you will find beneath it
a living splendor,
woven of love, by wisdom,
with power.

❧

Fra Giovanni

Acknowledgements

This book is the product of hundreds of hours of effort, volunteered by dozens of individuals who share a common desire: to promote awareness, understanding, and appreciation of people with Down syndrome.

I am deeply grateful to the sixty-three women who submitted their personal stories for this collection. It takes a great deal of courage and effort to capture one's experiences in words, especially when writing about such an emotional and intimate topic. I applaud their devotion to their children and their willingness to share their lives with such candor.

In particular, I thank those contributors who joined Segullah Group for the purpose of supporting this endeavor: Catherine Finn, Jennifer Graf Groneberg, Tara Marie Hintz, Stefanie M. Miller, Rebecca Phong, Carla Reeves, and Robin Roach. Each has dedicated hours of effort to producing and promoting this book, and I have treasured their unfailing enthusiasm and friendship.

I thank Martha Sears for contributing the foreword and for offering her continued support for this endeavor. I thank Sheri Heath for contributing the beautiful cover photo.

I appreciate the efforts of those who maintain the online forums relating to Down syndrome. Without gathering places such as Downsyn.com, BabyCenter.com, UnoMas.com, and Trisomy21Online.com, this book could not have been created.

I thank my agent, Kate Epstein, of The Epstein Literary Agency for her expertise and encouragement. I thank the staff of Woodbine House, especially Nancy Gray Paul and Fran Marinaccio, for catching the vision of this book's significance.

Finally, I express my love and gratitude for my husband, Reed, and my seven children, who have cheered me on and buoyed me up during the course of this demanding project. And I give special thanks for my son, Thomas, the inspiration for it all.

Contents

THE GIFT OF DELIGHT

❦

THE GIFT OF LOVE

Foreword

"YOUR LIFE WILL HAVE flashes of color you never knew possible." These wonderful and welcome words were written by Mary, the mother of a child with Down syndrome in my husband's pediatric practice, on a baby card I received seventeen years ago, congratulating us on the birth of Stephen. Out of the dozens of cards given to us by friends and family, hers was the only one that made my heart soar. It lit the spark of hope I so needed. Her son, Byron, had been born several years earlier, so Mary knew what she was talking about, and she knew what I needed to hear.

I'm sorry now that I didn't take the time to learn more from her or from the moms in our local Down syndrome support group. Reaching out for help was not easy for us. Maybe I was just too "proud"—after all, this was our seventh child, and we two "experts" were supposed to be used to parenting challenges. Surely we could manage on our own, I thought. And we did manage, but had we connected with other parents, we could have thrived.

That is why I am excited about this book. When Stephen was born, we sought information from books, but the only ones we found were textbooks or manuals with lists of symptoms and problems, and they were not written by parents. As eager as I am now to read and rejoice in each family's story, I would have grabbed onto this book like a lifeline back when Stephen was born, inhaling it for the courage and support it offers.

As with all our children, our parenting of Stephen has been a series of ups and downs, and I'd like to write the whole story someday. Stories, like the ones in this book, can help further the cause of getting our children the place they deserve in society, and seeing them welcomed as the uniquely valuable individuals they are. This welcoming seems to take place naturally as people take time to get to know our children. (Just ask the staff at the golf club where Stephen and his dad, Bill, play several times a week!)

This book makes it possible for many people to take that time—to get a glimpse into the ups and downs (but mostly ups) in the lives of sixty-four children and their families. More and more people will be getting to know children and young adults with Down syndrome, either by giving birth to one, or by meeting them in schools, places of worship, or in the workplace. Having that privilege will bring "flashes of color" to all our lives, and you will begin to see what I mean when you start reading this book. Be prepared to be amazed. And when you finish reading, share the experience with others. These GIFTS must not go unopened.

Martha Sears, RN
Author, *25 Things Every New Mother Should Know*
Coauthor, Sears Parenting Library; Little, Brown
Capistrano Beach, California

Introduction

Gifts: Two Birth Stories

THE BLUISH-WHITE GLOW from the laptop screen was the only light. It was late on an autumn evening and I was alone in my hospital room. Twenty-eight weeks pregnant, and scared. I had been put on strict bed rest a few days earlier, when my preterm labor finally had stopped, leaving me dilated to four centimeters.

On the laptop screen was a chart showing the most common complications resulting from premature birth, and their likelihood of occurrence based on gestational age. Respiratory failure. Cerebral hemorrhage. Severe intestinal infection. I couldn't help imagining how awful it would be to face any one of them. I knew the short-term crisis itself would be a nightmare. My last baby had been in the NICU for three weeks after birth, and it had taken me a full year to recover from it, even though the baby sustained no long-term complications. That was a lot less likely this time around. What if the baby had brain damage, or chronic lung disease? What if he needed multiple surgeries?

What kind of a life would that be for this child? What kind of a life would that be for me?

I thought of the last item listed on the chart of complications: Mortality. Facing the possibility of the baby's death was terrifying. But as I sat in that dark hospital room with tormenting fears in my head and a time bomb in my uterus, facing the possibilities regarding his life felt just as threatening—or even more so.

What happened next is difficult to describe. A deep sense of calm began to steal into my heart; the dark, dense cloud of fear began to shrink and dissolve. My mind was still imagining all the challenges the baby might face, all the trials I might have to endure. But somehow, those didn't seem to matter much. I felt awareness growing deep inside of me, awareness of something good, something real, something stronger than dread and pain: The beauty of life itself. As it sprouted up within me and burst into bloom, I was filled with profound peace. *Life is a gift*, I suddenly understood. *A good gift.*

Two weeks later my contractions started again, and after a difficult labor and delivery, Thomas was born. Before I could even see him, he was whisked into the NICU. My husband and I waited silently for the Apgar scores. We sighed with relief when we heard the good news: a one-minute score of eight, a five-minute score of nine. Our son was breathing room air, all on his own. We looked at each other, hardly believing our good luck.

But before long, two doctors entered the room with solemn faces and sobering words: "We think your son has Down syndrome."

It seemed like months, but was really only a few weeks, before I was sitting in front of the computer monitor again. Emails were streaming in from friends and family members in response to the birth announcement we had mailed out the week before. To their credit, our loved ones were full of cheer and encouragement regarding Thomas's arrival. But I felt resentful and even angry about their easy words of goodwill.

"I'm glad Thomas has come to such a special family."

"I had a neighbor with Down syndrome, and he was the sweetest thing!"

"I'm sure he will bring you great blessings."

Easy for you to say, I thought.

And then instantly, I felt guilty. I certainly didn't want people to feel sorry for me, or horrified by the diagnosis. I had faced a few negative reactions soon after Thomas's birth, and the shock and pity expressed had made me furious. I wanted to celebrate Thomas's arrival—so why did I resent others who were doing the same?

Because I had too much to process, too much to adjust to. I wasn't ready to hear about how great my life would be, especially not from people who didn't know anything about it themselves. My loved ones were speaking from a place far removed from the unfamiliar ground I was standing on. Their sentiments were genuine, their intentions were wonderful—but their words felt hollow. Thomas was stuck in a NICU isolette with tubes and wires poking into every extremity; I was stuck in a new reality that I could not yet understand or appreciate. And I felt so alone.

A few days later I received an email from Ellen, a dear friend from high school. She has an adult brother, David, who has Down syndrome. She wrote, in part:

"I have no doubts that you will love and appreciate Thomas as he grows and develops on his own timetable. I had the opportunity to have David at my house for most of the summer and fell in love with him all over again. (Crying now!) You are beginning on a journey with countless rewards and blessings. Thomas will touch so many lives and educate so many around him. What a wonderful gift you have been given."

A gift.

I remembered the wisdom and calmness that had graced me that night in the hospital room. Exhausted and bewildered, I tried—and failed—to reach that same wondrous, restful place within myself. But I believed my friend. I trusted her assurances that all was well. She knew—she had lived it. And her words planted seeds of hope that someday, somehow, I would find peace again.

The winter months following Thomas's birth and diagnosis were long and dark, in more ways than one. Thomas was home, but needed oxygen supplementation and a feeding tube. I had to seclude him from public places. All the usual stress of recovering from childbirth and adjusting to life with a new baby was compounded by the complex medical situation and the frightening unknown of what the future might hold for our family.

It's a sad irony that the times that we need help the most are the times we may be least capable of receiving it. I had so many options for finding support: parent groups, therapists, friends-of-friends, online forums. But I held back. I felt very fragile, as if every drop of energy I had was being expended in holding myself together, holding my world in orbit. I could barely manage brief telephone calls. Face-to-face conversations were exhausting. Engaging in online chats seemed impossible. Yet I desperately needed a way to orient myself to this strange new territory.

I reverted to my preferred method of learning (and of escape): reading. I could read privately, safely. I got my hands on all the information about Down syndrome that I could. Not surprisingly, my favorite material was the few pages in a popular parents' guide, *Babies with Down Syndrome* (Woodbine House, 1995), that featured snippets of families' experiences. As the president of a nonprofit organization that produces personal writings, I'm a firm believer in the power of the individual voice. This situation was a perfect example. The frank expressions of thoughts and feelings in the parents' guide helped me feel understood, accepted, grounded. Even if I didn't fully relate to the specific points of view, the words held a solid ring of truth. My only wish was that there were more reading materials that offered this comfort, strength, and intimacy. The short passages weren't enough to sustain me during the bleak days of winter.

As the light and warmth of springtime began to creep back into my days, my crisis began to abate in more ways than one. Thomas's health stabilized. My daily routine with him felt more and more like the familiar work of parenting a typical infant. Life didn't seem nearly as daunting. And, surprisingly, neither did Down syndrome. There were still challenges, such as trying to treat Thomas's hearing loss, and juggling visits with specialists and therapists. But Thomas himself was becoming more and more delicious to me. As my friend's letter had predicted, his arrival in our family was already bearing many positive changes. But his sheer presence was the greater blessing. Over time the influence of his gentle spirit brought me that longed-for, deep-seated assurance that all was well. That life is a gift—and specifically, that my son's life is a gift.

As the days lengthened into summertime, the last wisps of darkness that had clouded my thoughts and feelings slipped quietly away, and peace again unfolded into full bloom.

Thomas is nearly one year old, now. As I look back on our early months together, I find it remarkable that such a rich experience is developing out of a situation that seemed so undesirable. And as I have ventured into the extensive community of families touched by Down syndrome, I've encountered many others who have discovered a similar dynamic in their lives. Yes, there are challenges that come with the experience, but the tenor of the voices I've heard is strongly positive. Given the fear and dread that commonly surround a diagnosis of Down syndrome, it's clear that these uplifting voices need to be heard by the world—and especially by parents facing this diagnosis for their child.

This conviction, coupled with my interest and background in working with personal writing, inspired me to collect stories that reveal the landscape of parenting a child with Down syndrome. My intent was to create the book I wished I could have read during the long, dark winter following Thomas's birth. The process began with posts on popular Down syndrome-related Internet sites. I invited potential contributors to write about a specific blessing that their child has brought into their lives, and I suggested five broad topics for consideration:

- The respect that we gain for our children as individuals, for others, and for ourselves.
- The strength that they show us, instill in us, and require from us.
- The delight that they enable us to feel: laughter, surrender, awareness.
- The perspective on life's hidden beauties and realities that they make possible.
- The love they call forth from the deepest wellsprings of our hearts.

Early in the process of gathering submissions, I met another mother, Robin Roach, who was collecting personal stories from the members of the Down syndrome forum at BabyCenter.com. We combined our efforts, and with the help of several others with a deep interest in the project, the news of this opportunity spread quickly online. A group of mothers devoted to promoting Down syndrome awareness joined me to form a production staff. In a few short weeks, we had sixty-three wonderful stories in hand. And after an intense period of revising and polishing the stories, *Gifts* was born.

I've been impressed by several themes that surface repeatedly in this collection. One is the current of surprise which runs through the book. Many of the contributors describe feelings of grief following their child's diagnosis. Yet there is a significant gap between the life they envisioned in those early days and weeks, and the life they are actually living. Most of the traumatic possibilities they once feared do not come to pass, and the difficulties that do arise are far outweighed by the rewards that also come. For many mothers, the ultimate surprise is their discovery that they love their children without reservation, without limit.

I've also been fascinated by the dual themes of sameness and difference that emerge in these stories. The children featured here share a common diagnosis; many of them face similar challenges to their health and development. Yet each is an individual with a particular blend of strengths and weaknesses, likes and dislikes, talents and dreams. These are not "Downs children;" they are children with Down syndrome. And they are both alike and different from each other, just as they are both alike and different from typical children. Through the eyes of the people who know them the best—mothers—we see the beauty of these differences and the reality of these similarities, revealed to a world that is slow to acknowledge either.

This duality also holds true for these mothers themselves. The stereotypes regarding parents of a child with a disability are just as false, and harmful, as those regarding the child. Every mother facing a new diagnosis with Down syndrome will react in her own way; each will form a unique relationship with her child. We are not necessarily saintly or strong or special, and we are individuals, just as our children are. The contributors to this collection have diverse personalities and perspectives, and draw from a wide spectrum of ethnicity, world views, and religious beliefs. Some are parenting within a traditional family structure; some are not. Some never considered terminating pregnancy; some struggled with the decision. Some were calm at the time of diagnosis; some were traumatized.

But in the midst of all this variety, there is one thing each of us holds in common: we know that the life of our child with Down syndrome is a life worth living. Whether we believe it is granted by the supernatural, or bestowed by Nature herself, we've come to understand that life—including life with an extra chromosome—is a gift. A good gift.

Gifts. The title reflects the value of the deep emotional effort each contributor invested in her story. It captures the refrain commonly heard from parents of children with Down syndrome—the lives of their children are cause for celebration. It reflects key points in my own experience as a mother of a child with Down syndrome. And finally, it points to a vital aspect of the project's purpose: all royalties will be used to provide complimentary copies of the book to parents in need of support.

We know that these pages may not be a magical shortcut through fear and uncertainty and sorrow. But we want parents facing a new diagnosis to know that they are not alone on the pathway opening before them. To this end, we offer words that ring with the singular truth of personal experience. And we trust that these words will plant seeds of hope regarding the destination that awaits. Hope that will blossom in due time. Hope that, one day, will bear the fruit of peace.

Kathryn Lynard Soper
South Jordan, Utah
September, 2006

THE GIFT OF RESPECT

1

Aidan's Gift
by Valle Dwight

Aidan Campbell

I THINK IT'S SERENDIPITOUS that my second son's birthday is so close to Mother's Day. When Aidan arrived, I had already been a mother for more than three years. My first son, Timmy, a strong-willed, inquisitive boy, had taught my husband, Phil, and me many things—like how to survive on four hours' sleep, the best ways to navigate through a tantrum, and how to hide vegetables in chili. But I don't think I came face to face with the true range of what motherhood means to me until Aidan entered our lives eighteen months ago.

It was the first day of spring when Phil and I checked into the hospital. Shortly thereafter, Aidan came into the world looking very much like his brother—howling, arms and legs flailing, a mop of wild red hair matted to his head. But when the midwife handed him to me, I looked right into his tiny face and stopped for just one instant. *Hmmm,* I remember thinking, *his eyes look a little strange.*

I quickly rejected that thought—*no, everything's fine*—and turned to Phil. We reveled in the afterglow of what had been an easy birth, and talked about how lucky we were. We were filled with gratitude for the beautiful family we had created, and looked forward to getting home and starting our lives together.

Then the nurse arrived to tell us that she needed to send the baby to the nursery because he was a little cold and they wanted to warm him up. She took him away, and we began to call family and friends to share the good news about our eight-pound, thirteen-ounce newborn son.

But when Aidan still hadn't been returned an hour later, I had a nagging feeling that something was wrong. I didn't want to ruin the moment—or lend weight to my fears—so I said nothing to Phil.

The midwife arrived. She told us that there was a possibility our baby had "chromosomal problems." I refused to let it sink in. *Oh, a chromosomal problem,* I thought. *I'm sure they can fix it.* Although my mind hadn't registered her meaning, my body must have, because a chill ran right to my neck. Phil was silent. Maybe one of us asked what she meant, exactly. Maybe she spotted our look of obvious misunderstanding. So she spelled it out: "The nurse thinks he may have Down syndrome."

From where I sit now, I can split my life in two. There's the time before we heard those words, and the time after. Before, we were probably like most people. We knew we were lucky. We were healthy. Our little boy, Timmy, was funny and strong and happy. We had jobs and a loving family. But until we were hit with those words, I don't think we had any idea how fragile that luck can be.

I knew nothing about Down syndrome, but I had lots of frightening preconceptions. My first thought, even as I nursed him in the hospital, was "How will he get a job?" My instinct right from the start was to hold him tightly against a world that seemed irreversibly changed.

I thought back on my pregnancy, which had been uneventful. Because I was over thirty-five, my doctor had advised me to have an amniocentesis. So I'd made an appointment for the prenatal test that was to determine whether my baby had a chromosomal abnormality or spina bifida. I got as far as the ultrasound. Just before the doctor started the test, I changed my mind. I told the doctor I didn't want to risk a miscarriage.

"Well, your chance is one in one hundred that you'll have a baby with Down syndrome," she said. "I've had ninety-nine other women in here this month and none of their babies had Down syndrome. You might be the one."

I had been ambivalent about the amnio from the start. Driving to the appointment, I'd told Phil that I didn't want to terminate the pregnancy no matter what the amnio revealed, and he'd agreed. We'd planned to have a second child, and there was no going back.

"Even if the baby has Down syndrome," I told the doctor, "I won't terminate the pregnancy, so what difference does it make?"

"Well, that's what everyone says," she told me. "But they change their minds when they get the test results."

I was offended by her flippant attitude toward my baby. "Well, I'm not changing mine." And we left, clutching the ultrasound photos of our beautiful baby.

Now here I was five months later, holding my blue-eyed baby who suddenly seemed so distant. We took Aidan home and waited a week for the blood test that would tell us for certain whether the doctors' suspicions were correct. Meanwhile, we stared at him, wondering. We compared him to pictures of Timmy as a baby. And we went back and forth with each other: Did he look the same or different? And were the differences we saw a result of Down syndrome, or because he was a different person? I kept thinking about the moment he was born, when I'd noticed something odd about his eyes. But other times I'd reassure myself that he was no different from Timmy, that everything would be fine. It was an agonizing period.

By the time the results were in, I thought I'd resigned myself to the worst. But the news sent me reeling. I cried for two days. I was grieving for the baby we had expected, the only one we thought we were prepared for.

When the tears dried, I began the long learning process that will continue, I imagine, for the rest of my life. Having resolved to find out everything I could, I went online, I read books, I talked to people. I was surprised to discover that everyone in the world, it seemed, was either related to, went to school with, or grew up next door to someone with Down syndrome. Everyone but me. I discovered an Internet support group for parents, and at the urging of one of them, I posted a message announcing Aidan's birth. The fact that he had Down syndrome was understood. These parents wanted to know the truly important things, like our baby's height, weight, and hair color, and their interest put things into perspective for me.

Within days we had received more than fifty congratulatory notes—not one "I'm sorry" among them. Our spirits soared. Friends and family had been very supportive, but, let's face it, they knew as much about Down syndrome as we had. And they were all a little sad, too. But these other parents weren't sad at all. They felt that their children were a great gift, Down syndrome or not.

As I pored over the books and talked with these other parents, I found the factual side of Down syndrome fairly easy to piece together. Also called Trisomy 21, it is caused when a person is born with three of the 21st chromosome rather than the usual two. This extra chromosome, and all its associated genes, alters the development of the body and brain. What this would mean for Aidan specifically would be hard to say, but he would be developmentally delayed to some degree (most people with Down syndrome fall in the moderate to mildly mentally retarded range) and would have low muscle tone. This would make it tougher for him to crawl, walk, and talk. The list of the other potential problems was daunting: heart defects, hearing loss, vision problems, small airways making children prone to upper respiratory infections, and on and on.

In fact, it seemed that we spent the first few months of Aidan's life in the offices of endless medical specialists, most with titles longer than our baby's tiny body. By his first birthday, Aidan had seen a pediatric cardiologist, pulmonologist, ophthalmologist, audiologist, and an orthopedist, to name a few.

Of course, there was nothing in those reference books that could fully explain the other side of the story—the ups and downs of raising a child with Down syndrome in our society. That's what we've been learning from Aidan himself, and it's been a lesson filled with wonder. Aidan's life so far has been more complicated than Timmy's was. There are more ongoing appointments—he has physical therapy, a play group, and a teacher once a week. There have been challenging days and frustrating moments as we've all struggled to learn about each other.

But we've come to recognize that we've had trying times with Timmy, too—they've just been over different issues. Timmy never slept. Aidan goes to bed at 7:30 p.m. and wakes up laughing. Timmy threw tantrums to beat the band; Aidan definitely knows what he wants, but he's generally much less stubborn. We're learning, as all parents discover with the birth of their second child, that each child presents a unique set of challenges.

Aidan is actually more like other kids than he is different. He will learn to walk, talk, read, sing, and dance (you should see him rock to "Itsy Bitsy Spider"), although he will have to work harder than most kids to reach those milestones. And we will have to slow down and allow him the extra time. Beyond that, he will have skills, talents, and quirks all his own. He already does. He scoots around the house using his bottom, two hands, and one foot faster than any crawler I've seen. He can find his Barney doll no matter how well we've hidden it. And he's already using sign language, predating his eventual use of words.

When Aidan was newly born, all I could think about when I looked at him was "Down syndrome." But now I see that the syndrome is just a small part of who he is and what he will become. Aidan has shown us that contrary to stereotypes, kids with Down syndrome aren't always sweet angels. When he does get angry, he can throw a tantrum to rival his brother's. When he doesn't want to eat, he sweeps his vegetables off the table with a stubborn flourish. And he hustles away with a backward glance and devilish giggle when he knows he's put something in his mouth that he shouldn't. Like the rest of us, kids with Down syndrome have a range of personalities, moods, and temperaments.

The future for people with Down syndrome is brighter than it has ever been, which makes me hopeful for my son's adulthood. Early intervention, medical advances, inclusive schools that educate all kids together, and new therapies mean that people with Down syndrome can live longer, achieve more, and contribute to their communities in meaningful ways. Most of them graduate from high school; many live independently, marry, and have jobs. So while I wondered on Aidan's first day of life how he would even find a job, now I dream about the possibilities. Will he love the theater the way his father does? Maybe he'll want to work at a newspaper, as so many generations of my family have. Perhaps he'll be wiser than his parents and find work that actually makes money.

It has been only a short time since Aidan came into our world. To a degree, we're still on an emotional roller coaster. We have days of unadulterated joy over our family and what Aidan brings to us. And more wistful days when we wish that life was simpler, though these come less and less often. Sometimes I get sad about the might-have-beens, especially on the days when Timmy makes plans about things he and Aidan will do together, and I wonder which of those dreams will come true. Many days I feel guilty and unsure as to whether we're doing enough for Aidan. Would he be better off if we could afford this program, those vitamins, or that new therapy? And sometimes I get scared about what's down the road, especially when I think of the struggles he may face making friends in those horrible junior high years, or making his way in a culture that places such high value on convention and looks.

But as we head into year two of Aidan's life, I've long since realized that our luck did not run out the day he was born. Not at all. In many ways, our lives have been transformed. We have found loving support from people who used to be strangers. We look at the world differently and consider ourselves lucky to be able to. We have an appreciation for a slower pace, we take greater delight in each small step. And we have a newfound understanding of the preciousness of all people.

Valle Dwight, a freelance writer and editor, lives in Massachusetts with her husband, Phil, and their two sons, Aidan and Tim. Valle is currently writing a blog at ParentsConnect.com called "A World of Difference," which focuses on issues of disability, special education, and inclusion.

2

What To Do With A Boy
by Jessica Capitani

Jessica and Caden Capitani

"A BOY? WHAT DO YOU do with a boy?" I asked my husband and mother as I lay on the ultrasound table with cold blue imaging gel oozing down my pregnant belly. The technician had just shown us the baby's male anatomy on the screen. With three sisters and two nieces, this was going to be new territory for me. This was my first pregnancy so I wasn't sure how long this procedure was supposed to last, but it seemed even slower with the technician's silence. I was off in my own thoughts anyway. Frank and I had been trying to conceive ever since the day we wed nearly two years earlier. I had finally made an appointment with a fertility specialist, but two weeks before the appointment I found myself gagging over the toilet. I took a pregnancy test, but was so sure I couldn't get pregnant that I threw out the positive results as a fluke and didn't bother to tell Frank. When the nausea became more pronounced and my breasts became tender, I took another test just to be sure. And another. And another.

Now here we were watching the baby punch the placenta. It seemed surreal. We were finally starting a family. I wasn't concerned when the technician left the room briefly and upon returning explained she needed additional images. In my naïveté, I thought that the main reason for an ultrasound was to determine the baby's sex. We had an appointment immediately afterwards with my OB but still found time to call my father and Frank's parents en route to share our delight.

"Is it okay to videotape in here?" my mom asked when the doctor entered the small examining room.

"You probably don't want to tape this," he stammered. "We found three things during the ultrasound that suggest a genetic abnormality. First, there was a larger than normal measurement within the brain that indicates hydrocephalus."

The blood in my body froze. I felt faint and numb. I tried not to surrender to sobbing so I could absorb his medical monologue, but my brain had shut down and I didn't hear the other two findings. Thankfully, Frank appeared to be holding himself together enough to ask questions. I held tissue after tissue to my face until the doctor offered me the whole box.

Though we had previously declined amniocentesis, it now seemed worth the risks. We were escorted back to the imaging room for the test. Before we left, the doctor advised us to consider the options if a genetic abnormality was discovered. We could terminate the pregnancy, we could continue and keep the baby, or we could give him up for adoption as there was a waiting list for infants with special needs.

During the week while we waited for test results, Frank and I rejected adoption. If someone else had the strength and love to raise a disabled child, then we would find it too. As for the remaining options, it would really depend on the prognosis. Above all, we didn't want the baby to suffer. He had been very active the last few weeks, kicking all day and night. Was he in pain, or was he trying to alert us he was fine? Based on our ages, we had already discussed the risk of a child with Down syndrome before getting pregnant. We agreed to proceed if that was the finding. Realistically, I didn't know that much about the condition other than recognizable facial features and mental retardation. The genetic abnormalities other than Trisomy 21 were of more alarm to us. I wondered what was growing inside me.

When the doctor called me at home with the results, I knew it would be bad news. He identified himself by his name rather than professional title, like we were old friends. "I know this isn't what you want to hear," he said slowly, "The baby has Trisomy 21, Down syndrome." He also confirmed that the baby was a boy, though the information no longer brought joy. I was immobilized by the echo of the diagnosis. The reality of combining Down syndrome with hydrocephalus, and possibly more, suddenly seemed unfathomable.

The doctor had used the phrase "quality of life" more than once. He said we needed to make a decision quickly. If we opted to terminate, there wasn't much time to legally get it done, since I was already at twenty weeks' gestation.

Terminate. Abortion. A baby was moving around in his mother's womb while his mother considered those words. I found it ironic that I had always described myself pro-choice, but now I wanted no share of this choice. I questioned what our world had come to, that a mother would be put in this position. I couldn't stop my tears, grieving for the health of my child. I didn't know what to do. I stared at the ultrasound image. Would this be the only picture I ever had of my first child?

Our initial action was to educate ourselves. We didn't know anyone with Down syndrome or hydrocephalus. I wanted to understand the range of symptoms with each. The more we researched, the more we realized that other serious medical problems had yet to be ruled out. It was too early to tell what might develop from the enlarged abdomen and cardiac white spot that were also found during the ultrasound. How would the multiple issues interplay? What if we went through this whole pregnancy and lost the baby anyway? There was an endless stream of possibilities with more unknown than known. There seemed to be a ridiculously small amount of solid information on which to make a decision regarding the outcome of a pending life. We turned to our families.

When I saw my parents for the first time after the diagnosis, their eyes were reddened. They struggled to remain composed. My mother felt that with all the medical problems, there was too much stacked against the baby. Frank and I enjoyed being active, loved traveling and exploring new places. My parents were afraid our lives would be drastically altered with a seriously disabled child. They worried for our new marriage. They didn't know what we should do, but said they'd be behind us either way. I greatly appreciated their support, but still felt lost.

We had a dining room table discussion with Frank's family. His forty-six-year-old sister has severe cerebral palsy and has always lived at home. This has taken a toll on my mother-in-law, who didn't soften her delivery as she addressed us. She was heartbroken that her difficult parenting experience might be repeated by one of her own children. When one of my sisters-in-law mentioned that our child would be born an angel, Frank's mom stated that there was already an angel in the family and we didn't need any more. She apologized for sounding so negative, but it was the kind of candid dialogue I sought. Her comments left a haunting impression and I wondered if I was witnessing my future self. She had made tremendous sacrifices for a child that had never kissed her or called her mommy. I doubted that I could be so tenacious and dedicated.

As my mother-in-law hugged me goodbye she said that whatever we decided, we would not be judged by the family. I was relieved and surprised to hear those words. I was concerned about making irreparable damage with Frank's Catholic family if we terminated. I was not religious and feared I would receive the bulk of the blame. I dreaded appearing with that elephant in the room at every family gathering. Though calmed by the clemency, I was still no clearer on what we should do.

Many people said they were praying for us. I wondered what outcome they were praying for. I was absurdly told to calm down because the stress was bad for the baby. I stopped writing in my pregnancy journal and began referring to the baby as "it." Each night Frank and I cried ourselves into a semblance of sleep. My pillow and hair remained undried. At times there were lengthy, though not uncomfortable, silences between us. There were just no more words to add, no breaking information to ponder, no fresh outlook to discover, no new sentiments to share. We were pressured by the necessity of a sooner-than-later choice, but were stalled by the significance of the consequences. How could I determine the quality of my boy's life only halfway through the pregnancy?

I wished my doctor would tell us what to do. As a professional, he surely had been through this many times before. But he remained neutral. In response to my questioning, he did inform me that ninety-two percent of similar pregnancies are terminated. I was stunned that so many others were able to make the difficult decision and continue with their lives. I felt weak in comparison. Who were these people? It wasn't exactly a topic people overtly discussed. I imagined driving nearly two hours to the closest hospital that would perform this procedure. I considered how horrible the time there would be. How would I feel driving home? Relieved? Devastated? In the midst of passivity, I even pondered how much easier it would be if I lost the baby in a car accident along the way.

My best friend since I was ten years old was also pregnant with a boy. In fact, our due dates were only days apart. She was devotedly seeking resources for me. One Down syndrome website she forwarded had a discussion board. I felt like a peeping Tom, but I couldn't stop reading the posts of the parents there. They appeared so proud and genuinely happy. I showed Frank the pictures of their beautiful children. Their shared support and stories unknowingly presented us with our first hint of hope. They seemed like normal families doing normal things. Could that be us too one day?

Finally we could delay no longer. The next appointment with the doctor was our last opportunity to choose termination. As we lay in bed the night before, Frank and I wavered. I didn't want to give

up on my baby, but needed to know that Frank wanted him unconditionally, too. We discussed how our marriage would change if we
continued the pregnancy. Socially, we might lose friends. Financially,
it would be a strain. I wanted to dedicate myself to the improvement
of our child's life and health. In my interpretation, this required being a stay-at-home mom and thus one less income. We examined every aspect of our lives that might be impacted and nothing seemed so
insurmountable when broken down individually. The crux was the
wellbeing of our child. How could I, or anyone else, determine the
quality of a life? I couldn't condemn one not yet attempted. There
would be no guarantees of his health, but there were none for any
child. Our pregnancy was no different from any other in that aspect.
In addition, we had some definitives. We were assured of his sex and
trisomy. I felt privileged with such knowledge and was bolstered by
its security. It might not be much, but to me it was enough.

"I want to keep him," I declared.

"Then no going back," Frank eagerly replied, "We just go forward from here." I hugged my tummy and told my son that everything was going to be okay. Frank told him he loved him and tried to
find his head to kiss. Finally, we knew what to do with our boy.

*Jessica and Frank live in Hershey, Pennsylvania. They have one perfect
child, Caden (2005). Caden's hydrocephalus and other prenatal findings vanished at birth and he was only born with an extra chromosome.
Jessica is a University of Virginia alumna and a fulltime mother and
advocate for Caden.*

3

On His Thirteenth Birthday
by Jodi Reimer

Heidi and Kellen Reimer

DEAR KELLEN,

Thirteen years ago when you were born, I could never have imagined you as a teenager. Your dad and I were so busy adjusting to the news of your extra chromosome, your heart defect, and your colon disorder. Babyhood was scary enough without trying to imagine how things would be when you were much older. As time went on and you met your medical challenges one by one, we did try to imagine the future. It was still scary, but as we talked to and met other parents of children with Down syndrome, a flicker of hope began to burn in us. We realized that if we worked hard—together—it was possible for you to have a good life.

We've been through so many things—open-heart surgery, learning to communicate, learning how to help you get your needs met. School stuff. Behavior challenges. The time that you were nearly hit by a car when we were on vacation. The two times that you escaped the house on your tricycle and I couldn't find you. (Some kind person stopped their car, got you out of the road, and called the police. I swear you have had angels protecting you.) I am so glad that you have outgrown some of those things!

You are growing up to be independent and responsible. Please be patient with me as I learn to let you experience the world without my protection.

Lately we've been practicing this independence at Costco. When I am waiting in line to pay for our groceries, I give you two dollars and you head over to the snack bar. I watch from afar while you wait in line appropriately. Before I know it, you are heading back over to me with your hot dog, your pop, and your beautiful "proud of myself" smile. You are satisfied because you were able to articulate your order to a stranger and make yourself understood. Happy that you know how to operate the pop machine and put the lid on your drink. You are proud because you are doing such a grownup thing all on your own—you even remember to give me the change back. I am proud, too, because it is one more step toward independence.

But I'm mostly proud because it means so much to you.

Have I ever told you how much I love the look that you get when you accomplish something new on your own? It is a half-smile, kind of a smirk. Ever since you were a baby, you showed your emotions with your entire being. You didn't smile with just your mouth, but with your whole body. This look is no exception. You show your pride in yourself with the way you hold your head, the way you walk, the way you look down with your eyes (with feigned humility), and that winning half-smile.

When you were a baby I used to think about what life would be like when you grew out of your "cute stage." Would people treat you harshly? Would people want to take the time to get to know you? Sometimes I thought it would be nice if you stayed small and adorable forever.

But I didn't realize how fun and fascinating it would be to see your gifts, talents, and personality develop. Your sense of humor often takes me by surprise. Remember when your teenage sister was getting emotional about something or other and you said under your breath, *"Drama queen"*?

Or the morning the whole house was in turmoil before the school bus came and you went and put on your lifejacket?

Or that other morning, after I had worked so hard helping you get ready for school, when you mysteriously disappeared into your bedroom? Two minutes before the bus was scheduled to arrive I went to look for you. To my dismay, you were no longer in your school clothes, but in full pirate regalia. Even though there wasn't any time to spare, I just had to stop and laugh.

I'll never forget the time last summer when you came to work with me. You sat at my desk with paper and pen, as you had done many times before. Usually, you scribbled or made rows and rows of letters. On this day, I looked up from the work I was doing and looked over at your paper. To my amazement, you had not scribbled; you had sketched an incredible, detailed spider. I didn't have to ask you what you had drawn. I could look at those articulated hairy legs and see for myself. You surprised me so much. I didn't yet know you had artistic talent. It gave me so much hope and encouragement to see this emerge from you.

We worked with you since you were a preschooler on learning to swim. When you were around five years old you had group swim lesson—during one of them, you splashed a little girl and made her cry. You wore your turquoise swim ring for a few years. When you outgrew that, we bought you a flotation belt to wear in the pool. Finally when you were eleven years old, something clicked and you learned that it was fun to hold your breath under water. You figured out how to paddle harder so that you could keep your chin up and not swallow so much water. It was so exciting that you were able to accomplish something that you had wanted to do for so long.

What you've taught me is that when you are really interested in learning something, you find a way to learn it in your own time. When something is not important to you, we either need to find a way to pique your interest or let go of our expectations.

You have taught me so much about letting go.

Your Dad explained it like this: there are a few things that we thought you might be able to do by now. Things like riding a bike, conversing with us, verbally expressing your feelings, and reading more fluently. Instead of getting caught up in disappointment that you aren't doing these things, we have learned to correct our "compass setting" by looking back to you. By bringing our bearing in line with yours, we are able to celebrate what you *are* doing. Instead of mapping out your path, we join you on your journey.

As I think about your future, I want so many things for you. I want you to work at a job you love, one that interests you and allows you to use your abilities, in a workplace where people know you and are glad to see you.

I want you to have lots of people in your life who love you and are willing to invest themselves in you. People who are willing to get involved. Friends and family who will include you in activities. Friends who will accept you and embrace you, idiosyncrasies and all.

Mostly, I want you to love your life. I want you to have things to look forward to—reasons to get out of bed in the morning. Is this too much to ask? Sometimes I wonder if it is. I hope and pray that it's not.

Kellen, I want you to know that I am so proud of you. I know your life is not easy. I know how many struggles you've had so far and I can't even fathom how many more you still have to face. I've learned that I can't take those away. As much as I'd like to protect you and shelter you and keep anyone from hurting you, it just isn't possible. More importantly, if I were able to take all of your problems away, you wouldn't be allowed to develop as a person. Part of being human is our struggles and how we overcome them.

I want you to be strong and have faith in people. There are good people out there—once you find them, hold on to them. Always remember how much your dad and I love you. Remember that we are in your corner and that you can make a difference in the world by just being who you are.

Happy Birthday.

Love,
Mom

David and Jodi Reimer live in the Seattle area with their daughter Heidi (1987) and son Kellen (1991). Kellen was diagnosed at birth with Down syndrome, an AV canal heart defect, and Hirschsprung disease. Jodi works as the Parent to Parent coordinator for The Arc of King County, providing support and information to parents of newly diagnosed children with special needs.

4

Belonging
by Rebecca Phong

Rebecca and Elainah A'Jhinae Phong

WHEN I FIRST LOOKED DOWN at my daughter's beautiful almond-shaped eyes, the deep pools of brown intoxicated me. She looked back at me with a peaceful expression, knowing she was in the arms of her mother.

My last child. My baby girl.

So many times, I had dreamt about what her arrival would be like, what she would look like. Her birth was exactly what I had imagined, free from the sterile environment of a hospital. But while there were many joyous moments, there were also a few that were unexpected.

My midwife quietly approached me and whispered, "Do you think her appearance and features are consistent with the other children?"

I looked back at her and calmly replied, "No, I think she has Down syndrome."

She was a sleepy little one, unconcerned about the world around her; there were no typical bursts of crying that I had experienced with the other children. When I brought her close to my breast and attempted to nurse her, she was uninterested. Still, her tiny body seemed to be as much a part of me as it was prior to her birth. The sweetest hand wrapped around my finger felt as soft as silk. Upon careful inspection, I traced the long line down her palm as I glanced at my own hand and reflected upon the differences.

These differences didn't matter. She belonged with me.

I called the pediatrician's office the next morning to inform them of her birth and request an appointment. During the night hours I had encouraged her many times to suckle, but was unsuccessful. I had slept little that night, believing she would eventually wake up, crying and hungry. But she never did. When the receptionist told me to come in the following week, I insisted that the baby be seen immediately. A few short hours later she was admitted to the hospital. I remember looking down at the doctor's orders and reading "failure to thrive" as the reason for hospitalization. Just next to this was a note, marked with an asterisk: "Down syndrome."

Her first cry came when they drew her blood. I watched as my peaceful little sleepyhead became a virtual pincushion. Her nose was crammed with breathing apparatus, her body connected to so many wires. Protectiveness reared up within me. I had to keep myself from screaming, *Get away from her, can't you see you are hurting her?* On occasion, I would burst out of the room into the hallway in tears, helpless and unable to do anything to comfort her. Hourly heel sticks, medications, and a feeding tube had replaced the candlelight and aromatherapy that welcomed her into this world. She did not belong in this place—surrounded by strangers, subjected to pain.

My exits from the hospital were always a complicated, emotional project. I needed to shower, I needed to see my other children. But each second that passed during the elevator ride down, through the long corridor to the exit, felt like an eternity. The humid July air always greeted me at the door. The air in my car felt stifling, and it was difficult to breathe. I would open all the windows and the sunroof and begin to cry, driving as slowly as I could. Just blocks before the house I would attempt to gather my composure before seeing the other children, but sometimes this was impossible. They did not want me to leave again. They wanted their little sister home. We belonged together.

I would drive back to the hospital with vigorous speed. I could not get back into her room fast enough. I could hear my heartbeat pounding in my chest. I rushed about the hallways as if there were an emergency, only to find my baby waiting for me to return. Seeing her put the whole world at peace, all the uncertainty gone. Anything seemed possible—anything. She was just perfect, and nothing could change that. She belonged to life.

Her first year tested my coping abilities many times. She accumulated nearly three months in the hospital, weathered numerous health complications, suffered discrimination and difficulty of many kinds. I stepped up to the challenge as her greatest advocate. I learned the medical jargon and described her health so well that people often asked me if I worked in healthcare. I spent hours doing research on Down syndrome. I became a professional in her care. She is my daughter; I owe her that.

I look back on the events of that year and marvel at all that has transpired. My pregnancy, rather unexpected, was problem-free. Her birth, the most amazing experience I had ever had. The fragility of her health, something I did not expect. Her life, extraordinary in many aspects, provides me with reason to challenge the world on so many levels. Her sheer existence brings real life rewards that I never envisioned. Yes, there have been many surprises to face, many differences to cope with. But she is who she is, as she was intended to be.

She belongs with me. We belong together. She belongs to life.

❦

Rebecca lives in Michigan with her five children, Marcus (1990), DeAndra (1991), Hannah (1993), Chandler (2001), and Elainah (2004). Elainah was diagnosed after birth with Trisomy 21. Rebecca was instrumental in editing the photos and gathering participants for this book. She is actively involved in promoting Down syndrome awareness and currently maintains a personal blog at www.alwayschaosaroundhere.blogspot.com

5

Oh, Yeah?
by Robin Roach

Bryan Roach

AS I SAT WAITING FOR my Level II ultrasound, I felt something was not quite right. I couldn't put my finger on it, though. Every doctor's visit had been normal and uneventful, unlike my other two pregnancies, which were plagued with problems. My husband, Kevin, and my sister, Kelly, were there with me for the exam, excited to find out the baby's gender. My mother was at home awaiting the big news—would she be getting her first granddaughter, or another grandson? All I could think was, *Please let the baby be healthy.*

"A boy," the technician said soon after the exam began.

A healthy boy is good—I wouldn't know what to do with a girl anyway, I thought. My husband popped about five buttons of his shirt with the swelling of his pride, and I finally felt safe.

"I'm having a hard time with the heart so the doctor will take a quick peek," said the tech. This had happened with my other two, so I was not alarmed. The perinatologist came in to take over. As she scanned she said everything looked great.

Then the bomb dropped.

Your son has a bright spot on his heart," she said. "Did you have an amniocentesis?"

"No," I said.

"And no blood work?" She shook her head with great displeasure. "At your age (thirty-eight) you should have had one earlier in the pregnancy, in case you need to terminate."

I almost threw up. *"What?"*

"Well, that is a soft marker for Down syndrome. With your age, your chances go to one in sixty-nine. You should have an amniocentesis tomorrow. How about 9:00 a.m.?"

I was shocked—she never even gave us a choice. I left, feeling sick. I crawled into bed and cried for what I thought was all night.

When I showed up the next day, the perinatologist told me not to worry about miscarriage. I felt the outcome was in God's hands at that point.

"This is a FISH test. The results will come back quickly; you'll have a week to terminate."

Why did she keep saying that? No one asked me if I even wanted to.

A few days later I got up and went to work, fully expecting the results to come in that day as positive for Trisomy 21. Sure enough, the call came, and I immediately went into my OB's office.

"Your son has Trisomy 21," he said. "I understand from the perinatologist that you would like to terminate."

"No," I said, "I don't know what to do." I was confused, sick, and hurt. I called Kevin at work. He was dumbfounded and extremely upset. He had been so sure that everything was okay.

I went straight to my pastor and had a two-hour conversation with him. That was what I needed—some breathing room where I could talk through my fears and not make a knee-jerk decision. As my head began to clear, I was angry that the perinatologist had been so aggressive and intrusive in my private affairs, especially at a time when I was so vulnerable to the power of suggestion. My husband was furious as well. It was like the doctor was following some script from a textbook, with zero respect for our individual situation. *She wants to terminate*, I could imagine her telling the OB. *Oh, yeah?* I wanted to shout in her face. Kevin and I discussed both options. After shedding many tears, we decided this was the hand that we were dealt and that we would accept it. We called our families to tell them about our decision. Then I called my OB. "No way will I terminate," I said. "I believe you made the right choice," he replied. "Here is the number of a parent who delivered a baby with Down syndrome a few months ago. Give her a call, and let's get on with this pregnancy."

I felt so relieved to leave the option of abortion behind. My parents were relieved, too, that we were all moving forward. They were so excited for their grandson to be here with us.

Not long afterward, my mother became very ill. When I was at her hospital bedside one afternoon she told me something I will never forget. "One day you will forget about the Down syndrome and remember the boy. He will succeed in life. I know he will."

Two days later she passed away. And six weeks later, my son was born.

Bryan arrived via c-section on a cold February morning. He was big—eight pounds, thirteen ounces—and handsome as could be. All Kevin and I cared about was this sweet little boy with blue eyes and dark hair. Our son. Thankfully, he had no serious heart defect, just a murmur (PDA) that would resolve on its own in time. But he was only a few hours old when the predictions started.

He will have trouble feeding.
He will have communication issues.
There will be developmental delays in all areas.

Yet another script from some all-knowing textbook. I think I know what Bryan thought when he heard all this: *Oh, yeah?* He started to defy the odds right away. His suck was perfect; he fed like a champ. No obvious health problems; no NICU. The doctors were very surprised. And this trend has continued until the present day.

Bryan is now seventeen months old. He seems just like any normal little boy; it just takes a little longer for him to do some things. Other than needing ear tubes, he hasn't had any health problems. He uses words and signs to communicate, crawls like crazy after the dog, and can stand on his own for a few minutes. He loves music, Blues Clues, and Thomas the Tank Engine. He does "Itsy Bitsy Spider" better than most toddlers I know. He holds his own bottle, can drink from a cup, and is learning to sip through a straw. He can eat and throw spaghetti with the best of them—in fact, lately he's been eating anything not nailed down. My motto for him is the same as for any toddler: Do not leave food unattended!

Bryan is curious, bright-eyed, and happy, and always has to know what is going on. He adores his older brothers—he lights up at just the sound of their voices or their steps as he hears them come into the room. He has more perseverance and guts than most adults I know. Watching him is like watching the Little Engine That Could.

As I think back on the list of predictions that were made about Bryan, I see that some of them were accurate and many were not. More importantly, that list could not predict his personality, his unique attributes, and the way he affects the people around him. Doctors deal with facts, but children are much more than a collection of facts. They defy expectations; they do their own thing. We must never limit them based on some set of statistics, or define them based on a diagnosis. The same goes for mothers (a fact Kevin and I would like to share with that perinatologist). The same goes for everyone.

Bryan has not just taught me these lessons. He has taught my other sons, and his cousins. Last year my nephew Dylan befriended a boy in his class who has Down syndrome. He has changed his grandfather's perspective on life—Poppy is so proud of Bryan's skills, and Bryan loves to show off for him. Today Bryan did something new and wonderful—he crawled over to my father's photograph and said "Papa"! His aunts and uncles have great respect for him and love seeing him grow and progress. Our whole family has benefited in ways that no medical book could have described.

Kevin always says to the boys, "It's not the size of the dog in the fight that matters, it's the size of the fight in the dog." I'm a big believer in that now. Whenever someone tries to tell me how things will or won't be for Bryan, or for anyone in my family, I have two words for them: *Oh, yeah?* And I know my mother is up there somewhere, saying the same thing.

Robin and her husband, Kevin, have been married for ten years. They are parents of three boys, Danny (1998), Kevin Tyler (2000), and Bryan (2005). She is the PTA president at her older children's school. Robin was instrumental in helping to coordinate the stories for this book. She is actively involved in promoting Down syndrome awareness.

6

From Generation to Generation
by Debbie Ellenbogen

Binny Ellenbogen

Binny's Grandfather,
Ben Hershberg

MY PATERNAL GRANDFATHER, Ben Hershberg, was born in 1901 in Russia. The second-oldest of six children, he came to America at the age of four and settled with his family in Albany, New York. He married, fathered three sons, became a civil engineer, and began his own business. He worked well into his nineties. Even after his retirement, he would call into the office daily to check up on the employees.

Grandpa Ben had a rich personal life. He was a sportsman, a member of his college track team, an avid golfer who insisted on walking the course even in his eighties, a sharp bridge and gin player, and a true-blue New York Yankees fan. But in addition to paying regular visits to the health club and taking two or three daily walks around his neighborhood, he also told off-color jokes, smoked a pipe, ate greasy potato chips, and preferred cheap scotch to the fine single malt that my father would offer him.

He was a generous man, giving gifts for birthdays and holidays both major and minor, and making frequent donations to *tzedakah* (charity) both in his home community and in the greater Jewish and world communities. For as long as I can remember, I looked forward to seeing my Grandpa Ben at our Friday night *Shabbat* (sabbath) dinner table. He had twinkly blue eyes, a whiskery face, and was always interested in his grandchildren.

Grandpa Ben died at the age of 101. Soon thereafter, our fifth child was born. It is a tradition among Jewish families to name new babies in memory of deceased relatives, thereby preserving and honoring their names. In doing so, one hopes that the new child acquires some of the good qualities of the beloved family member. During my pregnancy, my husband and I had discussed various names for the baby. After my grandfather died, we were both aware that if the baby were a boy, he would be named in honor of my grandpa Ben. If the baby were a girl, we were still undecided on a name. Despite several ultrasounds, we had chosen not to learn the baby's gender. We preferred to be surprised.

At a routine ultrasound in my first trimester, choroid plexus cysts were found in the baby's brain. Follow-up testing revealed other worrisome details—elevated AFP levels, clubfeet, polyhydramnios (excess amniotic fluid). The perinatologist went so far as to say, "I can't see anything definite, but I have seen a lot of babies, and my gut tells me that there is something wrong with this baby." Despite all of the negative information, my husband and I decided against any invasive testing, in part because of my absolute dread of needles, but also because we would not consider termination. Avoiding testing also let us live with the illusion that all the frightening prenatal predictions were wrong. I did have two fetal echocardiograms as well as numerous level II ultrasounds to try to detect any medical issues in the baby, so we could be prepared for treatment at birth, if necessary. I spent much of the latter part of my pregnancy in a state of suspended worry.

When our baby was born, it was obvious to us that he had Down syndrome, even before his genetic testing was completed. He had a head full of hair falling down to his chubby neck, a sweet round face, and deep, thoughtful, blue eyes. Because he had difficulty maintaining his oxygen saturation levels, he stayed in the NICU for a little more than a week before he was discharged with a trunk full of medical equipment.

I was full of doubt, full of worries, full of sadness. Down syndrome was a vast unknown for us. Would my family find it an honor to name our child for Grandpa Ben? Or would they think it an insult to his memory? Grandpa had been smart, witty, athletic, industrious, generous—what could we hope for from our new baby? Full of uncertainty, I emailed my father to see how he felt. His prompt, direct reply still makes me cry when I read it.

"I would be honored with a new Ben, Benjamin or Binyamin in the family tree, especially the beautiful baby who to date has been known affectionately as 'Baby Boy Ellenbogen.' Of course, by all means please use your grandfather's name. I am certain that this special child will be raised in a loving, caring, nurturing environment and will be afforded every opportunity to develop to the maximum of his potential. What better way to honor your grandfather's memory?"

And that is how Binyamin Amichai Ellenbogen—Binny for short—got his name. At his *bris* (ritual circumcision), while he lay cradled in his father's arms, we proudly announced the name of our newest child to our gathered family, friends, and community. *Binny* for my grandfather, whose Hebrew name was Binyamin. *Amichai*, which means, "my nation lives," indicating that Binny holds a place in the long chain of our Jewish history. He is a sassy blue-eyed bundle of mischief who loves books, bubbles, blocks, sand, water, and anything with wheels. When he was born, our vision was clouded by confusion and lack of knowledge, by health concerns and worry. At the time, we focused on all the things that might stand in Binny's way—the stumbling blocks that other children do not face, the difficulties and differences that would prevent Binny from attaining the kinds of things that all parents expect and want for their children.

Now with the gift of time, we can see a little more clearly— clear enough to know that there are many possibilities for Binny, and that, like every child, he holds amazing potential inside of him. We have for him the same dreams that we have for our other children—a life of happiness and satisfaction, love and friendship, goodness and joyfulness. We hope that Binny grows up to be a *mensch*—knowing the difference between right and wrong, and able to act accordingly. Will he grow to emulate the positive characteristics of his great grandfather? Truthfully, we don't know what he will be like as he matures, but what parent does? All we know is that we will raise him to the path of righteousness. We hope his life will be a blessing; an honor to the memory of my Grandpa Ben.

Debbie and Hershel Ellenbogen live in Sharon, Massachusetts, with their six children. Hershel is a dentist and Debbie is an early childhood educator, and they are both active in local communal and educational organizations. Binny (2002) attends a Jewish day school early childhood program in addition to the local inclusive public preschool.

7

Different
by Tammy Hodson

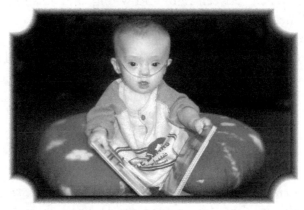

Parker Hodson

EARLY IN MY PREGNANCY with Parker I had a feeling that there was something different about him. I didn't know what. When I first saw him on the ultrasound monitor, the feeling grew even stronger. Then, when I was twenty-four weeks pregnant, I had a level II ultrasound. While most exams at this stage show a little black-and-white image sucking a thumb, mine showed Parker swimming on his back, with his hands flat at his sides, his tush sticking straight up in the air, and his legs floating over his face. From that time on, I stopped thinking about him as different. *Yup,* I thought, *that's a*

Hodson boy alright! Only a Hodson kid would consider mooning you from the womb.

Yes, Parker was born "different," meaning he has an extra chromosome. He also has several health issues, most of which are not common in children with Down syndrome. He has spent a lot of time in hospitals—you might say he's on the PICU frequent flyer plan. During our doctor visits I am always asked what Parker's diagnosis is. I run through the list of things Parker deals with. But the doctors always have to ask me again, "What is Parker's diagnosis?" It is only then that I realize they want me to tell them about his extra chromosome.

I always wonder why it is that Down syndrome is at the top of their list of concerns, when he has so many other urgent conditions to consider. And while I accept that there are some legitimate ways in which Parker is "different," I wish more people would see him the way our family does. To us, Parker is just Parker. He's the littlest Hodson boy. The one whose hair grows straight up. He's the kid who is learning to sign, and to identify the sounds his favorite farm animals make. He loves to laugh and play and be a part of his world, just like any other kid.

Unfortunately, that extra chromosome tends to be a barrier for many people, even more so than the medical problems that Parker has. People tend to be uncomfortable when they are around somebody different. They are not sure what to say or how to act. It is as if one teeny extra chromosome creates an invisible expanse that few are willing to bridge. People tend to make themselves more comfortable by assigning words such as *special* when they refer to Parker—as in, "That special little boy the Hodson family has." And while I appreciate their well-meaning intent and understand that their hearts are in the right place, the label still sets Parker apart from his peers. Why can't they refer to him as that cute little boy, or the incredibly courageous little boy? Let's face it: *special* is a word set aside for those who are different. I wonder if this perceived difference will influence how much association they or their children will have with Parker. Will he be invited to birthday parties? Will play date invitations be accepted? Or will he just be too *special?*

It is as though society is trying to abolish the opportunity to embrace anything or anyone that may be different. Not a surprise, given the history of the world. Wars have been started over someone's religion being different. Hate and violence have been spawned over someone's skin being a different color. People's worth as human beings has been defined by what is different about them. People feel threatened by "different." They want to get rid of it and replace it with what is acceptable to them. So much misery, all because someone or something is different. And now, through earlier and earlier prenatal testing, we can predict differences and eliminate them, before the world even knows that a new member of society was ever on its way. To make it even easier, the mother is praised for taking the higher road by not bringing into the world a child who is different. Gives a whole new definition to the term "throwaway society."

Once, while Parker was experiencing yet another hospital stay, his nurse came in and, after telling us how beautiful Parker was, told us something even more heartwarming. She said that after watching my husband and me with Parker, she knew she could have a child with Down syndrome and be accepting of him or her. She admitted that before meeting Parker, that would never have been a possibility. Parker enabled this transformation within her, just by being himself.

Parker is more like my other kids than he is different. Yes, he is much slower in learning how to crawl. He is slower in learning how to talk. But like my other kids, he loves to be cuddled and tickled. He loves to be the center of attention. He wants to do what his brothers and sisters are doing. He loves to roughhouse and be thrown into the air by his dad. And he will do something that he knows is naughty and then try to use his heart-melting smile to repent—the same exact smile and attitude that my oldest son uses so effectively to get his way. He is, in more ways than not, just a typical Hodson boy. Like the rest of us, he was born with his own combination of limitations and talents. And just like the rest of us, he deserves to be accepted and appreciated for the unique impact he will have upon the world.

Tammy and her husband, Reed, live in Utah with their six children, Bailey (1986), Brant (1988), McCall (1991), Rigel (1995), Kensely (1998), and Parker (2004). Tammy holds degrees in early childhood education and elementary education. She spends her free time being Parker's advocate, as well as blogging on issues that affect the medically fragile child with Down syndrome. Her blog can be found at www.prayingforparker.com

8

It's Better Than Good
by Janine Steck Huffman

Jeff and Nash Huffman

Nash Huffman

"BYE, POOPYHEAD!" Those parting words from our son, Nash, were tossed to his dear dad from the open window of my car, as Nash and I headed to camp yesterday. I glanced in the rearview mirror and saw Jeff was standing on the front porch, waving to us as we drove off, and grinning ear to ear.

Grinning, you ask? *Why, I would be punishing my son as such language is not tolerated in our household!* That's what I would have said too, before Nash was born. Instead, I silently count the number of syllables he has just spoken, smile in amazement at the clarity of each letter, and laugh at the wonderful sense of humor our son has. I quietly thank our speech therapist for giving us the tools to guide Nash to this step in language, and drive onward. You see, when Nash was diagnosed with Down syndrome shortly after his birth, I had so many questions about his future, especially regarding his speech development. When he was two, I would have given the world to hear any clear words from him. Now that he's five, I sometimes wonder if he will ever be quiet!

I wish that the public would abandon the negative stereotypes about Down syndrome, and that those facing this diagnosis prenatally were better informed about the bright future possible for their child before they decide whether to terminate. Why? Because both of these issues affect how the world perceives my son—from the medical profession, to the school system, to his social environment. When assumptions based on ignorance or outdated information abound, they perpetuate a society that will not embrace or even accept differences.

I understand these misconceptions all too well, because I was once one of "them"—one of those people with a drive to perform, to reach perfection, to always be the best; one of those people with the preconceived notion that a diagnosis of Down syndrome brought nothing but pain to the families involved; that children with the syndrome have no purpose in life and grow up to be adults with no joy or friends.

On April 9, 1982, a baby was born in the Bloomington Hospital in Indiana. This baby was born with an esophageal atresia, and also had Down syndrome. If the parents ever gave their baby a name, it was never known, so he was called simply "Baby Doe." The surgeon explained to the parents that the operative mortality rate for clearing the obstruction was fifty percent, and the attending physician told the parents that Baby Doe would be severely mentally retarded. The parents were told that their child would not be "normal," that some of these children were mere "blobs," and the alternative to surgery would be to do nothing. Based on the doctor's information, the parents decided that they would not proceed with the surgery, and would withhold further nourishment and medical attention. The matter proceeded to court, and on April 12th, Judge John G. Baker of the Monroe County Circuit Court held that the parents "...have the right to choose a medically recommended course of treatment for their child in the present circumstances." The Indiana Supreme Court upheld the parents' right to make this decision, stating that a starvation death was legal. While an appeal to the United States Supreme Court was being pursued, Baby Doe was placed in an isolation room where he died without treatment or nourishment seven days after his birth.

At that time I was a senior at Indiana University in Bloomington, and an intern for Judge Baker. I was asked to research the right to die issue, and that research resulted in legal conclusions that supported the parents, not with those that wanted to adopt Baby Doe. This information made me think that letting this baby go, since he will be a "blob," might be the right thing to do. Facts that assisted Judge Baker in his ruling that parents have the right to choose a medically recommended course of treatment for their child in the present circumstances—circumstances that would later become part of my life.

I graduated from law school, went to work for a living, and put having children on the back burner. My life was full with career, husband, travel, friends, and a fun social life. I figured I had lots of time to have children, and that it would happen when the time was right. But it never seemed to be the "right time." It was after my first marriage ended that I made up my mind—I *did* want a family. My future husband and I met, of all places, on the Internet. Via email, I found we grew up only ten miles apart from each other. He was a high school football star; I was a cheerleader for a rival school and into all sports. Our families actually knew each other. Yet we had never met. We knew it was fate—something I never believed in before. Now I know differently. We were married a little after a year from our meeting.

After trying the usual trying-to-conceive tactics, we suffered several miscarriages. Each was devastating, and created even more doubt as to the possibility of becoming parents. When I finally had a pregnancy continue beyond the first trimester, we were elated!

My OB asked what prenatal testing we wanted to have, and Jeff and I had a thorough discussion. We both agreed to avoid an amnio due to the risk involved. My history of miscarriage was one factor, but even more important was our conviction that we would embrace any child who came to us. Jeff felt very strongly about this. Just that morning, while driving to work, he had been listening to his Zig Ziglar "Success Without Guilt" audio tape. In the Ziglar tape, there is a discussion about a couple, Bernie and Elaine Lofchick, and their son David, who was born with cerebral palsy. Thirty doctors advised the Lofchicks to put David in an institution, saying he would never walk or talk or count to ten. But David's parents never gave up on him, and with a specialist's assistance, they helped him, stayed beside him, and most importantly, believed in him. Ziglar explained how his friend Bernie told him, "I'm not a buyer, I'm a seller." Instead of believing the negative prognosis the doctors had given him, Bernie focused on what he could do to help his son be strong, healthy, and happy. Today David is one of the top real estate producers in Winnipeg.

After relating this story to me, Jeff explained, "I too am a seller, not a buyer. If we have a child with a disability, we both will put our heart and souls into that child, disability or not, we know that." So the decision was final: no invasive prenatal testing.

We did decide to have a level II ultrasound conducted at twenty weeks to prepare us for any problems. Jeff was sure we were having a boy and was excited to have this confirmed. During the exam he asked the doctor, "Do we need pompoms or footballs?"

The doctor scanned for a bit, not saying a word. Then suddenly he announced, "Football!" Jeff and I were ecstatic.

The perinatologist was thorough and found no markers for any disorders. He even explained, as he scanned our son's little finger, that many babies with Down syndrome have only two joints in that digit. Ours had three, and no heart chamber problems or short femurs or other markers. We went home happy and celebrated with a takeout steak dinner from Outback, my pregnancy craving of the day.

The week after the ultrasound, I had an appointment at the hair salon. A girl about eight years old with Down syndrome was seated next to me. She was adorable, although uncomfortable in her perm curlers (who wouldn't be?). I smiled at her, and she gave a big grin back. Inside I was thinking, *I'm so happy that my son won't have Down syndrome. Jeff and I decided we could deal with any problems that we might face, but I don't know how I would cope.* And then, incredibly, "that feeling" hit. I suddenly *knew* I would be having a child with Down syndrome. I tried to keep the thoughts out of my mind, and didn't even tell Jeff about it.

This premonition became reality fifteen minutes after Nash was born. It had been a stressful day—the birth had been induced at thirty-seven weeks due to my high blood pressure, and the baby had come by emergency c-section. Everything seemed wonderful, though, once we saw our beautiful boy. Jefferson Nash cried right out of the box, and got a nine on the Apgar test twice. But then the perinatologist came into the recovery room. After congratulating us, he related his suspicions that our son had Down syndrome. Despite the warning I had received in the salon, I was in shock. Images ran through my mind of the baby I thought we would have—the baby we *wanted* to have—and tears started flowing.

I wish I had known then what really lay in store for us. Nash is our source of amazement each day. He is one smart little boy and could recite his ABCs and basic colors, sight read more than ten words, and use at least 130 signs of American Sign Language before the age of three. More importantly, he has taught me a lesson I still work through every day—that the value of a life, of a human, of a child, is measured not by how much he or she can accomplish, but how much he or she can teach others about what really matters. Like how to accept people with all kinds of different "abilities."

Our life is better than good. Sure, we have our tough days, but they have nothing to do with Down syndrome. How can this message be understood by those who don't have a person with Down syndrome in their lives? I don't know. I was one of "them" and I still don't know. But I will continue trying to build that understanding.

Nash is here for a reason, we know that. It is fate that I was involved in the Baby Doe case, that Jeff and I met, that he listened to Zig Ziglar that day, that the adorable little girl was next to me in the salon. We are advocates now for Nash and for others with Down syndrome. We also know that Nash will be his own advocate, and that he will make a difference in the world.

He's making a difference already. On the elevator, as we headed to the seventh floor for a routine ENT checkup, Nash made a point to look each passenger in the eye, shake his or her hand, and say, "Good morning." What an impact these interactions will have on society's view of people with Down syndrome!

One of the women in the elevator looked at him in surprise and said, "Well, hello dear!" then turned to whisper to her friend, "*They are always so sweet!*" Nash looked at her and saw fit to do another bit of advocacy as we walked off the elevator—

"BYE, POOPYHEAD!"

Janine and Jeff are proud parents of one son, Jefferson Nash (2001). Janine is an attorney with the Indiana Office of the Attorney General in complex litigation. Her husband Jeff is CEO of Janus Developmental Services, Inc., which provides services to children and adults with developmental disabilities. Both Jeff and Janine are active advocates within the Down syndrome community. Janine is on the Board of the Indiana Down Syndrome Foundation (IDSF) and is the IDSF Parent Network Chair. Jeff assisted in founding the Dads Appreciating Down Syndrome (www.dadsapprecitatingdownsyndrome.org) (DADS) group that is now spreading nationwide, and is a member of The Arc of Indiana Governmental Affairs committee. He is a motivational speaker who also appears at national Down syndrome conventions with the DADS group. Janine's blog can be seen at www.mauzysmusings.blogspot.com.

9

Mommy
by Kelly Rimmer

Alexis Skye Rimmer

SOMETHING WAS NOT RIGHT.

It was 7:38 a.m. Our daughter Alexis had just been born, and I kept waiting for the nurse to hand her to me, just like the nurses did when my first two children were born. But instead, both nurses were bending over her. One called for the respiratory team. The other beckoned Dr. Wilson, my OB, to assist. He started suctioning Alexis's throat. Two respiratory therapists hurried in and took over. "Her lungs are still wet," one of them said, trying not to sound concerned.

My husband Shane and I were worried. "Why isn't she crying?" I whispered.

"It'll be okay," he said. Then Alexis was sent to the NICU, before we even got a chance to hold her.

"You'll have her back in an hour," the nurse promised. But one hour turned into five.

Finally, the NICU doctor came to see us. "She has a heart defect," he explained, "and she has Down syndrome. We have to fly her to Labonheur Children's Hospital immediately." Shocked, Shane jumped in our car so he could arrive as soon as possible after Alexis's helicopter landed. I couldn't go with him.

What was supposed to be one of the best nights of our life turned into complete hell. I cried all night, thinking I would never hold my daughter, or even get to see her. I prayed until morning, and didn't sleep at all. Shane stayed with Alexis all night. I felt so empty without her. I felt like it was all my fault.

The next morning, I begged to leave the hospital. As soon as I was discharged, I called my parents to come get me. My dad drove the eighty miles to the children's hospital as fast as he could. Once we arrived, I ran past the ER and through the halls to the NICU. Shane was waiting for me at the door.

I finally got to see my daughter. She was lying on her back with needles and tubes all over her. Her skin was red from the heat lamp. She was fast asleep. But as soon as I touched her hand, she started moving her arms and legs. The nurses got so excited. "She has been waiting for you," one said. "We have tried everything to get a response from her, but she has been so sleepy. All she needed was her mommy."

My heart about jumped out of my chest. When I was pregnant with Alexis I used to lie in bed, talking to her and listening to her heart beat on the monitor I had. I would dream about holding her. That's all I wanted now.

Right then the nurse asked, "Do you want to hold her?"

"Please!" I said.

She unplugged the monitors, wrapped Alexis in a blanket, and put her in my arms. I looked down at her face and she looked up at mine. I touched her little hands and kissed her cheek. I opened the wrap they had her in so I could look at her feet. I kissed her and told her I loved her. I stroked her hair and held her as close as I could. Then Shane handed me a tiny little bottle.

"We can't get her to feed," the nurse said. "You try."

I put the bottle to her mouth and she started to suck. And I started to cry.

What impressed me most about that experience was that Alexis was no different than any other newborn. A new baby knows her mother's voice and smell before even seeing her face. Alexis was no different. All she wanted and needed was her mommy. This taught me that although we are all born unique, we come to this earth needing the same things: love, affection, and security. No matter how different we may seem, we all deserve to be cared for and respected as human beings.

Alexis Skye Rimmer (2005) is the daughter of Shane and Kelly Rimmer of Atwood, Tennessee. Alexis has a sister, Paige (1992), and a brother, Aaron (1999), who were excited to meet her and bring her home to love. Alexis is a happy and healthy baby who brings her family great joy.

10

Acceptance
by Shari Adelson-Pollard

Brandon Pollard

WHEN I WAS YOUNG, I would sometimes join in with other kids who picked on those who were different. In my fifth grade class there was a girl who had a neuromuscular disorder. Her name was Michelle; she was a small girl, shorter than the rest of us, with long brown hair. We made fun of the way she walked. Then in junior high, a boy who was mentally retarded rode our school bus. Every day, the kids would tease him, throw things at him, and mimic his speech. He tried to ignore them, but you could tell he was really hurt by it. He would sit in his seat and keep his head down.

I wish I could say I increased my acceptance of people with disabilities over the years. But my attitude as an adult still left much to be desired. I clean houses for a living, and one of my clients has a teenage son who has a mental disability. I would dread the days that he was home from school because he would want to tell me all about his Yu-gi-oh card collection, and he was always afraid I would vacuum up his beloved Legos. I would have preferred to avoid his company. I had similar feelings for the young woman with a mental disability who works at our grocery store. I'm ashamed to admit that I used to dread her carrying out my groceries, because she would repeat the same story several times. And I was in too big a hurry to hear what she was saying.

Then I became pregnant with Brandon, my fifth child. Things seemed normal at first. I refused all prenatal testing, even though I was thirty-eight years old. I felt nothing a test could tell me would matter or change my idea of having a baby. But toward the end of my pregnancy, something seemed different. Maybe it was because I had suffered a tubal pregnancy six months before and was still skittish, or because I didn't feel as much fetal movement as I did with the others. Or maybe it was mother's intuition. Out of curiosity, I started checking websites for information on Down syndrome. Looking back on it now, it gives me an eerie feeling that this diagnosis was the only thing I ever researched, because when Brandon was born, he was diagnosed with Down syndrome.

During those first hours following the diagnosis, I was full of fear of the unknown. I was angry, sad, hurt, and felt lots of self-pity. Then of course, I wondered how this would affect my other children and how they would react to their new brother.

The day I came home from the hospital, the early intervention team called to tell me about physical and occupational therapy. I was astonished at all that was expected of my little son, and of me. I am the mother of four other boys; I thought nothing could shock me anymore! But I realized my new beautiful son was going to need our help and I was determined he would get it. This was my first step towards acceptance.

Two weeks after Brandon was born, my oldest son, Conrad, graduated from high school. In a class of more than 400, it is hard to stand out as one of the best. Only three students were chosen to give speeches during the ceremony. One of the boys chosen had Williams syndrome, a chromosomal disorder. I cried through his whole speech. Afterward, he was given a standing ovation. For the first time I thought to myself, *Brandon is going to have a bright future with plenty of friends.* This was another important step toward acceptance of Brandon's diagnosis.

My next steps were easier to make, because of the wonderful support I received from my family, just as I had my whole life. When I had marital problems and divorced, my parents opened their home to me and my children, letting us live with them until I was able to get back on my feet, which was a great help and comfort. Then I revisited the website I had sought out while pregnant, the BabyCenter.com Down syndrome bulletin board. Interacting with other women in my situation enabled me to relax a bit and to feel more confident.

As I took even more steps towards acceptance of Brandon's diagnosis and the changes it brought into my life, I regretted my previous attitudes toward people with disabilities. I still feel bad about my behavior toward those who couldn't help their circumstances in life. I wish I could go back and change the way I treated them. But all I can do is pay attention to how I react and treat people now. Now, when I see the young woman at the grocery store, I take the time to listen, to ask her questions, and to make conversation with her. Now, when my client's teenage son is home, I talk to him about his cards and ask him about his baseball team, and I really enjoy our chats.

These days I make a point to be friendly to other families who have a child with a disability. During a recent trip to Disneyland, while waiting in line for the monorail, I saw a child with Down syndrome in front of us. I started small talk with the parents, instead of looking away. Turns out they lived in our area, and we became friends. Acceptance has its benefits!

Best of all, I've seen how accepting Brandon's brothers are of him. My two younger boys don't even notice a difference in Brandon. My older two boys are already protective of him. My son Corey always says, "Brandon, you're going to be the smartest person ever with Down syndrome." I'm confident that Brandon's brothers will not have the same narrow views that I used to have regarding people with disabilities. I think they will be the kind of boys who will refuse to join in with the teasing so common in our society. I think they'll be more welcoming to the hardworking individuals who carry their groceries.

I want to offer hope to parents facing a new diagnosis of Down syndrome. I was and am where you are; and where you will be. Remember, the broken heart is in you, not your child with Down syndrome. Within a short time, your broken heart will transform into a heart filled with love and amazement at this incredible person. You, too, will find the peace of acceptance.

Shari and her husband, Austin, live in Omaha, Nebraska, with their five boys, Conrad (1987), Corey (1990), Trevor (1999), Travis (2001), and Brandon (2005). They were given Brandon's diagnosis a few hours after his birth by the doctor on call in the NICU, but Shari knew it from the start, just from seeing Brandon's little toes. They are a family constantly on the go. Brandon is always included, and loves to do things with his brothers.

11

Sunshine
by Jeanette Bollinger

Jeanette and Carter Bollinger

"HE IS AMAZING," the elderly lady said. "When I was growing up people like him were institutionalized from birth, and I never knew how alert and bright they could be! I wonder why those people were never given a chance to live their lives with everyone else. You could never tell there was anything different about him!"

I was at the mall with Carter, taking a shopping break on a bench, when I had noticed this lady watching us. I had given her a smile and she had returned it with a rather unsure one of her own. At that point Carter had looked at her and given one of his 500-

watt cheeky grins. Her face completely transformed. She beamed at Carter, who in turn batted his beautiful long eyelashes at her. I knew that once again Carter had changed a person's perception of Down syndrome, and as I do every time this happens, I started letting my mind drift back to when my sweet baby was brought in to my life.

Carter Evan James Bollinger was born on March 30, 2005, after a long, drawn-out labor. He was pink, chubby (nine pounds!) and absolutely perfect. I experienced such a feeling of peace and utter joy when I held him for the first time.

In Carter's eighth hour of life, I was standing in the hospital hallway looking through the nursery window. He was being kept in a warmer because his temperature kept falling. The halls of the hospital felt like a sauna. Even in the meager hospital gown I was wearing I was sweltering, and I was contemplating taking a walk outside for some air. I was watching the nurses take blood from Carter's heel, and out of the corner of my eye I saw the doctor coming towards me. For some reason I just had a feeling that she was going to tell me something that would change the course of my life. I was right.

I will never forget her exact words. She said, "Your son has some features that make us think that he has Down syndrome."

My world stopped. Suddenly the hall that had seemed almost stifling was frozen, an icy chamber. I couldn't move, I couldn't speak. I could say nothing in response. I simply nodded my head and walked back down the hall to my room, where my husband, Kris, was waiting. I sat on the edge of the bed and stared at the floor. I must have sat there for five minutes before I said anything.

"They think he has Down syndrome," I said numbly.

The hours after that were a blur of visits from friends and family and many trips down the hall to the nursery. The next thing I remember in any detail was the nurse waking me at 3:00 a.m. to say that Carter was being transferred by ambulance to Children's Hospital in Vancouver. That was when I "woke up" and realized that Carter had bigger problems than just the Down syndrome. He was having difficulties keeping his oxygen saturation levels up, and his temperature continued to drop. I suddenly knew that I had to focus on him getting well instead of thinking about his possible diagnosis.

I followed Carter's ambulance to the children's hospital and didn't leave his side until the following evening. The special care nursery was a terrifying place. All around me was this atmosphere of helplessness and depression, and the only way that I could escape it was to focus on my sweet baby. I would hold him and rock with him for ages, singing softly to him. "You Are My Sunshine" seemed to be his favorite song. He would watch me intently, and gradually his beautiful blue eyes would start to droop and he would fall asleep in my arms. I never wanted to put him down. Even the busy nurses loved to hold him.

In the back of my mind I kept thinking that the pediatrician was wrong, and that the test for Down syndrome would come back negative. So when we got the blood work back from the lab with a positive result, I was in complete shock and denial. I knew that I would never be able to handle a special needs child, and I panicked. I suffer from clinical depression, and knowing how difficult that already made my life, I wondered how I would handle anything else. Thankfully, Kris took the diagnosis much better than I did, and was able to comfort me while I struggled with the news. I never would have been able to get through those difficult times without his love.

When I finally brought Carter home from the hospital I began to notice that people had a very strong reaction when they met him for the first time. It didn't matter what sort of mood or frame of mind they were in, as soon as they met Carter they seemed happier and just wanted to be around him as much as possible. All he has to do is smile at a person once, and he has them wrapped around his cute little crooked pinkie. He has a peaceful, happy presence that is very contagious. I learned quickly to give myself extra time when planning errands, because wherever we went, people invariably came up to us and started chatting. Everyone wanted to hold him, and more than a few people jokingly threatened to keep him for themselves!

The "Carter effect" is especially apparent in his older brother Aiden, who is three. Whenever he gets in an owly, grumpy mood, all it takes is a few minutes around Carter, and he'll let a smile accidentally slip out. Before long, he's his cheerful self again. Aiden loves participating in Carter's therapies, especially meeting any specialists we go to see (there is always a pile of toys to play with). He is Carter's biggest fan and cheerleader. When Carter sat up on his own for the first time, Aiden practically screamed, "He did it, Mommy, he did it! Yayyyyy, Carter!" I thought he was about to jump right out of his pull-up!

Five years ago, if I had been told that this was how my life would be, I never would have believed it. People have asked me whether I would take the Down syndrome away if I could. My answer is always no, because that would mean changing Carter, and I would never want to change him. If I can make life easier on him I will, as would any parent for their child. But he is perfect, just as he is.

I do still have days that are difficult to get through. I am on medication for my depression, but there are some days that are extraordinarily tough. There are times when I just want to shut myself in a room somewhere and hide from the world and everyone in it, or maybe to just scream and scream until I finally feel calm and empty. But with the support of my friends and family, and especially with the sunny love that radiates from Carter, I manage to make it through each day. And I still sing "You Are My Sunshine" to Carter every night, while he drifts off into a sweet sleep.

I often think back to the elderly lady that we met at the mall. I think of all of the children from her generation who were locked away in institutions, and it makes me so sad to think that their sunshine was shut away behind dark, steely clouds, instead of lighting up people's lives, like Carter lights up mine. If only these children had been given the opportunity to spread their rays of joy and peace. If only people had given them a chance. But they weren't given that chance, and I know that it is up to me to help Carter share his sunshine with the world.

Jeanette lives in Abbotsford, British Columbia, with her husband, Kris, and her two sons, Aiden (2003), and Carter (2005). She is a stay-at-home mom who spends her spare time working on scrapbooks.

12

Who's Winning?
by Sandra Assimotos-McElwee

Rick, Sean, and Sandra McElwee

AT AGE ELEVEN, SEAN HAD played Special Olympics golf for three years. His father was his usual partner for the "every-other-shot" annual tournament. But this year as the tournament date approached, Dad was out of commission due to recent surgery. We had to ask for a volunteer to be Sean's partner.

The big day arrived, a typical southern California spring afternoon. A fresh ocean breeze was gently blowing across the immaculate fairways at the Tijeras Creek Golf Club. After six weeks of practicing with high school and college golf students, forty-five Special

Olympians were ready to show their talents. Resident golf pro Marty LaRoche was directing the group, all decked out in the white shirts and khaki hats that Marty had donated.

Sean's volunteer partner was a woman who had recently retired and wanted to learn the game of golf. She was petite and blonde, in her late fifties, wearing an expensive golf shirt. Her golf bag looked like a pro's. Her husband, a scratch golfer, was paired with another Olympian; together, they made a tournament foursome. I watched her intently from my spot on the golf cart (as part of Sean's gallery, my husband and I got to ride in style). I could tell she didn't know many people who had Down syndrome. At first she spoke slowly and loudly to Sean, as if he had a hearing impairment.

Sean had the first drive off the tee, and hit the ball squarely, straight down the fairway about sixty yards. His partner apologized, lowering her voice, "Oh Sean, I am so sorry. I'm not as good as you are." And she wasn't. She was to hit the ball from where it lay, directly in the middle of the fairway. Poor lady, she topped the ball, and it dribbled about ten feet off to the right.

Sean patted her on the back and said, "Good try, you will do better next time." He then hit the next shot around fifty yards, once again straight down the fairway, sunk the putt on the green, and they headed to the next hole.

For nine holes Sean encouraged his volunteer partner. She really did stink. But he would not allow her to beat herself up. When she did connect with the ball he would say, "See, you did it! Great job!"

At the awards ceremony, Sean put the bronze medal on his volunteer's neck, shook her hand, and thanked her for playing with him. She put Sean's medal on his neck and gave him a big hug. After it was all over, she told us she was very impressed with Sean's sportsmanship and ability, and that the day had gone much differently than she'd thought it would.

I am always amused when people first meet Sean and don't know what to expect. When I first met him, I didn't know what to expect either. The day Sean was born and the doctor told me he had Down syndrome, I had no reference point, no preconceived ideas of what that diagnosis meant. My husband, Rick, and I simply decided we would give Sean every chance, and never give up on him. Ironically, it is Sean who has taught me to never give up.

One Friday afternoon around 3:00, I was thinking to myself, "I should just give up and go home." As a sales executive, I had made over a hundred cold calls that week and had fulfilled fifteen sales appointments, but was posting a zero in the "Accounts Sold" column. Discouraging, to say the least.

Then I remembered what Sean has taught me about persistence.

Sean struggled to roll over, sit up, and crawl. But once he started walking, it took no time for him to start to run. A gifted athlete, Sean picked up sports quickly. He could hit a pitched baseball when he was only four years old. He was the strongest kicker in soccer, and could serve over the net in volleyball when many other kids couldn't even hit that far. He has natural ability in every sport he has tried. Except for one: Basketball.

When Sean was six years old, we signed him up for a community basketball league. It was the kind where the kids practice and learn the basics of the game for the first half-hour, then play a game the second half-hour. Nobody loses, everybody wins. But Sean really struggled. Even though they had lowered the net to eight feet, Sean could not even hit the rim with the ball. For eight weeks, he tried and tried to just get the ball high enough to touch the rim, much less make a basket.

He never got discouraged; he never gave up.

At the very last practice, he finally made ONE basket. All the other kids on the team gave him high fives over and over again. All the parents watching cheered and cheered. The coach put him up on his shoulders and paraded him around the court.

How could I give up on myself, with a son like that?

So, that Friday afternoon at 3:00, I made one more cold call. I convinced the owner of a small business, who was reluctant at first, to agree to a sales presentation. After I met with him at his place of business, he was so impressed with the presentation that he asked me to pitch it again to his two partners. At 4:45 that afternoon I signed a major account, because I didn't give up, I didn't get discouraged.

Following Sean's example is a good way to succeed in business. But much more importantly, it's a vital way I can show him the respect he deserves.

I chuckle today thinking of the story that Sean's golf partner must tell at dinner parties: How she arrived on the scene as the "charitable one," the nice lady on hand to encourage her unskilled partner, only to walk away as the one who was uplifted and encouraged. Although Sean had bested her at golf, she walked away the real winner.

I know exactly how she feels.

Sandra lives in Rancho Santa Margarita, California, and is a medical device sales representative. She has been happily married to Rick McElwee for fourteen years. The day Sean was born, Sandra wrote a description of his diagnosis to include in his birth announcements. This developed into a speech, which counsels parents of typically developing children on what to say to parents of a child with a disability. The speech was published in essay form in the anthology, You Will Dream New Dreams, and is available in its entirety at http://www.leeworks. net/DDS/speech.html. Sandra is working with the Down Syndrome Association of Orange County to develop a program for physicians to better deliver the prenatal and postnatal diagnosis of Down syndrome. You can find her website for parents at www.leeworks.net/DDS.

THE GIFT OF STRENGTH

13

Notes From the Deep End
by Jennifer Enderlin Blougouras

Nicholas Blougouras

I WAS THIRTY-SEVEN YEARS OLD when my husband and I decided it was time to have a baby. We had been married nine years, together for sixteen. We had put off parenting for all this time in order to focus on careers, travel, fun, ourselves.

My job was pretty glamorous: Vice-president of a big publishing company in New York City. My life was filled with interesting writers, fascinating trips, sparkling conversation, fine wine, speaking engagements. I saw having a baby as something to check off my list of "Things To Do In Life." And besides, a baby would go well with my new black suit.

So I signed up for the Gwyneth Paltrow version of motherhood. The Kelly Ripa woman-on-the-go scenario. The version of motherhood that gets glamorized in *People* magazine. But in my heart of hearts, I was scared. Terrified. I knew my life was going to change, and I didn't want it to.

Still, I had the anticipation of regret and I thought having a baby would be "good for me." So picture this: Parenthood, to me, was like a giant swimming pool. I saw other people in the pool and they looked okay. But I didn't want to get wet. I was hesitant to even stick in a toe.

Other parents said to me, "Going into the pool can be really scary. But it's all worth it."

I thought to myself, *If they can do it, so can I.* And, tentatively, I put my foot in the water.

Suddenly, someone grabbed me from behind and threw me in the deep end of the pool. In the deep end! How unfair! You don't take the person most frightened of the water and throw them in the deep end! Throw another person in the deep end, someone who's used to the pool! Someone who knows how to swim!

How did this happen? Who did this to me? Gagging and coughing and choking and sputtering, I railed against the shock of the cold water, the unfairness of it all. My head went under and panic set in. *I'm going to die,* I thought. But instinct kicked in and clumsily, I moved my arms and legs. And I did not drown.

Now I was treading water. After a few big breaths I looked around and noticed there were other people in the deep end with me, and they were offering to help. But I didn't want to be in their Deep End Club. And besides, I didn't think I even belonged here. It was only a matter of time before someone told me it was all a mistake and I'd be pulled out of the pool to safety. I should have left well enough alone. I should never have tried to go into the pool, I thought. But since nobody came to my rescue, I continued to tread water. And I did not drown.

Soon I started to float. My panic subsided. I knew I could survive, although it surely wouldn't be pleasant being stuck at this end of the pool. I was able to rest for short periods, suspended on the surface of the water. I felt pretty much alone. Yet I did not drown.

Then I noticed there was a little boy in the deep end with me, a little boy named Nicholas with eyes that crinkle up like half moons when he smiles. A little boy named Nicholas who loves Bruce Springsteen and Puccini's *La Bohème* and 1940s Big Band music. And Nicholas could swim.

Looking at him, I began to realize that someday, I might be able to do more than float. I might be able to swim. And I might even enjoy it. Perhaps I'd even love it.

As I watched Nicholas I discovered that the deep end allows for underwater somersaults, and in the deep end, it's possible to dive. You can't do that in the shallow end. And I realized that perhaps someday, with Nicholas at my side, we'd both wave to the parents at the shallow end of the pool and say, "You don't know what you're missing, here in the deep end."

Jennifer is Associate Publisher at St. Martin's Press in New York City. She lives in New Jersey with her husband, Arthur, and their two children, Nicholas (2005), and June (2006).

14

For Such a Time as This
by Emily Vesper

Logan Vesper

I REMEMBER IT LIKE IT was yesterday—the very moment God planted the dream in my heart. I was eight years old, doing what most children do after getting home from school—eating a snack and watching TV. I usually didn't pay attention to the commercials, but that day a little girl in one of the advertisements caught my eye. Wearing a pretty pink leotard, she walked across a balance beam, looking down at her feet with deep concentration as her gymnastics instructor cheered her on. When she reached the end of the beam, she lifted her head up and gave the most amazing smile. She was so proud of herself, and I instantly fell in love with this little girl. Her big almond eyes were as beautiful as her contagious smile. I asked my mom why she looked this way.

"She has Down syndrome," she said.

Looking back to the TV and watching the little girl hug her instructor, I knew what I wanted to do when I grew up: I was going to be a teacher of children with Down syndrome. I began telling my dream to anyone who would listen.

Throughout my teenage years, my dream never died, but life didn't go exactly as I had planned. After I graduated from high school, I got married and got a job. I put off college for a few years, planning to go back and get my special education degree later. But then a beautiful baby boy joined our family, and then another. My college plans were put on hold for the time being. When I became pregnant a third time, I realized that it might take many years to fulfill my dream. But I was content to wait, and enjoy being a mother.

Fast forward nine months to the day everything turned upside down. "It's a boy!" I heard the doctor say, confirming what we had already known. The baby, who we named Logan, was crying and wriggling around in the warmer. He looked great and I was soaring. My third precious baby boy!

I was so full of joy, pride, and love that I didn't even notice my husband and doctor talking in hushed tones at my bedside. Once I noticed them inspecting Logan, I began to listen.

"He has a small cleft palate that will need to be fixed with surgery," I heard the doctor say. I was stunned, but reminded myself that a cleft palate wasn't the end of the world. I knew lots of people who had had surgery for that, and were just fine now.

"I also think we need to order a FISH test, to look at his chromosomes." I didn't understand. Did he think there was something wrong with my baby? I couldn't talk; my voice wasn't working.

Then my husband asked, "How sure are you that he has Down syndrome?"

"About ninety percent," the doctor answered.

The room started spinning; my eyes were burning with tears. I felt like I had been punched in the stomach. Surely, I hadn't heard him right. It just couldn't be. I had never imagined being a mom to a baby with Down syndrome. Teaching children with Down syndrome from nine to five was one thing; having to live with and parent a child with special needs every day was quite another.

Thoughts were racing through my head like a train out of control, things like:

Will he live with us forever?

He is never going to be able to have kids.

People are going to look at our family "funny."

His care is going to be way too expensive.

Is my husband going to be mad at me?

As these questions collided with each other, I heard our doctor say, "Don't worry, everything is going to be okay." I pulled back into reality and began listening to him. This doctor was so supportive. He sat with us for over an hour telling us what an amazing journey we were going to have. My heart began to calm as I accepted this new reality in my life.

Over the course of the next few days, I fell madly in love with my son. After we went home from the hospital and the busy routine of my new life set in, I had a poignant conversation with my sister-in-law, who also happens to be one of my best friends. We'd grown up together and she knew of my dream. She was talking about how ironic Logan's birth was, since my childhood wish was to be involved with kids with Down syndrome. Then she said to me, "Em, you got your wish. Your dream came true. You get to be the ultimate teacher of a child with Down syndrome." It was all I could do to not break down and cry on the phone with her. She was right. God had granted my dream. And in that moment, I realized that He is the one who put my dream in my heart in the first place.

It has been more than a year since Logan's birth, and he has taught me many things. I have learned not to be upset when my plans don't always happen the way I think they should. My plans are filled with selfish desire, but the Lord's plans are perfect. As I see my own child's amazing almond eyes and contagious smile, I am reminded of that little girl I had seen so many years ago. My childhood dreams have matured; God has chosen this path for my life and sometimes I still don't understand why. Even still, I know that along my journey, He will always prepare me "for such a time as this."

Emily lives in Olathe, Kansas, with her husband, Todd. Married in 1997, they have three children, Zachary Isaiah (2000), Aiden Michael (2001), and Logan Todd (2005). Emily stays at home with their children and Todd works for a large company in the Kansas City area. As a family, they enjoy cooking, biking, and taking walks, to name just a few activities. They also enjoy their local church.

15

Travels With Brendan
by Tammy Westfahl

Brendan Westfahl

THERE IS AN IRISH SAINT known as "Saint Brendan the Navigator," because he's rumored to have traveled the Atlantic spreading the gospel. Admittedly, my Brendan is no saint. Being a toddler, Brendan finds it amusing to hide his shoes, empty every drawer within reach, dump the food from the cats' bowls, and bathe in the dog's water dish. But just like Saint Brendan, my Brendan is a navigator. Lucky for me! Since his arrival in my life was also a departure into unfamiliar lands, I need someone with his skills to help guide my way.

Brendan's quiet strength has helped me maneuver the course of many bumpy roads. It's helped me manage the foreign medical jargon thrown at us in the early days of his life, when we first heard many ugly terms, such as "Necrotizing Enterocolitis" and "Hirschsprung Disease." They were such big, scary words, with unknown meanings and unclear implications. There were numerous consultations, x-rays to view, and options to discuss. It was so easy to become engrossed in the situation and to forget that we were discussing a baby, our baby. But the minute I'd walk up to Brendan's bed, I was thrown into the reality of the situation: I was the mother of this beautiful creature sleeping peacefully, totally oblivious to the chaos around him. This baby, who was fighting for his existence, was a part of me. If he could fight to survive, then surely I could fight through my fear and anxiety to find the answers to help him.

Brendan's sense of calm has guided us through the tumultuous weather that sometimes strikes this new land. Even on the worst and scariest days in the hospital, I knew everything would be okay. I could sit by Brendan's hospital bed and instantly feel calm. His peaceful ways continued to influence me even when his medical crisis had passed. On his first birthday, our family was asked to be in a news story promoting the local Buddy Walk. During the interview, whenever I felt myself becoming overwhelmed, I would look behind the camera to see Brendan waving at me. Instantly, I knew I could do it. I could do it for Brendan.

His perseverance has given me the strength to keep trying, even when steep hills seem too tall to climb. Overcoming enormous obstacles seems to be Brendan's specialty. He is a hard worker and isn't bothered by what he can't do. Time and again, I've watched him work tirelessly to learn a new skill. He just keeps trying until he gets it. When he was younger, he spent day after day working at his shape sorter, until he finally mastered it. I'm learning to be more like him. Writing this story has been incredibly difficult for me, but like Brendan with his blocks, I kept trying until I finally got it.

As we travel, Brendan doesn't let me miss anything. He points out the beauty, love, and grandeur in the landscape around us. He's taught me to enjoy the journey of life. He savors every bite of food he eats—we all know how much he enjoys it by the long "mmm" that follows each taste. Before he came into my life I never saw the beauty of bubbles blowing across the back porch at dusk. I didn't know how delicious a graham cracker could taste, especially when it's shared with a blond, blue-eyed toddler. Now I understand the delight of neglecting chores to play ball. I've discovered the peace and serenity of sitting in a rocking chair, sharing a book, and singing songs. I know the sweetness of baby hugs.

Brendan's openness to new adventures has been invigorating. He has forced me outside my comfort zone and has enabled me to try new things and think in new ways. Now, I accept that it's okay to need or want help. I'm learning to open up and share myself with others. Thanks to the many stops and starts of our travels, I've made new and wonderful friends, including other families with children with Down syndrome that we see each month at play group. Because I want the best for my son, I'm learning to be an advocate for him. I'm becoming involved in organizations like our local Down syndrome association, and other groups that work toward a better future for all of our children.

Brendan has shown me he is in charge of his future, and that my job is to follow his lead, support him, and give him the best opportunities I can. Often, my attempts at guiding or helping Brendan are met with a firm "no." I sometimes even get a gentle toddler push that tells me, "Back off, I know the way." As a navigator, Brendan knows the importance of staying the course. His stubbornness has gotten our family through many trials and tribulations, including medical issues. When I question our path and try to influence his direction, he just digs in and stays the course. I've learned to step back and give him the lead. Even at the age of two, he has an enviable sense of self. He's confident in his ability, and projects that confidence to others. That confidence has helped us, as his parents, to trust that our family cannot only survive this trip, but will also flourish in this new land.

When I stand in the middle of the road feeling lost and knowing I must have made a wrong turn, Brendan comes to my rescue and gently sets me on the right path. He never scolds or says *I told you so,* he just corrects me with love. There are times that we think he can't do something—until he shows us he can. He loves proving us wrong. There are times we trust medical professionals more than our own hearts—until Brendan reminds us that we need to look within for answers. I'm sure there are many other ways that I have erred with Brendan, but I know he accepts my imperfection as part of the journey.

Sometimes I get tired and think I'd really like to reach the end of this experience. I feel my journey has taken too long, and has been too hard. I become overwhelmed and feel burdened with all the places yet to see, and all the things still to be learned. Then Brendan will give me a bear hug, or he might plant a wet, sloppy kiss on my cheek. He may say something as simple and sweet as "mama," or make the sign for "daddy." He might even just smile at me. It's then that I realize I'm not ready for our trip to end. I realize that there are many more great things to see and do.

And I know that with Brendan at my side, I will never regret these travels. It never fails to amaze me that even without a map, Brendan knows the way. He doesn't always pick the easiest path, but he picks the best one: the road that leads home.

Tammy lives in Yukon, Oklahoma, with her husband, Chad, and their son Brendan (2004). They received Brendan's diagnosis at birth from their pediatrician. Brendan had some significant health issues that they found more difficult to deal with than the diagnosis of Down syndrome.

16

For James
by Leilani Lucas

James Lucas

WHEN I WAS THIRTY-ONE, everything I had ever dreamed of was finally coming true. My husband, Wally, and I had just purchased our first home, a beautiful, white, single-family house at the end of a cul-de-sac with a huge backyard for our dog, Rusty. Two weeks after moving in, I found out I was pregnant. We were both excited and scared at the same time. We had been married for five years, and this would be our first child.

Wally was such a proud father-to-be. He came with me to all of my doctor appointments, and he enjoyed listening to our baby's heartbeat and seeing the ultrasound images. Wally decorated our baby's room with little airplanes and cars on the wall. My tummy was nice and round and everything seemed to be perfect. Then the Triple Screen came back, showing a high possibility of Down syndrome. We were shocked at the result and denied it could be true. This can't be, we thought to ourselves. *No one in either of our families has any children with disabilities or health problems.* We decided we weren't going to worry about it, and would simply look forward to our new arrival.

Wally was there holding my hand as they took our child from my body and brought him into this world. I couldn't stop crying with joy as I heard James's little cry. They later took James away to run some tests. When I awoke a few hours later, Wally was leaning on my bed, holding my hand. "The doctors think James has Down syndrome," he said.

I said "no" and started to cry, and I couldn't stop crying. We cried together and hugged each other. "No matter what," he said, "James is our son and we will love him."

We told our friends and family that our little boy was healthy but different. The support and compassion we received was overwhelming. We put James into early intervention and therapy programs. Wally and I both worked full time; I was on active duty in the military and he worked as a sales manager for a local car dealership. We split our household responsibilities fifty-fifty, and took turns bringing James to day care. The only problem was that we forgot to take care of each other along the way.

A month after James's first birthday, Wally walked out the door.

He said he wasn't happy anymore. We argued like most couples do, but I thought it was just a phase that would get better. He never came back home. I was angry, mad, scared, and so lonely. How was I going to manage everything by myself? How could he do this to me, and especially to our son? James needed both of us.

James and I moved to Washington, DC, and made a fresh start. I had no family there and no friends to help at first. Luckily, I had a little boy who needed me to be strong. That kept me going through the many challenges we faced together.

James's education was a top priority, and I was disappointed with the school district we moved into. The schools were housed in old, rundown buildings and were underfunded and understaffed. James's special education teacher was very sweet as well as competent, but she was overwhelmed with a large class and a lack of teacher's aides. The school environment was noisy and the staff was not providing the special services and therapies James required to fulfill his individualized education program (IEP). I would have never realized these things if I hadn't been involved in his education. I visited his school and asked questions, followed up on his schoolwork and activities, and kept in close contact with his teacher.

I found a wonderful child advocate, and with her help, we took our case to court. After numerous meetings and court appearances, and countless letters from my lawyer to the school system, we finally won our case: All independent evaluations and attorney fees would be paid by the District of Columbia Public School System, and provisions for various therapies for James would be written into his new plan. Best of all, starting in the fall, James would attend a brand new charter school designed for kids with special needs. James's willingness to learn and his ability to adjust and adapt to change gave me the courage to fight the school system.

Another battle I faced was with the childcare development center (CDC) on the military base where I live. They gave me a hard time about accepting James into their program. They had a waiting list, but normally single, active-duty members have first priority on this list. James had been at the center at our last base, and had done well there. I wanted him in a similar safe, structured environment where he could socialize with other children his age. After months of persistent inquiries, I finally had to get my First Sergeant involved. It was determined that the CDC had prejudged James because of his disability. Finally, we were offered a slot for James. The staff learned to accept him for who he is. They made modifications to their program, such as changing the staff-to-student ratio when James was in the class, and training their caregivers on how to attend to the special needs of a child with Down syndrome. This experience has not only enriched our lives, but also those of the other children and staff at the center.

Many people don't understand what it's like to be a single parent with a special needs child, as well as an active duty military member. There are so many times I wish we lived closer to family, so James could play with cousins and see grandparents and aunts and uncles. There are times I wish I had someone to talk to, someone to help me make some of the tough decisions with James, someone to help manage school, work, doctor appointments, and all the little things around the house. These are things most people who have loved ones nearby take for granted. Wally calls every week and has come to visit James, but for the most part, I'm on my own. There are times when I don't want to be the strong one. I want to cry, because I'm feeling overwhelmed and there is no one here to help. But James always inspires me to keep going. He gives me comfort when I feel alone in this great, big world. He is my light in the darkness, and I am his.

Leilani is currently serving in the United States Air Force. She is stationed in Washington, DC, and works at the Pentagon. She's been on active duty for twelve years and would like to retire at twenty years, to pursue a teaching career. She enjoys going on day trips, reading magazines and books, listening to different kinds of music, talking to family and friends on the phone, and bargain shopping. Most of all, she loves spending quality time with James (2002).

17

Nourishment
by Deborah Minner

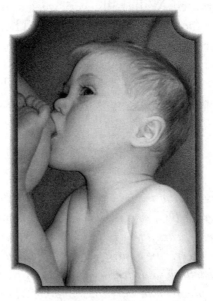

Sean Minner

"HE'S NOT BREATHING! He's not breathing!"

I opened the shower and saw my husband, Doug, holding our three-week-old son Sean, who was covered in mucus and milk and turning purple. I jumped out of the shower and began wiping off his face. I had Doug get the nasal aspirator and I used it to suction Sean's mouth and tiny nose. After a minute, he was gasping and crying. I held him close and tried to calm him down. He was breathing, but it was very ragged.

I got dressed and we took him straight to the doctor's office. The receptionist sent us in immediately. The nurse asked me to undress him and when we did, we saw that his hands and feet were purple, his body was mottled and his stomach was very distended. She rushed to get the doctor. He looked briefly at Sean, then picked him up and said, "We are taking him to the Emergency Room."

Ten minutes after we arrived at the hospital, I received the surprise of my life. The ER doctor said, "Has anyone mentioned to you that Sean has physical traits of Down syndrome?" I was stunned. The room spun. I started crying and said, "Down syndrome? What are you talking about? NO! He doesn't have Down syndrome, he just spit up really bad."

The doctor calmly and gently showed me the characteristics of Down syndrome that Sean had. He said that they would do a blood test to confirm the diagnosis, but it was highly unlikely that Sean did not have it. He gave me a handout on newborns with Down syndrome. As I read through it I saw "difficulty breastfeeding, difficulty maintaining suction resulting in milk leaking from mouth" among several other things that we had been through in the three short weeks of his life. Suddenly everything made sense to us.

Sean was eager to nurse from the moment he arrived, with a perfect latch from the beginning. He nursed and slept, nursed and slept. Everything seemed fine at first, but then things began to unravel. His glucose levels dropped rapidly, he wasn't maintaining his body temperature, he had an irregular heartbeat, and the nurse tried more than thirty times to do his hearing screen, without success. My doctor ran an EKG, took a chest x-ray, started an IV line for glucose, and called the children's hospital to ask for advice. They told him that it sounded like Sean had "early term/rapid birth" irregularities and that it should all even out within a week.

During that week, Sean was treated for jaundice and both of us were treated for thrush. He continued to latch on and breastfeed through this time, but he would tire easily during his feedings, and milk would run out the side of his mouth. I was determined to make breastfeeding work with Sean, as I had already experienced the powerful bonding it creates with my first son. For our family, breastfeeding was more than nourishment; it was an important part of our family uniting together.

My husband and mother arrived at the hospital and I broke the news to them about the doctor's suspicion of Down syndrome. Sean was admitted to the hospital so they could run the tests required for infants with Down syndrome, and to find out why he had aspirated. Over the next three days, we had mostly good news about his diagnosis. He didn't have any major health complications. His hearing was fine, his digestive system had developed properly, and he had just a small hole in his heart (ASD) that wouldn't require surgery or medication. His oxygen levels finally evened out and he was given a prescription for acid reflux medicine to help prevent future aspiration episodes.

Throughout his stay, I used the hospital breast pump to keep up my milk supply, and to express breast milk for Sean to drink in bottles. He was hooked up to so many monitors that nursing him was too difficult, and the doctors wanted to watch his intake to make sure he was getting enough food. I met with the lactation consultant after Sean was finally "wireless" so that she could watch him latch on and nurse. She was very reassuring and said words that I longed to hear, "You two are a beautiful nursing couple! You are doing everything right for him and he is going to be just fine." She said I could nurse, pump, and bottle feed for awhile, until Sean had time to grow and become stronger. My toddler had nursed through my pregnancy with Sean and I was now told this would be a big plus, because he could help maintain my milk supply better than just the pump. I so desperately needed to hear that things were going to be okay, that Sean would be able to nurse, and would grow and develop in his own time.

We went home and over the next three months, we followed the advice of the lactation consultant. There were times when I was so tired—tired of pumping, tired of trying again and again to get him to feed at the breast. I cried, I wanted to quit, I wanted someone else to be the caregiver of this child that I couldn't connect with. I kept telling myself, *one more day, I'll give it one more day. It has to get better, not only nursing, but the heartbreak too.* I loved him, he was such a sweet little newborn, and I was proud of his budding strength and personality. It just took time to grow to know him and accept the new world he introduced us to.

We reached a turning point when he was four months old. He woke in the night to eat, and instead of getting up to get a bottle ready, I decided to try to nurse him first. In his sleepy state, he managed to latch on and stay on for the full feeding. With his tummy full, I held him on my chest to burp him and give him time to digest. We drifted off to sleep together, and I knew that everything was going to be more than alright. I felt like I had found my son and he had found me.

From that night on, Sean nursed exclusively and only took bottles when he started daycare at six months old. I continued to provide expressed breast milk for him to have at daycare until he was twenty-two months old.

I would love to be a stay-at-home mom, but need the income to provide for my family. Taking the time at work every day to pump milk gives me a quiet moment to think about my son and to look forward to when I get to see him after work. It makes me feel like I am still with him, still connected to him when he isn't near me. Sean will be two soon, and he still nurses frequently when we are together. He loves to lie in bed to nurse, and often lifts his limber legs up to rest a chubby little foot on my face or breast. When he's full, he smiles up at me with those beautiful, shining, Brushfield-sparkling eyes. I'm grateful for the strength that has come to both of us through our nursing relationship. Our bond has developed not in spite of, but because of the challenges we faced together. Sean is my world, and I am so pleased to be part of his.

Deborah lives in Hutchinson, Kansas, with her husband, Doug. They were married in 2000 and have two sons, Aidan (2002), and Sean (2004). Sean was diagnosed with Down syndrome when he was three weeks old. Deborah and Doug work together with Doug's parents and brother at the family-owned insurance agency.

18

Matthew's Secret
by Katy Shapro

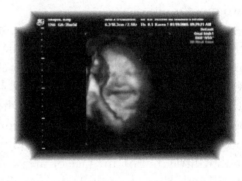

Matthew Shapro

THIS IS THE LONGEST WAIT of my life.

My son, Matthew, is on an unseen operating table, having the two holes in his heart repaired. He suffers from pulmonary hypertension, which makes this surgery an urgent matter. He is only five months old. As I sit with my husband in the waiting room, I can't stop thinking about the papers we signed the day before, acknowledging that we knew what could happen during this surgery.

The surgeon appears and reports that the surgery was successful. Anxious to see Matthew, we head for his PICU room. When we enter, I am astounded by what I see—so many people moving around him, and too many machines to count. My eyes fall on my little baby, lying naked with tubes coming out of everywhere. I am so shocked that I have to sit down. I thought I had prepared myself, by reading all I could and by watching the instructional video supplied by the hospital, but nothing could have prepared me for this sight.

This is not the first time I have been caught unprepared. My thoughts turn back to the day after Matthew was born, when the pediatrician came in my room with the results of his physical exam. This was my third child and I expected things to go just as they had before. I figured the doctor would report on how wonderful Matthew was doing. But this time was different. When he entered the room, he sat down. That seemed a little odd. Then he told me he had noticed a few markers during Matthew's exam that could indicate several different conditions. One of them was Down syndrome.

Down syndrome. I immediately froze. I could barely hear the doctor, who was sitting right by my bed, and I started to feel nauseous.

When I was able to regain my composure, the doctor described Matthew's low muscle tone, the single crease on his left palm, and the slight flatness between his eyes. He had ordered a chromosome test; it would take two weeks for the results. I was stunned. How could this be happening to me? I was twenty-eight years old. Down syndrome only happened to older women.

My pregnancy had been typical, with regular checkups, and routine tests that all came back normal. I'd had several ultrasounds, all normal. During one of these exams, we saw the most amazing view of the baby, smiling. The technician caught the image and produced a photograph for us. We couldn't take our eyes off that face, that smile. It was like he had a secret and shortly we would all be in on it.

Down syndrome. I didn't know this was Matthew's secret.

On Matthew's third day of life, the pediatrician came into my room with more upsetting news: Matthew had a heart murmur. An echocardiogram and an EKG were ordered. It had been difficult to wrap my mind around the diagnosis of Down syndrome, but this was far worse. You can live with Down syndrome; you can't live without a heart.

After many tests, it was determined that Matthew's heart problem did not pose immediate danger. We were discharged from the hospital, and went home to await the results of the chromosome test. As far as I could tell, Matthew was a typical baby. I prayed every night that this was all a mistake. But as the days passed I felt a peaceful resolve settle within me. Regardless of the test results, Matthew was my baby first. Yes, I worried and feared the unknown, but he was my son. That's what mattered.

At Matthew's two week checkup we received the test results: positive for Trisomy 21. His pediatrician could not have been more patient or kind. Still, all of our misconceptions about Down syndrome came rolling in. I always thought that Down syndrome meant he wouldn't learn the same as typical kids, or do typical things. How naïve we were! I read as much as I could and I soon discovered that as far as disabilities go, we won the lottery. Matthew will do the things typical children do, just at his own pace. He will be able to run and play with his brothers; he will be able to do whatever he chooses. My mother gave me words of wisdom that I still repeat to myself to this day. She said, "You have two typical children already. Matthew is going to be your adventure."

An adventure. I am brought back in time to the current moment in the PICU. Recovered from my initial shock, I hold Matthew's hand and speak softly to him. Watching him lying in his crib after all he has been through, I realize how much strength and courage he needs from me. He has shown amazing resilience, and I must do the same. Through the remainder of his hospital stay, which requires four weeks and three additional surgeries, his strength continues to fuel mine.

We check out of the hospital exactly one month after we checked in. Driving home, I am eager to take up life again. I am filled with hope for Matthew's future and for my own. I think again of that smiling face in the ultrasound photo. This is Matthew's real secret— that together we can face whatever our adventure has in store.

Katy and her husband, Sam, live in Myrtle Creek, Oregon, and have three sons, Peter (1997), Owen (2002), and Matthew (2005).

19

Lifting Each Other
by Anita Minor

Jason and Brittany Minor

I FOUND OUT I WAS PREGNANT in July of 2004. I was thirty-eight years old. I was excited and scared at the same time. To be honest, my first thoughts were that my husband and I would not be able to afford another child. We already had two children together, and my husband had a sixteen-year-old from a previous relationship. Then, the Tuesday after Thanksgiving, we found out that the baby had Down syndrome. Dealing with an unplanned pregnancy was hard enough, but the diagnosis made things even worse.

One of the first things I did when I found out was go on-line and look for information and pictures of children with Down syndrome. I was looking especially for African-American children, because I needed to know how Down syndrome "looked" on people with my complexion. I could barely find any! I did not see a lot of these children out and about, and I was shocked at how few of us were in print. I felt like we were the only ones in the African-American community going through this. One lady I know said I should play the lottery—to her, that's how rare it seemed for black people to have babies with Down syndrome

It was a difficult time at first. Not only did I feel alone in society, but also in my marriage. My husband in his darkest moments wanted me to terminate the pregnancy. At the time, he felt there was no way to handle the financial burden of a fourth mouth to feed, especially a child that might come with a myriad of health problems. I had contemplated the thought a few times when I first found out, but found my heart would not allow me to do it. I would not have been able to live with myself if I had.

This caused some very difficult times for us as a couple. At one point, I suggested that if he could not deal with my decision, then he could vacate the marriage. I was so angry with him, because I felt like he was forcing me to do something against my will. There were moments when I wanted to physically harm him. We spent a few days seething at one another. I cried a lot, and I think he did too. I did not want to lose my husband and I felt like I would. But as much as I loved him, I could not change my mind, no matter what the outcome was.

I soon discovered that standing firm when we both were down is what helped make the right decision for us. My husband had lifted me at times in the past. He was always the one who said everything will work out, no matter the situation. He held me together when our oldest child suffered a severe head injury at six years of age. He helped me make it through the difficulty of my mom's bypass surgery and my dad's diagnosis of Alzheimer's disease. This time, it was my turn to lift him. I just let him know how needed he was, not only by me and the kids, but especially by the new baby. I told him I understood how scary this was, and that it was okay to feel the way he did, but that we would make it through this. He is a great father, and I have to believe this baby was meant to be with us.

A diagnosis of Down syndrome can test even the strongest and most faith-filled marriages. But it can also lead to a depth of love and commitment that the couple had never experienced before. Our marriage was superglued by the addition of Jason. As soon as he was born, my husband thanked me for all of his children and has thanked me many times for Jason. My husband said his only wish is to love Jason and help him become the best person he is capable of being, and every day I watch him do just that.

Lifting each other is so important, not just within families, but within society in general. Even the briefest and smallest encounters with others can spark unbelievable moments of hope and encouragement. When Jason was six weeks old, we had a visit from Vince Schmidt, who runs the Janssen-Schmidt Tennis Academy for kids with Down syndrome. He brought along his four-year-old son Jonah, who has Down syndrome. This was the first child with Down syndrome I had ever met in person. He was beautiful and bright and friendly, and my husband and I felt so uplifted at that moment. That encounter help alleviate some of our stereotypical fears about DS.

My experiences with Jason have inspired me to start a support group in North St. Louis County. With the help of the Down Syndrome Association of Greater St. Louis and the St. Louis Christian College, I am working on organizing a play group for children with Down syndrome, and hope to eventually create a social club for adults and teens with Down syndrome. I want Jason to grow up included in the mainstream, but I also think he will benefit from group functions with others with Down syndrome, especially as he grows into adolescence.

Our family is living proof of the strength that comes through lifting each other, and this same strength can be found in communities if we come together to help each other. Making this journey alone can be very discouraging. Having people to turn to who truly can relate to your situation can lift you to a mountaintop of possibilities and hopes.

Anita and her husband, Winfred, live in Missouri with their children, Brandon (1994), Brittany (1997), and Jason (2005). Anita works as a clinical research coordinator at Washington University School of Medicine, and spends her spare time taking Britt and Brandon to their sports activities. To relax, she loves to go with Brandon to the batting cages. They love all sports and hope Jason will be a standout at the Special Olympics. Albert Pujols is their favorite athlete.

20

The School of Life
by Ann Bremer

John Bremer

IMAGINE A CHILD AS the dean of a college. It sounds funny, but that's exactly what my son is. When my son was born with Down syndrome, it felt as though someone had enrolled me in college: The School of Life. I didn't want to be in school, but my son was in charge. He knew exactly what I needed to learn.

The first class I took was Expectations 101. This class taught me that there are no guarantees in life. It included information about mourning the loss of something you never had and crying harder than you've ever cried. I learned how to host a first rate pity party with only one guest: me. I gave a great speech titled, "This Kind of Thing Only Happens to Other People."

That first class was quickly followed by others. Appearances 101 covered everything I needed to know about what a typical family looks like. After much study it seemed apparent that I was no longer the mother of a typical family. I then tackled the many assumptions I held about families of kids with special needs: The parents were patient and compassionate. They were advocates. They were saints. By the end of the course I came to the conclusion that many of my assumptions were incorrect, my lack of sainthood being the obvious indicator.

Health 105: Since children born with Down syndrome are more likely to have special health concerns, I learned about the many medical problems my son could have. I studied diagrams of the human heart. I made mental notes about the symptoms of leukemia. I learned what an otolaryngologist is and how to spell "ophthalmologist." There was a long chapter on genetics and reproduction.

When I felt overwhelmed by the number of credits I was expected to carry, I discovered a large community of people who were also attending The School of Life. I signed myself up for Support 104 and realized there were other new students struggling with their coursework just as I was. But there were many more who had already completed the classes I was taking, so I went to them with questions. Each and every one of them understood completely the difficulty I was having, and each assured me I would pass my courses with excellent grades. They also said my son was the best teacher I could have. I looked at the tiny baby in my arms and doubted that this could be true.

Acronyms 201: This class covered the many new acronyms I would need to know: ASD, VSD, PFO, GI, ENT, EI, PT, ST, OT, IEP, IIIP, ASL, PECS, SMO and AFO.

Advocacy 203: When I first saw the title of this class I assumed it would require rousing speeches, fist pounding, and the making of demands on my son's behalf. It all seemed very intimidating. What I learned, however, was that advocacy could mean something as small as taking my son to the mall and letting him be a baby as unremarkable as any of the other babies in their strollers on a quiet weekday morning. The coursework did get more difficult and included lessons on how to speak intelligently to medical professionals and service providers. The amazing thing about this class was that I was continually motivated to do my best by one simple thing—love.

Dealing with the Uninformed, or How and When to Educate Jerks 301: Thankfully this class was brief and only occasionally do I need to use what I learned. It taught me how to evaluate the asker of insensitive questions to determine the usefulness of explanation. I learned when to simply nod and smile and when to gently correct. This course also had a useful section titled, "Hold Your Anger Knowing that Life Will Deal with the Extremely Insensitive." It's a fact that The School of Life has many students who were once jerks. They struggle with their coursework, but ultimately become some of the best students because they must work harder than most.

Milestones 303: In this class I learned that milestones are simply markers on the road and that the goal is to reach the milestones, not to reach them faster than anyone else. Topics covered included how to help your child achieve milestones, patience, and how to properly celebrate when a milestone is reached. Included with the textbook was a package of party hats and noisemakers.

When my son was two and a half years old, he decided it was time for me to get my master's degree. Although I didn't feel I was finished with my undergraduate work, he knew that an advanced degree would solidify what I had already learned. My son, whose symptoms stumped several doctors, finally got the blood test he needed at my recommendation because I had taken such good notes about the symptoms of leukemia in Health 201. He was diagnosed with acute lymphoblastic leukemia. I felt sorry for the parents I met of typical kids with cancer because they hadn't completed any preliminary coursework. Their entrance into The School of Life was far more traumatic than mine had been.

My first two classes were Chemotherapy 501 and Bald is Beautiful 505. But the most important class I took in this phase of my education was Life and Death 503. It included information about suffering, accepting the possibility of death, and understanding that death is a part of life. There was a chapter in the textbook titled, "God's a Big Guy, He Can Handle Your Anger," and another titled, "Even if You Live to be Ninety-Five, Life is Short."

I am now in the process of writing my master's thesis. I'm told, however, that this won't be the end of my education. As my son grows I will be required to take continuing education credits. Some of these workshops will be difficult, but I don't fear the coursework like I once did. I now embrace what I was once afraid of. I even tutor new students. With gentle reassurance, I am able to guide students baffled by The School of Life. It gives me great satisfaction to pass along what I've learned.

I would never have chosen to attend The School of Life, but that's where I've learned some of the most important things a person can hope to learn. I was taken to my first class kicking and screaming and now wonder why. Why would a person not want to have a bigger heart, to love unconditionally and with abandon, to be a better parent, to see all people as having equal value?

What a small person I was before this little child came into my life.

Ann Bremer is a stay-at-home mom in a suburb of Minneapolis. She has been married to her husband, Tim, since 1993. Her son John (2002) is the fourth of five children. John was diagnosed with Down syndrome shortly after his birth. Today he is a happy, healthy, singing, dancing, walking, joyful teacher of all that's important in life.

21

Fight the Good Fight
by Joanne M. Crouse

Madison Crouse

I CAN STILL REMEMBER the tears, the sadness, the grief of my husband's words to me in the recovery room, after the birth of our daughter, Madison. His voice was barely audible as he said, "Down syndrome," and then he slumped across my chest as I lay on the hospital bed. It was just after midnight, August 23, 1988.

Scared and trying to understand what was happening to her—to us—my mind spun with confusion. I thought she was dying. I was only twenty-three years old. I had no idea what Down syndrome meant. When the doctor told us she was "mentally retarded," my worst fear was that her brain actually hurt.

The doctor wanted to keep Madison hospitalized for ten days, with the hope that we wouldn't want her and she could be given to one of many people on a waiting list. Sold, actually—for $30,000. All I knew was I needed to take her home—*immediately!* And I did.

That was the first occasion of many in which Madison inspired me to fight for what was good and right. The next came soon afterward. We ran into trouble with our health insurance company: they denied Madison coverage because of her diagnosis. When we applied for state medical aid, they denied coverage because Madison's condition wasn't severe enough. I fought the system for four years, insisting that Madison be entitled to the health care she needed and deserved. Finally, I won my battle with SSDI (Social Security Disability Insurance). I cried when I received the letter in the mail saying Madison was covered.

"Why are you crying?" my husband asked.

I replied, "Because now I know that we won't be turned away when Madison needs treatment. I know we won't go bankrupt because of medical bills. And I can die knowing she can go to the hospital when she is sick."

Madison's very existence gave me a reason to push forward with determination when things were difficult. And as I moved forward, I found that there were people on the path to guide me and strengthen me.

When Madison turned three, I went to sign her up at a Head Start preschool program and was told the classes were all full. I was blessed to have a terrific early intervention teacher from the regional center who marched me back into the Head Start office the next day and laid down the law—literally.

By age five, Madison was ready for kindergarten. With the recommendation of a young teacher who believed in her abilities, I met with the principal of the neighborhood school and enrolled her in a regular class. On the first day of school, Madi got to ride the "big bus" with everyone else.

The following day, the bus driver pulled up to the bus stop, hopped off the bus, and pushed her way through the crowd to where the mothers of the school children were gathered. I was waiting there with my toddler on my hip, my first grader at my side, and Madison holding my hand. The bus driver took out a piece of chalk, drew a big square on the sidewalk, and wrote "MADISON" in the center of the square. She then announced to all the parents and children waiting there, "No one can board the bus until Madison is standing in the square!"

It was one of my most humiliating moments. I told my oldest daughter to go on to school, and I walked Madison home, crying all the way. I had so many thoughts racing through my head. Would the neighbors be mad at me for holding up the bus, for making their children late for school? Would they be upset with me for trying to integrate Madison into a regular class with their children? My mind was reeling—what was everyone thinking? What was I thinking? I didn't even know anymore. I had lost control of my emotions. Just when the helplessness of the morning was sinking in, my doorbell rang and I could hear one of my neighbors telling me to open the door.

When I finally did, I saw not just one neighbor, but all of the neighbors from the bus stop. Each one of them had called the school district and the transportation department to complain about the bus driver. They weren't there to fight me, they were there to show me that they were fighting for me, and with me, for Madison. They urged me not to give up. They reminded me to be the squeaky wheel, to keep pushing on.

The person who has inspired me and helped me the most is Madison herself. As I have watched her, she has showed me how to fight the good fight, and be happy while doing it. I have watched Madison in the hospital fighting to take a single breath because her lungs weren't developed enough to battle the pneumonia, asthma, and stridor. I have watched her be handled by a myriad of doctors and nurses, and be subjected to countless tests and treatments, yet remain cooperative and friendly. I have watched her playing with the light switch on the wall, flicking it up and down to make the light go on and off—little things the books all said she wouldn't do. I have watched her sit outside in the cool breeze, alone, enjoying the simple things around her. I have watched her watch other people, smiling to herself.

I've heard dozens of times that children with Down syndrome are weak. They have weak muscle tone, we're told. There are many things they won't do, shouldn't do, can't do. But Madison has never been weak. She lives her life with dignity, grace, and strength. And with her help, I am learning to do the same.

Joanne lives in Elizabeth, Indiana, with her husband, Richard. They have been married for twenty years. Richard has two adult children from a previous marriage, Dylan (1975) and Amberly (1978). Richard and Joanne's children are Lindsay (1987), Madison (1988), and Rachelle (1991). Joanne opened their home to special needs day care when Madison was younger. She advocates for other parents and the family volunteers with Special Olympics. Joanne had a poem about Madison published in Challenging Voices, a book by Cheryl Gerson Tuttle, M.ED.

22

The Dream
by Rosemarie Aiello-Gertz

Jack Henry and Madeline Aiello-Kimberlain

I'D NEVER HAD A DREAM like it before, and I've never had one like it since.

It began with a visit to my college roommate's house. Immediately upon entering the house I see this little peanut of a boy. I can't tell you what his face looked like. Strange that the dream was so vivid, yet his visage was not. Though no one told me, I knew that his name was Henry. Henry was an amazing baby because he could already walk and talk. I looked at him and thought, *Oh, what an adorable little boy!* I just wanted to pick him up and hug him and dance him around the room. But I was a stranger to Henry, so instead I bent all the way down to him and spoke to him in my most friendly talking-to-a-small-child voice. "And who do *you* belong to?" I asked.

He replied, "I belong to YOU!" Then he stretched his little pudgy arms up to me and said, "Mama." My heart exploded with surprise and the purest joy I have ever known. I was so overcome that I woke up.

That dream was an incredible gift. At that time I was a single mom, in a relationship that couldn't last and shouldn't last, and I was pregnant with a baby that was to be less than perfect, a baby that I knew would have a damaged heart, and might have more problems as well. After the dream, I knew that Henry was my baby and his message to me was that he would be fine. In fact, he would be more than fine—he would be wonderful. He would amaze me, and he would bring me so much joy that my heart and soul would overflow. I felt safe then. I was no longer worried about my baby's survival. I was no longer worried about how I would manage things when this relationship ended. For the first time, in a long time, I looked toward the future with hope.

On February 24, 2002, Jack Henry was born. Jack's dad did not want to call him Henry for fear that he would forever more be referred to as Hank (though I wouldn't have minded). So I settled for Henry in the middle.

We had been warned that Jack Henry had a quartet of problems with his heart; we were now informed that there were other challenges ahead for him as well. Jack had Down syndrome and a bowel problem that infrequently accompanies it, duodenal stenosis. I wondered how that could be. The dream had seemed so real. He was supposed to be fine; he was supposed to be protected. Doubt set in, and I worried that Jack was not safe, that he would die. "I belong to you!" he had said to me. I held onto that message all through that day, and all through the next as he underwent his bowel surgery.

After a successful operation and a five-week recovery, Jack was finally able to come home. Then, even the shortest crying spell was terrifying, as it could deprive him of oxygen and turn him blue. Fortunately, Jack was a happy and patient baby. When he did cry, his four-year-old sister Madeline would sing him her sweet songs, which would soothe and quiet him. We had painted his bedroom a calming blue and softened it with white puffy clouds, and in this peace and comfort, Jack thrived. But every night before I went to sleep, I worried that his heart would not last until he was old enough to have it repaired. My fear would lift as I remembered the dream. *He will be fine, he will be more than fine, he will be wonderful and he will fill my heart with joy,* I would repeat to myself. Then I could sleep.

When Jack was four months old, his heart could no longer wait. But he was ready; the surgeon could attempt the full repair. For the first few hours of the surgery I reminded myself of the dream and then, exhausted, I slept until I was notified that the procedure was complete. He was breathing on his own again; his heart had restarted.

Ten days later, he returned home. The operations had taken their toll; it was as if he was a newborn again, unable to even lift his head. But he had energy in him that was not there before. With his heart repaired he was suddenly pushing himself to achieve with amazing determination. He made quick gains in every area and was soon rolling over and sitting.

Still, I worried. Although his heart operation was successful, his heart was not fine. In the future, his valves would not be able to support his growth. In ten years, he would need another major heart operation; in twenty, he would need another. Doubt set in, and I worried that Jack was not safe after all, that he would die. I started to wonder if my dream was just my own wishful thinking. My fear of the future felt so heavy. How could I go on living this way?

When Jack was eight months old, I received my answer. As I looked over at him sitting in his bouncy chair, he lifted his arms up to me for the first time, and for the first time he uttered, "Mama." *Whoosh!* The reality of my dream came rushing back to me, and I was again flooded with surprise and joy. He is the child from my dream. He is fine. Yes, he is more than fine—he is wonderful, and my heart is filled by this little peanut of a boy who I love so completely. And this time I was no stranger. I picked him up and hugged him tight, and danced him around the room.

*Rosemarie, a single mother of two, married David, a single father of
two, in 2005. They live with their four children in Racine, Wisconsin.
Rosemarie's youngest, Jack Henry (2002), was suspected to have Trisomy
21 prior to birth after a congenital heart defect (Tetralogy of Fallot) was
discovered. The diagnosis was confirmed after birth. Rosemarie works
in information technology as a business and process analyst. Her family's
interests include soccer, American Sign Language, and music.*

23

We Are Not Alone
by Michelle Adams

Matthew Adams

MY HUSBAND AND I stood on the threshold of the doorway looking into the room. It was bright inside and we could hear the sounds
of adults chatting and kids laughing. The smell of fresh-baked cook-
ies on the snack table drifted over to us. We stepped out of the cool
night and into the warmth of the room, another step further into our
new journey.

It was a journey that had started four months earlier when, in
the sixteenth week of my pregnancy with our second child, a simple
blood test had quickly been followed by a sonogram, a weekend of

tears, an amniocentesis, and a diagnosis. We were having a boy and he would have Down syndrome. We had come away with the disconcerting feeling that the professionals we had dealt with were expecting us to terminate our pregnancy. We had many discussions, wondering if we could raise this child, wondering what this might do to our family. We loved him already, but what could we expect? We had never felt so alone. Everyone we told wasn't quite sure what to say to us. No one really knew anything about Down syndrome, only vague things like "they are always happy." There were lots of tears shed from family and friends alike. Everyone was supportive and wanted to help somehow, but had no idea what to do for us.

We found ourselves wanting to tell people about the diagnosis and talk about our feelings, but it was so hard to know when to tell someone and when to just let it be. There was no one that understood what we were going through, no one to tell us what we could expect. I spent many hours poring over books from the library and searching the Internet for information. I found myself in a state of information overload—there was just too much information out there, and a lot of it felt so very negative. This list of things that could go wrong—would any of them happen to Matthew? Was this the way it would really be? A lot of the books were written a long time ago; how much had changed since then?

Our search for understanding is what brought us to this bright, warm room full of lively people. It was a meeting held at the public school offices for a group of parents of children with Down syndrome. The leader was Gina, the mother of a teenager with Down syndrome. When her son was born, she had seen a need in the area for a parent support group and decided to begin one. Her group had grown and grown since then. That night, we were a month away from Matthew's due date. We were so up and down about this pending event, and eager to be with others who knew how we felt.

Gina gave us a warm welcome and introduced us to the other families (so very many families!) that were chatting in little groups. We were hugged and congratulated. Looking around, I saw two sets of parents with very young babies, and many other parents with kids of all ages, ranging from several months old to teenagers. It was so nice to see the children with Down syndrome interacting with each other and their siblings in all the typical ways. We watched the families and saw the normalcy and love that was there. As the meeting started, we sat in a large circle and went around the room with introductions. It was wonderful to finally be with people who understood what we were going through and could help answer some of our questions. Most of all, simply observing what things were like for a family with a child with Down syndrome was so reassuring. We went home armed with a better understanding of what raising our child might be like. We began to realize that everything would be okay.

Matthew arrived one week later, and in a hurry. He had problems breathing at first, which landed him in the NICU for three days. We surprised the hospital staff a little by being adjusted to the fact that he had Down syndrome. We were also blessed to meet a couple in the NICU whose daughter, Josie, was two days older than Matthew. The Down syndrome had been a surprise for them and it was wonderful to be able to meet them with congrats and hugs, like we had been shown.

When we brought Matthew home later that week, we were still struggling with the issue of introducing Matthew to others. Would people be able to "tell"? Should we offer an explanation of his diagnosis? Our uncertainty wasn't helped any by the very large bump that Matthew had on his head. It was basically a bruise that had been present since birth, but it made our baby even more conspicuous. We found ourselves running into friends we hadn't seen in awhile and feeling awkward as we tried to explain. Once again, our friends weren't quite sure what to say. So it was a relief to arrive at the next meeting of the parent group with Matthew in tow. Everyone "knew" and was so glad to meet him. He was quickly scooped up, cooed over, and passed around to anyone who wanted to hold him. It was so nice to be welcomed without question and be hugged and congratulated without reserve.

Fast forward four years: We no longer wonder if people can "tell" (it just doesn't matter to us anymore) and are even surprised when someone recognizes the fact that Matthew has Down syndrome. We are blessed to now have two parent groups for Down syndrome in our area that have monthly playgroups, informative meetings, Easter egg hunts, Christmas parties, and annual Buddy Walks. The connections we have formed with other families are priceless. They are there for us when we need help with any of Matthew's meetings for his therapies and schooling, or if we need help with any advocacy. They are there to explain certain terms to us when we don't understand them. Often, at least one other family has been through any procedure or condition that we encounter. We don't feel alone anymore.

Every year in sunny, warm October at the Buddy Walk, we meet up with the couple that we had met in the NICU at Matthew's birth. We really enjoy catching up with each other and seeing Matthew and Josie together. Each time we see them, I love to take a photo of the two birthday buddies together and see how they've grown. Not only does my son have lifelong friends, but my husband and I do, too.

Michelle and her husband, Michael, live in Arizona with their children, Ryan (1997), and Matthew (2003). Michael works at the local airport doing line maintenance for a major airline. Michelle is a stay-at-home mom. She helps out in their boys' classrooms as much as possible, and is an avid digital scrap booker.

24

Where There's a Will, There's a Way
by Kelly Anderson

Will Anderson

I WAS AWAITING THE BIRTH of my fourth perfect child—emphasis on *perfect,* because my life was indeed perfect. Three beautiful children, a caring husband, a nice house, a stylish nursery, and a new son on the way. The whole spotless picture. There was no room for flaws in my life.

The delivery was routine. Happy banter from the medical staff. A painless delivery (my first epidural—wow, what a difference). It was all wonderful.

But soon after the birth, the banter stopped and things became hushed and businesslike. Will was presented to me all wrapped up origami-style in hospital blankets. And right away, I knew

Will's eyes. His slightly slanted, almond-shaped eyes told me a tale of a thousand words. Instantly, a pall was cast over a time that was supposed to be loving, quiet, bonding. My husband wouldn't believe the words I whispered to him.

Did I mention that my life was perfect? *Was.*

I grew up a quarter mile from a school and residence for mentally retarded children. As I held my minutes-old son, images of those polyester-clad, drooling children filled my mind and heart. They had been taken out of society and placed in that institution and there they simply existed, with all their odd behaviors. Those kids had scared me.

My life is over, I thought. If things couldn't be perfect, it was not worth the struggle. I wanted it to be over.

The next morning I visited Will, sleeping in an isolette in the special care nursery. I noticed an older gentleman with mannerisms that suggested a military background making rounds with a few residents. After being handed a chart, he boldly called across the room, "William? Where's William?" I raised my hand meekly at the same time the nurses directed him toward us. As he strode over he stated, loud enough for us all to hear, "Where there's a will, there's a way!"

I remember those words so clearly, but they were hard to actually believe. How could a positive outlook change the baby sleeping beside me? He had Down syndrome! I was still in shock. I still hadn't caught my breath. I had lost my will, and felt like there was no way.

The idea of telling the rest of the kids was something we dreaded. How much should we say? Were they old enough to understand? We told them about Will and what little we knew about Down syndrome, as simply and plainly as we could. My daughter started to cry when I said Will might look a little different. I showed her a picture of a little girl with Down syndrome on the Internet. "But she doesn't look any different," my daughter exclaimed.

When we brought Will home, my children greeted him with six open arms, all wanting to be the first to hold him. I realized they were seeing their brother—that's all. Their beautiful brother. But I was still unsure of who he was. When I looked at him I saw a diagnosis with all the misconceptions that were attached to it. I didn't take the time to inhale his new baby smell and to let my cheek run across the softness of his silky hair.

Within a few days, the shock of the diagnosis wore off, and I felt like I could breathe again. I started to regain my senses, and began actually thinking about getting a handle on this situation. And then, one bright, sunny morning, I woke up feeling more lighthearted than I had since Will was born.

The sunlight of that day seeped deeply into me, allowing me to see the reality of my life and my son. Somehow, all those terrible childhood images disappeared. Somehow, I managed to shed the preconceptions that society had burdened me with. I could see the truth. When I looked at Will I saw my son—that's all. My beautiful son.

From that point on, when I looked back at my life before Will arrived, I saw it much differently. I had thought my life was unique and amazing. But now, I realize how bland my life had been, as if shaped by a cookie cutter—a predictable family doing predictable things. And I had gone along with it, just as everyone had wanted me to. I'd been blind to the wonder that surrounds us, the glorious, everyday miracles that most of us pay no heed to, the precious people we have no time for. How self-centered our whole existence can be—unless we have a teacher. Will is mine.

My three older children have been affected by Will in such positive ways. They love to accompany Will to his preschool to meet the other kids in his class, many of whom also have developmental disabilities. They are not afraid of people who are different. My daughter's teacher took me aside one day to tell me what a wonderfully caring and sensitive person my daughter is. Even in the presence of his friends, my oldest son makes time to hug and play with Will, not caring if he looks "cool." I could never, as a parent, instill in them the qualities that Will has. But because of their brother's influence, they are becoming amazing human beings.

As for me, I know I am not "special," despite what many people say. I have often been told that God picked me to be Will's mother because of some extraordinary abilities I must have. I know these people mean well, but their words irk me a little, because I know that I am the same as everyone else; I think that if I was "chosen," it must have been because I needed to be fixed.

Will has taught me that I possess gifts that I never knew were there. He has shown me how deeply I can love and has revealed a part of me that can delight and marvel at even the smallest things. If I could give a message to a mother with a prenatal diagnosis, I would say this: You are greater than you could ever imagine. Your child is waiting to give you a very precious gift: The gift of yourself.

Will is now two years old. Our days are more joy-filled than ever, for every person in our house. And along we go now, down the road of our lives, bumps and all. We now travel equipped with the knowledge that within each of us there is greatness. We are greater than society will allow us to believe. We are aware that there may be different types of challenges to face, but we will be all the better for it. Traveling down our own road, not the one everyone else wants us to travel. Together.

And Will is showing us the way.

Kelly lives in Hudson, Ohio, with her husband, Mark, and their four children. She is a stay-at-home mother and an avid gardener, and she enjoys reading.

25

Emma Sage
by Tara Marie Hintz

Emma Sage Hintz

I CELEBRATED MY PREGNANCY with Emma Sage just as I did each of my previous pregnancies. I shared my joy with everyone, even though there was a possibility that our child had Down syndrome. It just didn't matter to me. There would be no blueprint—our baby proved that from the moment of her conception. Her determination tossed all of our birth plans aside, as she came quietly into my arms, in our own home. Her birth was pure bliss, and I felt so powerful, as a mother, a midwife, and the first to realize that she did, in fact, have Down syndrome.

Emma. *One who heals.*
Sage. *One with great wisdom.*

She met her best friend, Claudia, when they were both just sixteen months old. They were inseparable from the start. As they've grown older, they have learned many things about one another, many ways to work together to accomplish their goals. And they have found great comfort in each other's presence.

When Claudia struggled to write her name, Emma Sage led her by example, showing her just how easy it was to do. She believed in Claudia's ability to be successful and she was persistent in helping her get the job done. Emma Sage's dedication to her friend's success played a huge role in Claudia's achievement, and they were both so proud.

The roles switched when the girls went outside to play on the trampoline. Emma Sage, who is much smaller than Claudia, needs help to climb up so that they can bounce together. They've developed a routine to accomplish this, with Claudia climbing up first, then lying down on her stomach and reaching over to Emma Sage. They tightly clasp hands as Claudia gives Emma Sage just enough assistance to get her where they both want to be—up high, jumping!

Their bond of friendship shows in their ability to communicate with each other. It can take some effort for strangers to decipher Emma Sage's speech, but Claudia always understands what she is saying. Sometimes Claudia will even act as a translator, conveying messages from Emma Sage to another child or adult so that she is fully understood. Emma Sage always has a big smile on her face as if to say, "See, Claudia knows what I am saying, why don't you?"

The two have been taking dance lessons since they were three. From the start, they would practice their dance routine together every day, each helping the other to make sure their positioning and movements were correct. They danced and twirled and were more than ready for their first dance recital. The day of the dance recital, Claudia was stricken with stage fright. Emma Sage went over to Claudia and hugged her and told her to do "Chi," a relaxation exercise. Together, the two of them drew their hands up to their chin and breathed in deeply and released, allowing their arms to relax. The calming effect gave Claudia the nerve to move out of the wings. Once on stage, their friendship shone as brightly as the spotlights. I watched them smiling at each other and directing each other through the performance. When it came time to take a bow, Emma Sage and Claudia stood arm-in-arm before the cheering crowd.

As I watch this friendship blossom, I see a living treasure, a gift that builds and grows as the days roll forward. It is proof of the power of give-and-take. It is a celebration of each child and the beauty that is created when these gifts are shared. There is a slight difference in their genetic makeup, but that does not hinder their relationship. Instead, their strengths and weaknesses are bridged when they are together. They are unstoppable.

Imagine how the world would change if more of us embraced such partnerships. If we understood the power of give-and-take, and believed that beautiful things are created when different gifts are brought together. If we would come together as human beings, bridging our strengths and weaknesses, united in simple friendship.

I caught a glimpse of this possibility during a recent trip to the grocery store. As we traveled through the aisles picking up the things we needed, Emma Sage began singing her favorite tune. "The sun'll come out, tomorrow..." she belted out, full of brightness and cheer. Within moments, our eyes met those of a man and his daughter. We exchanged smiles, and they began to sing along. In the next aisle, we met an older man who joined us, singing with great gusto. By the time we arrived at the cash registers, my daughter's lovely song had taken hold. Cashiers, customers—all of us sang aloud, "Tomorrow, tomorrow, I love ya, tomorrow..." As I walked out of the store, I felt unstoppable.

Emma Sage. One with great wisdom; one who heals.

Tara Marie Hintz lives near Califon, New Jersey, and shares her life with her husband, Rick, and their four children, Katrina (1989), Greta (1991), Otto (1996), and Emma Sage (2001). A former media relations director, Tara Marie is celebrating the gift of motherhood and works from home. She is a board member of the ARC Foundation of Hunterdon County and the Down Syndrome Group of Northwest New Jersey.

THE GIFT OF DELIGHT

26

Surprise!
by Cynthia Yunke

Noah and Chris Yunke

I'M WASHING DISHES AND having a very difficult time, breaking glasses, knocking things over, stabbing myself with the knives. I think I have the flu. I'm coughing heavily, sniffling, aching, and *SO* tired.

My adult daughter Dana comments, "Mom, you look pitiful."

I give her a sarcastic, "Thank you very much," and say, "You know, if I didn't know better, I would swear I'm pregnant. I feel like crap, I'm clumsy, I can't concentrate, and I feel like throwing up."

Dana looks at me and says, "You're pregnant! Let's go buy a test!"

After much arguing and debate she calls her sister Nikki and says, "We are on our way over to take a pregnancy test for MOM!"

Understand the significance of this statement. I am thirty-six years old and have five children; the youngest is ten. I had become a mother at sixteen and a grandma at thirty-four.

When we get to Nikki's, I disappear into the bathroom with the test. Pee in a cup, dip the stick for five seconds. Put the cap on, lay it flat on the counter. Seconds later, there it is—the double blue line that means I'm expecting a baby.

I go back to the living room to wait the full five minutes, just to make sure. When the timer goes off I am afraid to move. My daughters run into the bathroom, followed by my twenty-month-old granddaughter Felicia. After hearing some whispering, Felicia toddles out and looks at me and says, "Gramma...baby!"

I almost pass out, at first, but within seconds, I'm so excited I can barely talk.

What a surprise!

Fast forward to March. I get a phone call from my OB's partner saying that my Triple Screen came back "grossly abnormal" for Down syndrome. She "strongly urges" me to have an amniocentesis. The nurse explains what the Triple Screen looks for and how it is calculated, and assures me it is probably a false positive—she has seen them many times before. I find out my chances are one in five. I'm a nervous wreck.

Two weeks later, we enter the room for the level II ultrasound and amniocentesis. The tech asks if we want to know the sex of the baby, and if we have a preference. I say we'd hoped to have a girl, but with the scare we'd been given we would take any baby—just let it be healthy. She says, "Good! There is his little nubbin!"

Then my doctor comes in to take a look. She is uncharacteristically quiet. She finishes her exam and sends in the perinatologist. When he comes in, he shows us that our son has a thickened nuchal fold, a cyst in his brain, a dilated kidney, and shortened femurs. We proceeded with the amnio, to confirm the results of the ultrasound before we told others, and so we could better prepare ourselves.

Another two weeks pass, and I get the call that the amnio is positive for Trisomy 21.

"What are you going to do?" the doctor asks.

"We're continuing the pregnancy," I say.

She mutters something about getting back to me in a few days because, "I don't think it is registering with you what I have just told you."

What a surprise.

I hang up. My three sons are staring at me. Ten-year-old Christopher is at my right side, sixteen-year-old Michael is in front of me, and fourteen-year-old Wally is watching me from across the room. I completely lose it. I cry and rant and rave, which scares my boys, at first. Then, Mike grabs me and holds me, rocking me and saying it would be alright. What a kid.

"Go take a nice hot bubble bath and relax," he orders.

I numbly do as he says. When my husband, Chris, walks in the door, I run into his arms, crying. He looks at me and says, "Cindy, what's wrong? We knew this could be true. Why are you reacting this way?"

His words are like cold water on me, waking me up. I realize he is right. I'm only crying for me. I'm wondering if my son will walk and talk and live a long life. And what about a meaningful life? I realize how little I actually know about Down syndrome. I decide to get educated—fast.

I learn that my son will indeed walk and talk and live a long life (outdated information put life spans of children with Down syndrome at about fifteen years, but today, it is closer to sixty). And meaningful? He already means more to me than I could ever put into words. I know I could not, should not, and would not try to place a value on this child based on his potential. I love him so very much, and want him with all my heart. His life already has meaning.

From that point on, I feel calmer. Although every morning for a week, I wake up thinking, "Please let that be a dream." When I remember that it is all real, I think, *Why me?* But then I quickly answer myself, *Why not me?* My sister-in-law's daughter once said, "If anyone should have a baby with special needs, it's Aunt Cindy."

I wasn't convinced this was true. "Should" anybody have a special needs baby, I wondered?

Whatever I think about it, it's happening, and I am ready for it. I'm glad I have the results to prepare myself and my family. We can do all our worrying and wondering and "getting over it" while the baby is kicking up a storm, safe in my belly.

Our family rallies around us and supports us in many ways. Since there were four in the family pregnant, we discussed baby names many times. Although we had made it known that we were naming our child Matthew Joseph (Matthew meaning, "Gift from God" as this is what our child was, and Joseph meaning, "to add a son"), we were surprised and hurt when our niece and nephew elected to name their son Mathew. We decided to name our son Noah Matthew Joseph, Noah meaning "restful" or "peaceful". It is family tradition to have two middle names so this helped ease the sting.

On the hottest, most miserable night of the summer, after a beautiful meal out with my husband, I go to our room and close the door. I strip down to my underwear and lie on the bed with a fan aimed at my aching, hot, tired body. I watch in amazement as Noah moves under the skin of my belly. A foot here, a shoulder there. I caress his form and sing him the songs that I have been singing to him since week fifteen of my pregnancy. Then I tell him how much I love him, and how I can't wait to hold him, and see his precious face, and nurse him.

POP! Just a small hint of a sound really, but it brings with it fluid. Lots of fluid. My water has broken at thirty-one weeks, six days. Boy, talk about Noah and the flood. It was the right name for him after all!

Hold on! I didn't mean I wanted to see you right away! I think. So Noah agrees to wait a bit longer, and a bit longer, and even longer. I am on hospital bed-rest for three weeks. Chris attends my baby shower in my place, and I get to see pictures of him wearing one of my favorite maternity tees.

So it goes until August 10, at 3:42 p.m., just a few weeks before our twentieth wedding anniversary, when we finally get to see our little Noah, weighing five pounds even and squalling his little head off. The most beautiful surprise I have ever seen.

Cynthia and Chris Yunke live in Roseville, Michigan, and are the parents of Nikki (1981), Dana (1982), Michael (1985), Wally (1986), Christopher (1990), Noah (2001), and Simon (2004). Noah is the proud uncle to Felicia (1999), and twins, Adriana and Ariana (2001).

27

Light the Way
by Alicia Culp

Kayla Culp

I FOLLOW THE LAST BUBBLE with my eye as the warm summer night's breeze blows it lazily beyond the trees. Kayla sits on Daddy's lap, kicking frantically for more. I'm blowing bubbles as fast as I can, trying to turn our backyard into a magic land for our baby. She loves the bubbles; she clasps her hands tightly together in anticipation. I catch one with the wand, holding it out for Kayla to pop it with her soft, pudgy fingers. The last of today's sun rays shine brightly through the big bubble, making it a spectacle of brilliant colors. Kayla's eyes grow wide with wonder as she pops it. Watching her, I wonder how we ever lived without her.

It was evident early on that Kayla was supposed to be here, to join and complete our family. In 2004, my husband and I had three teenagers, with no energy or plans to expand our family. In fact for many years, the idea of starting over and raising another child, after we were almost at the "finish line" with our other children, was a comical subject for us. But gradually, in the year prior to becoming pregnant with Kayla, my heart began to shift.

We hadn't really decided to attempt a pregnancy; we'd only discussed it a few times. Nevertheless, sixteen years after the birth of my youngest child, I became pregnant again. We were shocked and elated. Our teenagers were a little "grossed out" at first; I don't think they cared to think about how I got this way. Sadly, though, at eleven weeks' gestation, I miscarried. My husband and I were devastated and realized how badly we wanted another child. We decided to try again and I got pregnant immediately.

When the doctor held Kayla up for the first time, I knew there was something different about her. I saw the nurse whisper to the doctor and eventually, their suspicions were relayed to us: Down syndrome, with a possibility of a heart defect that could be life threatening. Kayla was quickly transported to a different hospital for testing. Those were our darkest hours. I felt so empty. There were no more kicks to feel inside me and no baby in my arms. I felt so helpless, because I couldn't protect her, or at least ease her fears when she went through whatever she might have to endure. I'd even coached my husband before the birth to stay with Kayla when she was being cleaned up, so she would always hear one of our voices. Having her taken away completely was beyond heartbreaking. I wanted so badly to run after her and hold her hand, let her know Mommy was here, but the epidural hadn't worn off; I wasn't even able to walk yet. My husband and I just hugged each other, cried, and prayed.

We were initially told Kayla would be admitted to another hospital. Amazingly, a few hours later the cardiologist called us and told us that Kayla only had a small hole in her heart that would likely close on its own. She would be coming back to us within the hour.

We were so relieved; we looked at each other and thought, *Okay, now all we have to deal with is Down syndrome—no problem.*

But that was easier said than done. I was terrified. I didn't think I was strong enough to handle seeing my child suffer. And in the beginning, that's all I could picture. It's difficult to keep your thoughts positive after forty-eight hours of labor and seeing your new baby, the little being that was moving around happily inside you only hours before, hooked up to monitors and tubes. I thought about kids making fun of her for the rest of her life, and how she would always be different. I wanted to protect her. I wanted to grab her and run.

I thought of parents of children with Down syndrome as saints; it just seemed like the most unlikely thing in the world to happen to us. We had too many faults to be good at this. When my husband and I met, we were both a little on the nonconformist side, sporting long hair and tattoos. Though age has smoothed many of our rough spots, I couldn't picture myself as the elderly, devout woman toting her grown, disabled child with her everywhere for the rest of her life. This was my only image of people who had Down syndrome—dependent and lonely. I couldn't bear the thought that my child might have such a bleak future.

Kayla spent five days in the hospital after birth. Despite the heartbreaking barrage of blood tests, oxygen tubes, heart monitors, and chaos, she was incredibly alert and focused from the start. She was stronger than the stressful situation that surrounded her. It was then that I realized that she had a light burning brightly within her that was much more powerful than Down syndrome.

Upon our return home, I tried to learn all I could about Down syndrome; I thought I needed to do this immediately. But sometimes the worst-case scenarios and bleak outlooks I read about left me in tears. I had just thought that Kayla would be slower to learn than other kids; I had had no clue about the long list of medical problems associated with Down syndrome. So on top of all the other emotions I had as my body recuperated from childbirth, I was also angry that she might have to deal with a lot more than just a learning disability. It seemed so unfair. Why did these kids get hit with so many medical problems on top of everything else? When my husband came in the room to find me rocking Kayla and crying, he'd ask me if I'd been reading too much again. When one of us broke down in those first few weeks, we would talk the other through it with positive thoughts. Kayla brought us closer than we had been in years.

Eventually, I was able to put the literature on the back burner and use it on an "as needed" basis. I also began to learn to savor the days with my baby—not "the Down syndrome baby," just my baby. The first year has had its challenges. Kayla isn't much of a sleeper. Some nights, with no medical explanation, she'll wake up every hour or so, and sometimes stay awake for an hour or two at a time. It's hard to be positive when I'm so exhausted, but Kayla looks and me and smiles and somehow, I find the stamina to keep going. I love to watch her face light up when she sees Daddy come home from work, or when her brother or sister walk into the room. I also love to watch their faces light up when they see Kayla.

Kayla seems to have an intoxicating effect on everyone she comes in contact with. My attempts at giving my husband and teenagers "alone time" with Kayla always end up with me perking my ears up and waiting until I can feel those thick little thighs wrapped safely around my hip again. When we visit my parents every Sunday, they describe her arrival as the "lights coming on"—and her departure as "being suddenly left in the dark." My mom asks me every other day if I can think of somewhere or something that I need to do, so she can baby sit Kayla. She claims to go through "Kayla withdrawals" if she doesn't get to hold her enough.

Now, as I watch Kayla stretching her arms out to catch the bubbles, with the sun shining down on her sweet little face, I still want to grab her and protect her from the world. But I also know that with the light that grows stronger in her every day, our path will always be brightly illuminated.

Alicia lives in Lynnwood, Washington, with her husband, Lenny. They were married in 1999 and together have four children. Kayla (2005) is their youngest child. Alicia has spent the majority of her career as a paralegal and is currently taking time off to spend with her children.

28

Blue Ribbon. First Place.
by Carol B. Mills

Archie, Jonah, and Maren Mills

I WAS ABOUT TO EXPLODE with pride when I saw the ribbon hanging from my six-year-old's very first science fair project. Blue ribbon. First place.

Months earlier, a newsletter had come home inviting kinder-gartners to participate in the science fair, which was mandatory for kids from sixth grade on. Jonah, my academically inclined, typical-ly developing child seized the opportunity. We spent hours poring through science project books and online science fair sites before he found the right project: How sweat cools the body. Sweat and six-year-olds—a perfect match. For weeks, he tested subjects, diligently recorded the results, and arranged his board. With pride he carried it into the auditorium. The deep blue ribbon was a well-earned validation of his efforts.

That afternoon, when I picked Jonah up, I threw my arms around him and congratulated him on his blue ribbon. He looked a bit annoyed and said, "But Mom, I won because I'm the only kindergartener who entered."

My heart sank. How dare someone burst his bubble and tell him something so horrible! "Who told you that, Jonah?" I asked.

"Nobody had to tell me that, Mom. When they announced the winners from each grade there were first, second, and third prizes. In kindergarten, mine was the only name they called." Ah, the insight of a child.

I wanted to cry. Jonah was disappointed. He didn't feel as if he'd "won" anything and didn't see the value of his own hard work. I stumbled through a few attempts to make him see the value of work itself—the honor of giving your all—but it didn't seem to register. We displayed his project at home, and life went on.

A few months later, his chromosomally enhanced younger sister, Maren, then a few days shy of four, had her first dance recital. For her, and more so for me, it was a big day. Right after Maren was born, I had seen some little girls in their dance costumes and my heart had sunk. *My daughter will never have a dance recital,* I'd thought. How little I knew!

So, there in her beautiful molasses-colored tutu for her role in "Candyland," Maren stood before 800 people, ready for her first performance at the Bama Theatre. She had her hair pulled into a bun, and wore just a hint of lipstick, blush, and mascara. Such a beautiful ballerina! My heart soared with pride as I saw my baby girl become a vision of grace.

But as the curtain came up for her number, Maren looked stunned. There was a different backdrop—a giant Candyland board—that hadn't been there during rehearsals. She was mesmerized by the eight-foot-tall peppermint sticks and enormous, brightly-colored lollipops. I could imagine her thoughts, her mind spinning:

How can I get those in my mouth? But her rapt attention was a problem. As most of the other girls in her group did their dance steps, Maren kept staring at the confections. My heart began to sink.

And then, as the music came to an end, Maren looked out into the audience and started to blow kisses. She gave a final twirl with great flair, and took a majestic bow. The audience went wild. Feeling their approval, Maren hammed it up with more bows and kisses. Her teacher lifted her high for her own round of applause. Her energy and delight captivated us all.

After the show, Maren leapt into my husband's arms and recounted her performance. "Daddy, I twirled, I danced, I jumped, I kissed!" She was as excited as a toddler on a sugar rush. She truly was on a dancing high, so proud of all her accomplishments.

People came to congratulate her, and tell her she was the star of the show. With each compliment, Maren grinned her biggest grin and said thank you. A few times, she even offered an encore of twirls. She walked from the auditorium hand in hand with her younger brother, Archie, who wanted a piece of the attention heaped upon his big sister. He, too, was beaming.

On the way home Jonah said, "Mom, Maren did an awesome job!" Given my never-ending need to turn every moment into a life lesson, I thought that this would be a great opportunity to show Jonah how hard things are for Maren, and how important it is that we give her every chance in the world to shine and grow.

"Jonah, did you notice that Maren didn't do her dance all the way through?" I asked.

"Yes Mom, I know that, but she did the best she could and that's what counts." I had to choke back my tears when he continued, "It's just like that blue ribbon I won for the science fair. Sometimes you are a winner just for showing up."

Apparently, it wasn't my day to teach a lesson. It was Maren's.

I often hear people ask "What's it like for a child to have a sibling with Down syndrome?" I simply tell them that the day Maren was born, her brothers won the ultimate sibling prize: A blue ribbon. First place.

Postscript:

It's been a year since Maren's first recital, and she has just had her second. Radiant as Ballerina Barbie from Switzerland, she danced her whole number this time and stole the show again. Just like last year, her fans rushed her backstage and the teenaged dancers who helped with the recital didn't want her to leave.

Her brothers, however, were the most proud. They walked tall, beaming, as they escorted Maren from the building. They can't wait for next year!

Carol holds a Ph.D. in communication studies and is an assistant professor in that field at the University of Alabama, where she teaches interpersonal and organizational communication. She provided a keynote address on the importance of person-first language at the 2006 NDSC convention in Atlanta. She lives with her husband, Jon, and their three children in Tuscaloosa, Alabama. As a family, they live by the Roald Dahl quote, "And above all, watch with glittering eyes the whole world around you because the greatest secrets are always hidden in the most unlikely places. Those who don't believe in magic will never find it."

29

The Buddha Bean
by Beth Crawford

Grace "Bean" and Beth Crawford

I WAS HOLDING MY BABY girl in my arms when I got the news. My daughter, I was told, is a reincarnated Buddha. The Bodhisattva, to be exact, come back to teach us all lessons of compassion. My mother-in-law was sure of it. For three months I had been grappling with how to think about this baby. She was my Bean, my Sweet Pea—a whole garden of cuteness—unique and perfect. Or maybe not so perfect, given the extra chromosome. I had spent hours struggling to reconcile my experience of her with all of the deficits that I couldn't see but was told to expect. I had thought of almost every angle on the problem, but I had not considered that she might be a major religious figure. *Hey kid,* I whispered, *no pressure.*

Few believe that my daughter is a god, but many expect her to be an angel, to be perpetually pure, innocent, and sweet. While reading the guidebook to new parenthood, *What to Expect the First Year,* I came to the section gently titled, "Of Special Concern," which describes the scary diagnoses. After a matter-of-fact description of Down syndrome, the authors add, "They are also usually very sweet and lovable." Such editorial comments do not accompany the other diagnoses, implying either that the kids with other conditions are not sweet and lovable, or that sweetness and lovability go without saying, except for Down syndrome. Actually, I don't think the authors intend either implication; they are just echoing a cultural tendency to idealize people with Down syndrome as being especially sweet and lovable, happy and uncomplicated. The stereotype may be true for all I know, but I'd rather reject it out of hand than construe my daughter's sweetness as yet another characteristic of her diagnosis.

I have resisted the pull to idealize or deify my daughter. I even qualify the seemingly benign, "She's a gift from God!" by adding "Yes, like all children." It is not that I am a staunch atheist, it is just that I want her to be seen as human (when I'm not calling her a legume). She is one of us after all, and accepting her as one of us means recognizing her faults. But that said, what new mom goes around avowing her child's faults? It seems more natural to insist that your baby is special, than to insist that she's not. This is just one of many mental contortions I have found myself in since her birth. It's awkward because, in fact, she is special, and not just euphemistically. Her smile, her cooing sounds, the peaceful way she drools—these things seem magical to me, and I revel in them as if they were supernatural gifts that no other mother has ever known. This has nothing to do with her diagnosis.

When my daughter was born, one of my many fears was that that raising a child with Down syndrome would diminish the experience of parenthood. It does not. Now, as she nears six months old, I cheer her on as she grows into the person she is going to be. I sigh over the poignancy of moving up to size two diapers, and I applaud her discoveries of laughter and feet. My Bean may not be a Buddha, at least not any more than anybody else is a Buddha, but she is my delight.

Beth lives in Richmond, Virginia, with her husband, Matt, and daughter Grace (aka Bean), who was born in 2006, and diagnosed at birth. Beth is an assistant professor of cognitive science and does research on emotion and spatial cognition.

30

A Hopeful Future
by Nancy Iannone

Gabriella Iannone

"I HAVE SOME BAD NEWS, but not the worst. Your baby has Down syndrome." My doctor kept talking, but my mind would not comprehend her words. Time stopped. "You still have time for an abortion."

Trying to keep my swirling mind in order, I said, "No, we would never do that. I'll be fine when I see you on Thursday." *My baby has Down syndrome. She probably has the heart defect the perinatologist suspected too.* I slammed the door in my brain to hold back the flood of grief that was threatening to take over, and I shut down to everything but pure logic.

Abortion. There it was, right in front of me. The thing I had said would never be a part of my life. Here it was, in my living room. And for a few minutes, it did not look like the monster I thought it would be. It looked like a solution, an answer. A way to make this pain go away. My brain scrambled like a rat in a maze looking for the way out, and abortion was right there, looking supportive.

I realized I had to think this through, but the thoughts came in short, logical bursts. Religion? Not an issue for me.

Ethics? I am pro-life, but like many women facing this decision, in my state of mind I'd change camps pretty quickly if a theoretical position was the only thing holding me back. I put that aside as my brain settled on the final question.

Capacity? Could I physically feel a baby kick then say, *Get rid of it?* Could I participate in my baby's demise? No. It was a physical impossibility. I simply knew that I couldn't do it.

The entire, logical sequence took less than a minute, and when I had my answer, the floodgates opened and the grief poured in. After an hour, I wasn't sure if the doctor had actually called me. I almost called her office to ask.

Why was I so upset? I had known people with Down syndrome, and never felt sorry for their families. They were happy and I never viewed their children as burdens. In fact, my parents welcomed those children into our home with open arms, and I thought I had a very positive view of children with special needs. I guess I never considered it on such a personal level before. Actually, there was not much considering going on. It was just sadness.

After a rough day and night, the cardiologist confirmed that the baby had a hole in the middle of her heart that compromised all four chambers. Her statements about "stellar success rates" faded to the background as phrases like "open heart surgery" pushed forward. Part of me was worried and concerned, while another part hoped for a miscarriage that would end the pain. To complicate things, I was also trying to ignore a thought that kept coming to the surface: what if my husband wanted to abort? He was pro-choice to my pro-life, and he had been silent when I told the doctors that I would not abort. Since there was no way I was going to terminate, I couldn't say anything to him. Suppose he said something that he would regret years later, whenever he looked into his child's eyes? So I ignored what I thought was the elephant in the room. On the way home from the cardiologist's office, my husband turned on the public radio station. There were two evangelical ministers debating the finer points of politics and abortion. The show lasted the entire ride home.

Eventually, my husband spontaneously made a statement that showed me he didn't want me to have an abortion. Theoretically, that issue should have been something discussed privately and put to rest, but it was not that simple. After the initial conversation with my obstetrician, I received three separate phone calls from other health care providers. Each opened the conversation with a reminder that I still had time to have an abortion. Then, the "buzz" started (What are they going to do?" or "Is she having an abortion?" or "I'd have an abortion.") I started to feel like I had the word "expendable" stitched across my maternity shirt. One woman offered to lay hands on me and "pray away" the Down syndrome. Basically, I felt like I was climbing "Mount Acceptance" and nice, well-meaning people kept telling me there was a quick way off the mountain just below me. I wanted to scream, *You're not helping!*

On the third day, I woke up and said, "Everything is going to be okay." And I knew it was. I could picture in my mind's eye my future, adorable three-year-old, and I felt a sensation of being comforted by my future self. Still, the rest of the pregnancy was an emotional roller coaster, complicated by pregnancy hormones, chasing after three other children, my then two-year-old's health issues (including chronic diarrhea, which she liked to use for finger paint, several endoscopic biopsies and other tests, and a severely restricted diet), and a history of preterm contractions. I spent a lot of time researching, but nothing in my reading truly prepared me for the reality of raising my baby, because nothing compares to actually holding the baby, the snuggling and the smiles, the laughing and the cooing, and all of the other things that make parents fall in love with their kids.

March 1, 2005. Miss Gabriella Louise was born with a lusty cry, weighing five pounds, six ounces. By then, we had accepted the diagnosis and moved on to optimism. However, in her newborn stage, we still felt a bit like we were "keeping our chins up." We had some feeding and weight issues that caused us to lose a lot of sleep in the beginning, and things were stressful.

Gradually, life went back to normal, and Miss Gabriella started shining brightly in our lives.

After a while, I realized that we had moved beyond surviving to truly living. Gabriella was amazing, endearing, loving, and beautiful. My three other girls—ages seven, four, and two—adored her, and my husband, who was originally nervous for them, saw that Gabriella would only enrich their lives. The heart surgery was anticlimactic, and Gabriella was home in three days on nothing more than Tylenol. A year after the surgery, the worry, fear, and anxiety are a distant memory, a blip on the radar.

Gabriella continues to amaze us as an adorable seventeen-month-old. She loves to sway to music, splash in the bath or the pool, and squeeze her sisters' faces. We went away this weekend and took Gabriella with us because she is still nursing. When we came home, a near-riot ensued as her sisters fought over her. To help Gabriella with language development, she is learning sign language at a pace that has amazed her sign teacher, and the other kids have picked up an impressive sign vocabulary, even looking up signs on their own and displaying them proudly. Though I delight in her physical and cognitive progress, the true joy I receive is seeing her shining, laughing face, especially when she thinks she is playing a trick on me.

Last week I finally received a copy of the genetic karyotype from the amnio. I had never actually seen it. I read it and suddenly felt so sad. Not for me or for Gabriella—life is good. No, I felt sad for the woman on the other end of the phone line, about to hear the news for the first time. I cried for her fear, and the pain of having to face the dark issue of abortion again and again. I wanted to comfort her and tell her that everything would be okay, that what she fears is a fiction, unrelated to this reality, and that life is great. Back then, I had the sensation of my future self comforting me, and it gave me a glimpse of a hopeful future. Today, I picture myself sending that hope back in time. And I try to give other parents a glimpse of hope, beyond the temporary grief.

After all, my baby is not a diagnosis, not a list of her potential woes. She is a beautiful person, full of laughter and grins. There is a world of possibilities laid out before her, and I love exploring those possibilities with her.

Nancy lives in southern New Jersey with her husband, Vincent. Married in 1993, they have four children, Samantha (1997), Maria (2000), Elena (2002), and Gabriella (2005). Nancy is a former lawyer and teacher, but has been home with the children since the birth of their second child. Nancy has joined the board of trustees of The Sensory Playhouse (http://thesensoryplayhouse.com/), an open-play facility designed for kids with special needs, which allows them to play and learn in an inclusive setting. Nancy hopes to provide comfort and hope to those parents receiving the diagnosis of Down syndrome.

31

Enjoying the Ride
by Leah Spring

Angela Spring

WE STAND AT THE TOP of the hill—Noah, Tyler, Angela, and I. It's a frosty January morning and the conditions are perfect for our new sleds. These are not your ordinary cheapo sleds. Wal-Mart was all sold out of those. No, these are "Super Fast Racer Sleds," $25 each, promised to be "the fastest sleds in the neighborhood." And this is no ordinary hill. It's about 200 yards from the crest to the bottom, with a good fifty-yard flat area beyond. We decide to send Angela down, with Tyler following behind so he can help her back up the hill.

She flies. She flies so quickly that Noah and I laugh at how fast and far she is going. She bounces along, hat blowing off and hair blazing out behind her, screaming and laughing, "Wheeeeeeee! I go fast!" She zooms past all the other sliders. Twenty feet…fifty feet…a hundred feet…my little girl on her super fast racing sled, guaranteed to be the fastest on the block.

And then I see it.

At the end of the "runway" at the bottom of the hill—and no sled ever makes it that far—is a two-foot drop to a pond. Most of the surface is frozen, but there is a four-foot-round circle of open water at the edge. And Angela is heading straight for it.

I panic. I start screaming. "Someone grab that kid! CATCH HER BEFORE SHE GETS TO THE POND!" But the two dozen or so adults that she raced past just watch her go.

With sleds zipping past me, I start running down the middle of the ice-glazed hill, trying not to take my eyes off her, sure she's going to go under. I can hear Tyler running and screaming behind me, and Noah behind him. Had someone had a video camera, it would have looked like one of those Chevy Chase movies. The kid is zooming down the hill at a hundred miles an hour. Cut to the fat mom, running in slow motion down the very steep, ice-covered surface, arms going like windmills, legs not quite keeping up, mouth open in a slow, distorted scream, and the teenagers coming from behind trying to bypass the screaming banshee mother.

I feel so very far away from her.

I watch as she drops off the edge, skims across the open water, and comes to a stop right smack in the middle of the pond, with her feet dangling over the edge of the sled. Laughing hysterically at her very exciting ride.

I'm still running, and screaming at her to not move. But I am slow. Tyler gets to the pond before me. He stands at the edge of the open water. I turn to look for someone else to help, but everyone has wandered away. Nobody even realizes we are here.

It occurs to me that I'm a horrible swimmer.

"Go get her, Tyler!" I scream, as I keep running. He looks at me like I am insane. Which, of course, I am. I know it's not a very deep pond—probably six or seven feet deep—but if Angela moves, she's going to go under.

Tyler cuts through the long weeds and snow to a different part of the pond, and as he steps on the ice, I hear it crack. He looks at me, clearly scared to death. I scream, "GO!" And he does.

In moments, Angela is safely back on solid ground.

I have never been so scared in my entire life. I had visions of a drowning kid and funerals and all the horrible things I could possibly think of. For me, the adventure is over. All I really want to do is go home.

Not Angela. She had fun and wants to sled some more! We keep one person at the bottom of the hill to stop her, just in case. But she never makes it that far again.

Angela's whole life has been like this. She wasn't supposed to live, and now she's ten. She wasn't supposed to be able to eat by mouth, and now I have to limit her. She wasn't supposed to succeed in school, and here she is, headed into the fourth grade. There have been so many times throughout our journey together when I thought Angela had reached her peak, only to have her show me, yet again, that she has no limits. The sky is her limit, not the image I have in my head, or what some doctor or therapist has told me about children with Down syndrome. It's like the roller coasters she loves to ride. While I hold on tight and often close my eyes in fear, wondering why in the world I agreed to do this, Angela has both hands in the air, eyes wide open, laughing hysterically and hollering for more. When the ride is done, she gets right back in line for another go.

Not too long ago I decided it was high time I take some lessons from my daughter: Start living life for the moment, and not worrying about what tomorrow holds. After all, she is having fun on this ride called life, so I might as well too.

But we're never going sledding on that hill again!

⚘

Leah and her husband, Dean, were married in 2005. They live in Eagan, Minnesota. Leah has three children, Noah (1987), Tyler (1988), and Angela (1996). Leah is a sign language interpreter and cued language transliterator, and travels the United States speaking to parents and educators about the benefit of using Cued American English with children who have Down syndrome.

32

Lost and Found

By Traci Cross Williams

Ashlyn Williams

THE NIGHT OF ASHLYN'S birth I felt so alone. My husband, Mike, was asleep on the couch beside me; I was awake, worried by what I was seeing in that sweet little face. My mother, my mother-in-law, and my sister had already left the hospital. I couldn't help but wonder, *Did they see it too?* The nurses didn't come out and tell me that they suspected Down syndrome but I knew that they did. One nurse came to my room and was giving me all of the information on caring for newborns. She slipped up as she told me, "Lay your baby on her side or back when she sleeps to prevent Downs—I mean, SIDS." I was crying inside. I didn't really want to think that anyone else saw it, and if I didn't ask, then maybe I was just seeing something that wasn't there.

Mike and I had been around people with Down syndrome all of our lives. Mike had extended family members with Down syndrome who I also knew. I had worked in special education classes while in college. I also remembered "the class" from elementary school that would play on the playground when I was in first grade. So when my suspicions regarding Ashlyn were confirmed, I wasn't afraid of Down syndrome per se, I was afraid because of health concerns. And I was afraid because this was our daughter. Even though I loved her from the beginning, she wasn't supposed to be born with an extra chromosome. The hardest part was telling friends and family. Once I saw that they still loved her too, it was easier for me to accept.

Four months went by and we had all settled into a routine. Breastfeeding was going well and I was back at work. Then it happened again—my feet were pulled out from under me. Ashlyn began having episodes of disturbing behavior. She would draw her legs up and crunch her arms into her chest, and would sometimes let out a cry. This would happen several times a day, every day. She looked like she had an upset stomach, so I would grab the gas drops and give them to her. Her pediatrician and I both thought she was having some type of stomach trouble.

These episodes continued for months. Gradually, Ashlyn's development regressed. She lost her smile and became noticeably weaker. I thought this was an effect of her having Down syndrome, and assumed that she was going to be low-functioning. Finally, when she was a year old, we switched pediatricians. Our new doctor quickly diagnosed Ashlyn with infantile spasms, a type of seizure disorder. A neurologist confirmed the diagnosis. I educated myself about the seizures and found that they were a nightmare compared to Down syndrome. My baby could possibly have these seizures forever, and might be in a vegetative state even if we were able to free her from them. The episodes were so hard on her body and robbed so much from her. Every time she jerked during a seizure, I would cry and hold her and rock her and pray that God would make them stop. It was horrible knowing that the seizures were taking away her personality and could be causing irreversible brain damage. *Please give me back my baby,* I prayed. *Give me back her smiles. I can handle Down syndrome, but please take away these horrible seizures.*

We tried several medications. None of them stopped the seizures and all of them had awful side effects. We eventually ended up giving Ashlyn daily steroid injections that I had to administer. I felt like this was our last hope, and if anything could get rid of them, this was it. This drug was a monster with horrible side effects and I was scared out of my mind to give it to her. We took her to church on Sunday and the congregation prayed over her little body that God would protect her from the side effects and keep her safe and free her from the seizures. We began to see improvement after the first injection. She became very cranky and irritable, which was an expected side effect from the drug, but I could see a difference every day. After a week and a half of injections, her behavior was alarming, but her seizures had stopped.

Once free from the seizures, she slowly began making cooing sounds, then started babbling again. Her beautiful smile came back and, at sixteen months old, she was finally acting like a baby again.

Some people view Down syndrome as an imperfection or a disease. I too may not have seen the worthiness of someone with Down syndrome before my daughter was born. I'm sad that it took me almost losing my baby to find the wonderful gift I had been given. I still give thanks daily to God that He gave me another chance to see all of the beauty He had given me at her birth.

Traci lives in Salisbury, North Carolina, with her husband, Mike. They have three children, Spenser (1994), Ashlyn (1999), and Mason (2001).

33

In the Moment
by Gina Vivona

Leo Woodrum

Photo by Marianne Lozano

I JUST LOVE GOING ON walks with Leo. He's two and a half years old, so the simplest of things is fascinating to him. And at this moment, he has a tree in his sights. Without taking his eye off of his goal, he reaches out his hand, knowing that I'm there to grab it. He holds on to steady himself, as he maneuvers over the gnarly roots twisting under the grass, and makes his way toward the magnolia tree in our front yard. When we get to the trunk, he lets go of my hand to pat the tree with his itty-bitty hand. Leo looks up at me. "Ah, tree," I say. Then he nabs my hand again and heads for the next tree. This is one of his games that he made up, and we play it often—sometimes for a whole hour. Walking from one tree to another. Patting the tree, then moving on to the next.

This picture of me is very different from the one three years ago. As a true task master, I always had a list of things to do. And while in the middle of my list, I would think about the next thing on my list, or what I had to put on my list for tomorrow. It was even hard for me to sit and watch a video with my husband. "Come sit down," he'd say. But I was too busy, up and down ten times during the movie to start a load of wash, write an outline for a proposal for tomorrow's meeting, or start another list. I was always ten steps ahead, which was why my business was successful, but it made it hard to fully rest at night.

Pregnancy had been at the top of one of my lists, but was the one thing that took the longest to accomplish. The timing was just not right for us, or I was just too busy, but after five years the happy day arrived and I was finally pregnant. I knew some things would have to change, starting with slowing down. I wanted to be calmer and take care of my body and mind for Leo. True to my nature, I checked off every item I could think of to ensure a healthy outcome. I ate well and got plenty of rest. I banned caffeine, even my beloved chocolate. No sugar, no aspirin, no artificial anything. Nothing unnatural for my precious Leo. I had a wonderful pregnancy and not even one sick day. I could feel Leo moving and I loved him already.

When he was born, he was so beautiful. He had his daddy's hands and eyes. I can't express how shocked we were to learn he might have Down syndrome. This little bucket of love couldn't possibly have anything wrong with him. It seemed much more likely that he had a super hero chromosome—Super Love Bucket, able to cure the world with a single smile.

Down syndrome! Couldn't it be called something else? I hated the negativity of the words. When the doctors' suspicions were confirmed, my husband went into research mode, while I held Leo tight and cried all day and all night. I loved him, but the news was heavy on my heart, and a million thoughts whirled in my head. My focus was lost.

One night, about three weeks into motherhood, I was breast-feeding Leo at 2 a.m. and stroking his tiny hand resting on my chest. I was so exhausted from the day's events and my endless thoughts nagging at me that I felt brain-dead. I became aware that I had no thoughts. My mental list was gone. There was only *being*—mine and his. In that one moment, I felt peace. Contentment. As I gazed at his preciousness, I realized that if I worry about tomorrow, I'm going to miss today; I would miss this very moment. I was overcome with joy and relief. *All I have to do is love him. Make him happy. It won't matter if he's at the top of his class, or if he gets a good job. He just has to be happy.* The weight was lifted from my heart. My focus was clear.

I hold onto this peace and focus as Leo and I explore the trees together. Leo has just let go of my hand, so this is my opportunity to slip behind the trunk. I peer out just enough so that he catches a glimpse of me. He thinks this is hilarious, and as he runs around the tree, I squat down and let him tackle me. He either thinks that this is the best game on earth, or that his mother is a big goober. Either way, I don't care. I'm just happy to be here.

My cell phone is ringing from somewhere deep inside the house, but I ignore it. After all, I'm very busy right now.

Gina Vivona is the proud mommy of Leonardo. In her spare time, she runs a successful graphic design business creating award-winning projects. She is encouraged and supported by the love of Michael, her husband of nine years.

34

Expecting
by Peggy Cooper-Smith

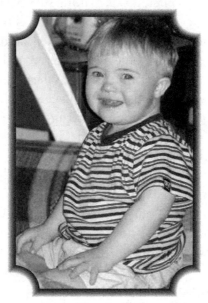

Cason Smith

I KNEW WHEN HE WAS just hours old that without a doubt, I would die for him.

I'm not sure that I would have admitted the same in the first few minutes of his life. We had gone through seven and a half years trying to get pregnant. Pills, injections, surgery, in vitro fertilization cycles, failure after failure, until the final attempt worked. I had felt so blessed with our long-awaited pregnancy, even though it wasn't an easy one. But this news was not what I was expecting. The doctor spoke the words into my husband's ears—those words that, once told to me, made me feel as though my child would never be good enough, would be thought of as an embarrassment, would never be worthy. How utterly disappointing, miserable, and embarrassing it is that I almost agreed with those thoughts. I quickly redeemed myself the moment I held him, looked into his deep blue eyes, and silently promised that I would always take care of him. I knew he was mine forever.

Which isn't to say that my struggle was over. There were medical obstacles to overcome: First, it was making sure his heart was healthy. Next, the battle to get off supplemental oxygen. The last struggle was jaundice. With each hurdle, I talked, coaxed, and prayed with my new baby boy so that he would heal quickly and be able to come home. This formed a connection from my heart to his, and I could feel our bond growing stronger and stronger as each minute passed.

But there were also emotional struggles. I cried, I prayed, I got angry. I was royally pissed off at God for not giving me the child I was expecting. My husband, Chris, was so "together" during those first few days, while I totally fell apart. For almost twenty-four hours after his birth, I was unable to see the baby. The strong pain medications I was taking caused a drugged sleep. Chris was the one who faced the geneticist, the neonatologist, the cardiologist, and the nurses, learning what to expect for our son. He kept me updated between my long sleeps, bringing me pictures and telling me how beautiful our baby was.

It was so hard and so different for me.

Even though it didn't feel like it at the time, we were lucky; our baby spent only six days in the NICU. All initial issues were addressed and cleared. He was healthy, weighing eight pounds, six ounces. Our son: Cason Alan Smith. We brought him home to begin life as a family, but my husband and I were now totally different people. We were the new parents to a baby with Down syndrome.

We were thrust into the world of early intervention services and therapies. I know now that therapy has helped Cason in many areas, but at first it was overwhelming. Physical and occupational therapy began for Cason when he was only nine weeks old. It's hard to imagine what one might do with a baby that small, but they always found things to do. Some days, I wished we could have stopped people from telling us the six different ways we needed to hold, feed, or lay him on the floor to play. Some days, I just wanted to yell, *Leave my baby alone!! He'll roll over, crawl, and walk when he's ready to. Quit disrupting our lives each and every week!* I wanted to enjoy and play with our son, without making everything a "therapied" activity.

Soon enough, I adjusted to the extra visitors in our home and began a routine. I learned to enjoy him as a baby first, and loved every milestone he met, no matter how long it took to get there. Time passed, and before long, it was Cason's first birthday. While it was mostly a happy time in our lives, it was difficult to realize that he really was delayed in his development—he wasn't walking yet, or really even crawling. I questioned whether the extra services were helping, or just taking up more time in our already busy lives, but we stuck with it.

Shortly after his birthday, Cason took off. He started crawling at thirteen months, and his speech blossomed. He continued to refine his large motor skills, and began pulling up and cruising along the furniture. By nineteen months, he took his first steps into his overjoyed, crying mommy's arms.

I just wish that I could go back to myself as a brand new mother and tell her, *Don't worry so much! Everything really will be okay. This child is going to mean more to you than you can ever imagine.* I wish I could convince any new mother of a child with special needs of these things, but I guess until you actually live it yourself, you don't realize how wonderful your new life can, and will, be.

Now at twenty-two months old, Cason is more like his typical peers than not. He can scale a couch, a recliner, or a toy box in no time flat, and he can demolish the living room in about three seconds. He looks at me with an ornery gleam in his eye and a big grin as I tell him not to do something, and then laughs hysterically as he does it anyway. He makes us smile every day, gives the best hugs and cuddles in the world, and terrorizes our cats any chance he gets.

It's funny. Sometimes I look at Cason and wonder, *Does he really have Down syndrome? Are they sure they read those tests right?* He is not what I was expecting at all; he is so much more. Sure, he has therapists who visit him a lot, and specialists we visit occasionally. We are aware of certain health issues associated with Down syndrome, and we will continue to watch for them in the future. Cason has some delays in specific areas. But this little boy can make your bad day a better one. He can carry on a toddler debate over whether or not he should touch his mommy's lamp, and he laughs knowingly at jokes and little teases. He wasn't the baby I was expecting, but he is the son that I deeply love.

Peggy and her husband, Chris, were married in 1996. They live in Lafayette, Indiana, with their son Cason (2004). Peggy is vice president and cofounder of the Lafayette Area Down Syndrome Organization (L.A.D.S.O.) that provides parent information, support, and friendship for families touched by Down syndrome.

35

Green Onion
by Cori Guillaume

Anthony and Brian Guillaume

WHAT'S UP WITH GREEN ONIONS? They're just your garden variety onion, right?

They can be grown in your garden, but they are a far cry from ordinary. The delicate bulb is pulled from the soil before it is fully developed, giving it a mild flavor that is appreciated by many. The succulent smell reveals itself even before you enter the room. We enjoy green onions in soup, salad, or by themselves. But whatever the color—yellow, red, white or green—an onion is still an onion.

Life is full of green onions—things that are just a little different than what we are accustomed to, things that strike us as a bit unusual. We tend to avoid these green onions, unless someone slips them into a recipe and we find ourselves enjoying their unique flavor.

"Excuse me, excuse me!" I called to the lady walking past me in the Wal-Mart aisle.

"I'm sorry, do I know you?"

"No, you don't, but I wanted to ask, does your son have Down syndrome?" I said. I figured if he did then I could share my story; if he didn't, well, then I probably wouldn't see this person again, so what did I have to lose?

"Yes, he does," she replied with a stern look on her face, ready to defend her child.

"My six-month-old son has Down syndrome too," I replied. Her face softened, and an immediate understanding passed between us. A friendship began that day.

When I first looked at this woman's little blond boy, about two and a half years old, I saw my son's future. I saw my future. And I was frightened! Not because this boy was disabled or different, but because he was so *normal.* He was trying to pull things off the shelves, trying to throw things out of the cart, and he was eating French fries. This was what I had to look forward to? How was I ever going to keep up with a two-year-old?

More important than my initial fright of this little boy's energy was the calm feeling that engulfed me. I looked at this mother and thought, *She is just like me. She is young, vibrant, and genuinely happy.* I could see wisdom and contentment in her eyes. I could tell that she was comfortable with her son; she knew who he was. She was not fazed by a diagnosis, or society's definition of her child. And from her initial response to me, I knew she was poised and ready to be an advocate for him.

That day in the Wal-Mart aisle, my life changed. Normally, I would have gone about my business, never noticing that beautiful little boy with his courageous mother. They would have sneaked by me without a second glance and I would have been deprived of the privilege of knowing them; would have missed the honor of being their friend. And here's the irony of the situation: Remember how I figured I'd never run into that woman again? Well, I am constantly running into my friend at Wal-Mart. It's been two years since our first meeting, and although our hectic lives don't allow us to visit as often as we would like, the times we do share are wonderful. We've enjoyed play dates at each others' homes. Whenever we peek in on the two boys playing, each appears to be doing his own thing, but the disarray in the living room suggests that they enjoy plenty of combined mischief.

I knew that being a mother would change me, that I would experience a love that words could not describe, that I would become a member of the "don't mess with my kid" club. I didn't know that being Anthony's mom would unlock another world, a world where I approach complete strangers because I think we may have something in common.

Tonight I will watch my green onion as he sleeps and thank him for helping me experience life's robust flavor.

Cori lives in Carlisle, Pennsylvania, with her husband, Brian. Married in 2000, they have two children, Anthony (2003), and Noah (2005). After a battle with jaundice and slow weight gain, Anthony was diagnosed with Trisomy 21 at nine weeks of age. The family enjoys hiking, fishing, and spending long weekends at their cabin in the Alleghany National Forest.

36

Big Sister
by Karen Roberts

Tanner, Kimberlyn, Sarah, and Gideon Roberts

"SARAH, SARAH, WHERE are you?" I'm lying in bed in the early morning hours of a summer day. My three-year-old son, Tanner, is calling for his ten-year-old sister. Lately when he wakes up he calls for her, not me. She isn't in her bedroom, so he starts searching for her, calling as he goes. "Sarah, are you watching a movie?" He finds her downstairs and joins her. A little later, she puts cereal in a bowl for him and pours the milk. Gideon, who is five, gets up. Sarah gives him cereal and milk, too.

While I'm downstairs doing laundry, the baby wakes and starts to cry; Sarah gives her the binky and winds up the mobile. She comes downstairs to tell me the baby is awake, then gets the diaper and wipes and talks to the baby while I change her. When I sit down to fold the clothes, Sarah sits down with me and helps sort and fold. "Sarah, can you play with the baby while I put these away?"

"Sure," she says, and then she plays and talks with the baby while I'm busy. She makes the baby laugh and laugh. When I put the baby in her seat and put on her bib, Sarah gets the cereal out of the cupboard. "I feed her?" she asks. She is very careful as she feeds her with the tiny baby spoon.

The little boys are hungry again. Sarah gets out bread, mayonnaise, ham, and cheese. She will start making the sandwiches if I am not in the kitchen.

People are usually surprised at how much Sarah can do. I am a little surprised myself, sometimes. I'd had no close interaction with anyone with Down syndrome before Sarah was born. My expectations swung between thinking she was going to be the most brilliant person with Down syndrome that ever was, to thinking maybe she won't be able to do anything for herself. When we decided to have a child after her, we thought that maybe he would be a little push for her. Someone to encourage her from below. I never thought about how she would watch over and teach him.

"Where is Sarah?" This question is asked many times each day. Sarah is outside swinging, playing her favorite music on her portable CD player. Her brothers run to join her on the swings. Or, Sarah is changing into her swimming suit, ready to play in the little pool. The boys go and change into their swimsuits to splash in the pool with her. Or, Sarah is out front riding her bike. The boys rush out to ride with her.

When the baby goes down for a nap and it is quiet time, Sarah will help pick out a video to watch, put it in the machine and make sure the TV is on the correct channel. When she turns up the sound, I call down the stairs, "Sarah, it's too loud, turn it down."

"OK." The sound goes down a bit.

It is time to do chores. "Whose turn is it to set the table?" I ask. Sarah runs to the chart. "My turn set table. Tanner feed dog," she says.

It might sound like Sarah is perfect. She is not. Sometimes Sarah doesn't want to play with the boys. "Go away," she says, as she closes her bedroom door. Some days when I say it is time to do chores, she says, "I don't want to." Or she might say, "Gideon not be nice to me," when her brother is teasing her. She can be suddenly hard of hearing, if I ask her to turn down her music. She sometimes stomps her feet when Gideon and Tanner want a different video than she does. "No, I don't want!" She might fling herself down and cry, upset that she doesn't always get her way. It is amazing how much she is like the other children in this way, having to learn to take turns and share.

Sometimes her abilities grow ahead of her understanding. She wants to play at a friend's house, but forgets to look before crossing the street. Or she doesn't come right home when the friend can't play. Usually her dad, her older siblings, and I watch out for her. But lately, some changes have been happening. The beloved older sister is being watched over by the younger brothers. "Mom," says Tanner, "I walked Sarah to Katie's house." I did not ask him to walk with her, he just did it on his own.

Recently, Sarah went to see if Katie was home. "Come right back if she isn't there," I said. The little boys wanted to walk with her, so I said okay. A few minutes later, Tanner came running home for Dad. "Sarah won't come home!" Sarah was down around the corner past Katie's house, upset because Katie wasn't home to play with. After Dad had brought the strays home he said, "Gideon was standing on the corner also." I asked Gideon what he was doing. "I stayed with Sarah while Tanner went to get Dad."

Where is this protectiveness coming from? We haven't yet told the little boys about Down syndrome. Sarah is just their big sister. And yet, they are starting to watch out for her while she watches out for them. When Sarah was born, I worried about what the future held for her. Would her siblings be there for her when her dad and I couldn't be? I worried, but I didn't need to. For the past ten years I have watched her older siblings play with her, protect her, and love her. Now I know the younger ones will do the same. But I think the thing that brings me the most joy is watching Sarah "in action" as the big sister.

Karen lives in Chubbuck, Idaho, with her husband, Jeffrey. Married in 1985, they have eight children: five daughters and three sons. The oldest child was born in 1987, the youngest in 2005. Their fifth child, Sarah, was diagnosed with Down syndrome after her birth. She had open heart surgery when she was seven weeks old to repair a heart defect (VSD). Sarah has three older sisters and an older brother and she adores them all. They love her, watch over her, and treat her like any other little sister. She also has two younger brothers and a baby sister who are featured in this story. The family likes to go for walks, talk, play games, and watch movies together. Karen is a fulltime mother who loves to read. She does her best to take care of the needs of all her children, from college student to baby.

37

Speech Therapy
by Kelly Schuh

Lee, Dylan, and Kelly Schuh

"OKAY, DYLAN, LET'S SEE how this tastes!" Julie, my son's speech therapist, is tempting him with a spoonful of peaches. It's a good thing she's so skillful with a baby spoon, because she's decked out in a beautiful outfit, as usual. I guess being a topnotch professional with no children has its privileges. Dylan is fifteen months old; he has been meeting weekly with Julie for two months, to improve his feeding skills. Dylan is always happy to see Julie, especially because of the stash of toys in her bag that he gets to play with at the end of their sessions.

When Dylan was diagnosed with Down syndrome the day after he was born, my husband, Lee, immediately began searching for information. I was reluctant to join in at first; I just wanted to enjoy my new baby. But as the months went by, I became deeply interested in finding out what we could do to help our son have the best life possible. Lee and I read many resources and gained much knowledge about Down syndrome, and this calmed our fears about our son's future. We realized that with the appropriate services, including speech therapy (ST), physical therapy (PT), and occupational therapy (OT), Dylan could make a great start in life.

Dylan began OT and PT when he was five months old. Our pediatrician wanted to wait on speech therapy until Dylan was at least two years old. I thought that was too late for Dylan to start, since he was having feeding issues. So I secured a speech therapist myself. We worked with several others before we met Julie.

We are diligent in applying the counsel of our therapists, especially in regards to speech and communication. After learning that we should encourage Dylan in all of his efforts to make sounds, we have been delighted with any noise he's been able to produce. Lately, he's made a new discovery: By pursing his lips together and blowing with all his might, he can make a great spitting sound. We, as parents, see this as an exciting learning experience!

All the effort is paying off, I think as I watch Julie spoon in the peaches. Dylan is doing a great job managing the task, which has been difficult for him in the past, because of tongue protrusion. He's so pleased with himself that he gets a telltale gleam in his eye. Uh-oh, I know what's coming. He puckers up, and out comes the loudest spitting sound ever. Strained peaches spray all over his face, his highchair tray—and all over Julie!

I try hard not to laugh as Julie grabs a cloth and starts trying to wipe off the orange blobs on her slacks. I'm remembering how Dylan sprayed me with bananas just a few days ago. Good thing I was wearing jeans.

"It's not a good idea to encourage those kinds of mouth noises," Julie says, looking pretty disgusted. I decide not to remind her that we were told to celebrate all of Dylan's attempts to communicate.

Instead, I wait until Lee gets home and tell him the whole story. We laugh and laugh as we think about dear Julie's "peach shower." Yes, every day there are new learning experiences to be enjoyed—and some are downright hilarious!

Kelly lives in Perrysburg, Ohio, with her husband, Lee. Married in 1996, the couple longed for children for four years before conceiving Dylan (2005). The prenatal Triple Screen was normal. Dylan was diagnosed with Down syndrome the day after he was born. Lee is a manager at a market research company. Kelly worked at the same market research company for eleven years before Dylan's birth. At that time, she chose to be a stay-at-home mom because of Dylan's special needs. Kelly recommends that every parent of a child with Down syndrome prepare to be an advocate by learning as much as possible about the subject. Kelly found wonderful support at BabyCenter.com and encourages all parents to join a similar support group.

38

Loving Emma Jayne
by Emily Zeid

Emma Jayne Abu-Zeid and Emily Zeid

I HAD EVERYTHING perfectly planned.

I met my husband eight years earlier while I was in college. I knew him as a friend long before I knew him as a lover. As our friendship grew into a love affair that surprised us both, our lives became more and more entwined. By the end of our first year together, we had combined our finances and our households. Shortly thereafter, as we moved across the country together, our commitment to each other solidified.

It was three and a half years before we got engaged, and another six months before we wed. Our marriage was a good five years in the making because as committed as we were, I did not want us to become legally obligated to each other until we were planning on starting a family. Since I didn't want to be too young for the responsibility or too old to spend the energy, I had to wait for the right time.

I had everything perfectly planned.

We had the loveliest wedding. Our wedding party was comprised of eight bridesmaids and seven groomsmen who flew in from all over the country. I authored and orchestrated a complex ceremony that involved the entire wedding party and both sets of parents, and was administered by a longtime family friend. We all celebrated long into the night, dancing to music provided by my father's band. We ate homemade cake and fawned over the handmade decorations and favors.

I had everything perfectly planned.

Shortly after the wedding we began our search for a home to call our own. We found the perfect house and sped through escrow—it was meant to be. There was an extra bedroom for our future children. Much to our happiness, we conceived immediately. In private we congratulated ourselves for our superior biology. (We now find our smugness ironic.)

Other than my constant whining, my pregnancy was uneventful. We underwent all the recommended prenatal screenings and diagnostic ultrasounds, and eagerly anticipated each doctor's appointment. Everything was normal and all measurements indicated excellent fetal growth and health. While I would have hypothetical discussions with other mothers-to-be about poor prenatal diagnosis or birth defects, I knew my opinions would be moot because my baby would be perfect. I wholeheartedly rejected even the slightest possibility that there would be anything wrong with my baby. I knew with certainty that she would be a genius.

I had everything perfectly planned.

At thirty-one weeks, our ultrasound technician was surprised to note that all of the baby's limbs measured the same gestational age; apparently such proportion is rare. That was also when we discovered that the baby was in the breech position—a position that I knew she would stay in. While we discussed how to help her move, with a sinking heart, I knew that I would be having a cesarean birth.

My perfect plans were beginning to disintegrate.

My c-section was scheduled for Friday the 13th. Our midwife couldn't imagine why this would make me uncomfortable. I spent the night before the surgery in a state of utter fear. Until then, I had no experience whatsoever with surgery. I was horrified to learn that I would be awake during the procedure, aware of the scalpel that was cutting into my body. And, if I survived, I would be rewarded with a little human that I was responsible for. While I knew that rethinking motherhood the night before I was supposed to enter it was probably not the wisest choice, my terror knew no boundaries.

Yet I gathered enough strength to show up for our appointment. Because my fear was seeping out of my pores, our surgical team did their best to put us at ease. Even though I cried like a baby throughout the surgery, our OB team did a fantastic job and before I knew it, our daughter had arrived.

I should have known something was wrong then. They neglected to hold her up after they pulled her from my womb. I saw my first glimpse of her when my husband brought her out after she had been cleaned and swaddled, en route to the nursery for her measurements. I remember thinking that her eyes looked strange.

I was then taken to post-op where I remained for hours while the drugs wore off. I still hadn't held my baby.

Finally I was taken to my room. On the way, we passed the visitors lounge where my family had been waiting patiently. I saluted them victoriously as they cheered for me. We all knew that I had conquered my fear and that everything would be okay.

Or not.

My husband was in the hall outside of our room holding our unnamed baby. As they wheeled me in, he asked me if anyone had spoken with me about our baby. My body was inflamed with fear as I asked him what he was talking about. With a quivering voice, he told me that the medical staff suspected our daughter had Down syndrome. It is the most vivid memory I will ever have. On my deathbed

I will remember every sound that was uttered, every breath that was taken during that endless moment.

I started sobbing and did not stop for days. I had been told that my baby was retarded before I had even held her. When I finally did get to hold her, all I could see was the Down syndrome. All I could see was that she wasn't perfect at all. My plans had been smashed into smithereens. There were too many pieces for me to even try to put them back together again. The doctor came to evaluate her and itemize the evidence of Down syndrome. To show me all of her imperfections. Every last one.

Through my teary eyes I saw the doctor whisk her to the nursery for a bath. Just then, some friends arrived at the hospital to meet our daughter. My husband took them to a viewing window of the nursery to point her out, but all he saw was a baby in an incubator. He told them that this wasn't our child, but it was. A nurse rushed out and explained that our baby girl had started turning blue due to a heart defect (PDA) that was causing persistent pulmonary hypertension. She wasn't getting enough oxygen, and couldn't even regulate her own temperature. To our dismay, she remained in the nursery for the next twelve days.

During this time, I cried and screamed as I alternated between grief, fear, guilt, and anger. The only image I had of Down syndrome was an outdated one of retardation and isolation. I can't stress enough how uninterested I was in having a retarded child and being a forced caretaker for the rest of my life. My husband and I both come from academic families that highly value brainpower, from a world where intellectual prowess is the most important survival skill one can have. The thought that I produced a daughter who would be anything less than brilliant was horrifying to me.

I spent the first few days of her life unwilling to bond with her. I did not want to name her because I didn't want her to be mine. But I didn't want her to be anyone else's, either. The thought of going home without her to an empty nursery was unbearable.

This was the most pain I had ever experienced. I had spent my life blissfully untouched by tragedy, and had to rely on every coping mechanism in my being to digest that pain. It hurt to breathe.

The hospital provided little comfort; they simply were not prepared for a Down syndrome birth. While they encouraged us to care for her, they were unable to give us any solid information or counseling. All they could give us were their best wishes, scant information downloaded from the Internet, and some pamphlets published by the National Down Syndrome Society.

My husband, thankfully, was an emotional rock. He loved our daughter unconditionally from the moment he saw her and was willing to spend his life giving her whatever she needed. He helped me see that I would too. He cradled me while I grieved, embraced my fear, and helped that hurt and fright evolve into love, acceptance, and hope.

As I watched her struggle in the nursery amongst a maze of wires, I began to see my determination in the outward thrust of her chin. I saw my lips, fingernails, and a pair of deep blue inquisitive eyes staring back at me with trust. I saw the possibilities of the future every time she gazed at me. I had created her life and I decided then and there that it would be a good life, a full and valuable life brimming with bliss. I would make it so.

She needed a name, a name that would foretell the strength that we would help to instill in her. We named her Emma Jayne, a sturdy name filled with personality. Though we were unaware at the time, Emma means "whole and complete" and Jayne means "gift from God." We were delighted to discover that her name so befit her, as she was, and will always be, a whole and complete gift from God. She was meant to be.

Today Emma is a happy and healthy six-month-old baby. She is active, alert, and eager to live. She smiles easily and laughs often. She becomes more beautiful with each passing day. I now see the beauty in the differences that I used to believe were flaws. Her upturned almond eyes are filled with wonder, the flat space across the bridge of her nose is a favorite kissing place, and her low set ears show off her ponytails perfectly. Her low muscle tone means that she works so hard to build her strength and endurance. Nothing is given to her, and nothing comes easily to her—she earns everything she has with hard work. Her determination is a source of inspiration and pride for me.

When she smiles, she smiles with her whole body.

I look back on her birthday, which is a surreal nightmare for me. The wound is still raw, but I no longer feel trapped, sentenced to a lifeless world of deadened dreams and excruciating disappointment. In my memory, I see my former self awash in despair and I desperately want to reach out to that lost and frightened woman. I want to embrace her and comfort her with the vision of today. I want to close her pamphlets and whisper gently into her ear that she will fall quickly and completely in love with her child. I want to shut out the doctors' medical babbling and tell her how her baby's differences will seem so minute and will eventually emerge into a huge source of motherly pride. I want to slip baby Emma Jayne into her arms and explain that once she gets acquainted with all of Emma's heart-melting ways, the idea of a lifetime together won't be so scary after all. I want to help her stroke Emma's face as I tell her that she will discover that a life with Emma Jayne is a wonderful way to live. That she will find in time, it is the only way to live.

But I can't, and that woman and her pain will exist forever in my memories. She is still part of me, but I am not part of her. Life with my sweet Emma has taught me so much and has fundamentally changed me. I am a better person today than I was yesterday, and the world is a better place with Emma Jayne in it. I have no idea what the future holds for her or my family, but I have no doubt that it will be filled with love and joy. I will strive to help Emma Jayne be the most she can be, and to be as independent as she is able, but in the end, Emma will be who she is. She will show me who she is and what her capabilities are. If she is destined to spend her life down the hall from me, well then, I honestly can say I cannot imagine a life more fulfilling than one with my Emma Jayne.

My plans are no longer perfect, because I've realized how futile the quest for perfection is. Humanity is a state of imperfection and to deny this fundamental truth is detrimental to our development. This truth is where compassion, empathy, and pride originate from. It is not the end of a life that defines its importance and worth, but the journey traveled during that lifetime. Words cannot capture how eager I am to embark on this journey with Emma Jayne.

This is the journey of my life. It is not going to be perfect. It's going to be better than perfect.

It is going to be amazing.

Emily lives in Minneapolis with her husband, Khaled Abu-Zeid, and their two children, Emma Jayne (2004) and Gabriel (2006). She works in real estate, but her passion is the arts. She spends the little personal time she has writing about disability issues and the nature of her life on her blog, www.wonderbabe.blogspot.com.

THE GIFT OF
PERSPECTIVE

39

Beginning
by Renee Sherman

Liam Sherman

WHEN THE DAY BEGAN it was a perfect morning for "treasure hunting." The weather was crisp but beautiful, and we had arrived early enough to beat the crowds. This citywide, outdoor sales event was held on a military base forty-five miles from home, where families moving on and off the base could sell their unwanted belongings in order to travel lighter. My husband, sister, and mother-in-law were there to help me pick out some things for the baby—my first—who was due in a few weeks.

After several successful purchases, we climbed a hill to another street full of tempting treasures. Weary and thirsty, a drink stand caught my eye. It was a bathtub filled with ice and cold drinks, and the sign above it read, "Liam's Pub Tub." I wanted to support such an inspired entrepreneur, so I picked out a clear soda, took a few sips, and headed off to the next house in search of more must-have items.

As I began walking down the driveway, I felt a sudden wetness. Confused, I stopped, and waited. Again, I felt the same sensation. I turned to my husband Gary and said, "I think my water just broke."

"No way," he replied with little certainty and a hint of sarcasm. He was remembering the same thing I was—the lesson in our pre-natal class in which we learned that first-time moms seldom deliver before their due date, and their water doesn't usually break before labor begins. It seemed that I was breaking the rule.

My heart was racing and my head was spinning. We were an hour's drive from home, and I was quite sure I didn't want to deliver at the military hospital. So we rushed to the car and tried to make our way off the base, but we took a wrong turn, and landed in the thick of traffic. This seemed to perfectly symbolize the chaos of the situation.

I remember looking into Gary's eyes for reassurance. For some weeks now, he had been kidding me that I needed to pack my bag for the hospital. And as unbelievable as it sounds, I really had intended to pack the next day. So my bag wasn't packed, the guest room wasn't ready, the baby items weren't ready—I wasn't ready! But things were out of my hands.

After three more turns, we came upon military personnel assisting traffic. Gary proudly declared through the open car window, "My wife's in labor, her water just broke."

"Congratulations, sir," replied the MP, as he pointed us to the highway.

Finally, after being admitted to our local hospital and hooked up to a plethora of machines, all required to monitor the birth, I tried to settle in and rest as Gary left to pack my bag and prepare for our baby's arrival. I controlled most of my contractions with breathing patterns learned in Lamaze class, but with the continuous beeping from the baby's heart monitor, and the awkwardness of dragging three machines and one towel with me each time I needed to use the bathroom, I began to lose focus. When Gary returned, I sent him to find the nurse to request an epidural, but regrettably, I was too far along to receive assistance with pain. Suddenly, I was on my side and instructed to push. After all the craziness of the day, in just four or five pushes, our baby was born.

We have a boy, and you should see his monkey toes!" Gary announced with excitement. He took our son to meet family members who were waiting just outside the door. When it was finally my turn to meet and greet our new one, I marveled at how small and soft he was.

Since we chose not to know the baby's gender before birth, we had delayed picking a name. Liam was on the list of names we liked, and after the day's adventures and visiting "Liam's Pub Tub," we were certain this was the name to choose. Too excited to sleep, we went to peek at our newly named son in the nursery and were thrilled to see him sleeping peacefully under the heat lamp, while the other babies in the nursery wailed. How lucky we were, with a beautiful healthy new son, a successful delivery, a healthy mom, and a proud dad! It was a perfect moment.

The next morning, the door to my room opened, a man walked in, and introduced himself as Liam's pediatrician. "I need to speak to you about your son," he said. We were both weary from the night's excitement and tried to look presentable in front of our new baby's doctor. He looked at us both with stark reality in his eyes, "He has Down syndrome."

The doctor continued speaking, saying something about "heart" and "healthy," but I couldn't focus on what he was actually saying. I looked to Gary—who seemed as stunned as I did—and thought, *This can't be true*. I finally asked the doctor to stop talking while I tried to take in what he had said: My son has Down syndrome. Impossible! I'd had a fabulous pregnancy, a healthy delivery, and our wonderful new baby had scored high on his Apgar test. *It can't be true*. I remember digging into the pit of myself and trying to remove this entire circumstance—to make it go away—to return to the time before Liam's doctor walked into the room, before our world had changed.

After the doctor left, the nurse tried to console me and offered to summon a representative from the hospital's spiritual counseling service. Not affiliated with a religion, my husband and I were hesitant, but desired to speak with someone. I was full of raw emotions and did not bother to hide how painful this diagnosis was each time we were greeted by another well-wisher. After a friend asked if we would have more children, I finally collapsed sobbing into my mother's arms.

Driving our new baby home from the hospital, we listened to a song that really hit home. *They say that all good things must end some day*, the lyrics rang out. *Autumn leaves must fall.*

Once home, we tried to settle into a new routine of life with baby. Breastfeeding, which I thought would be sunshine, rainbows, and butterflies, became a struggle to maintain my sanity. While I was supposed to be enjoying the most beautiful moment a mother and infant could share, I would instead look at my son and think, *I have a baby with Down syndrome.* Did breastfeeding seem impossible because he had Down syndrome? Was the painful gas that caused his rare colic outbreaks due to Down syndrome? Was my mental state and lack of sleep and hesitation to bond with my child all due to Down syndrome? When things didn't go the way I thought they should, I blamed everything on the diagnosis.

I found strength and comfort in my family. I poured out my feelings and my fears to my husband, and he became my lifeline to a world that I still wanted to experience. He encouraged me to see our son as I had before the diagnosis.

"What if people make fun of him? What if he can't make friends, understand our jokes, get into college, or live on his own?" I asked.

"I know your concerns and fears; I have them too," Gary empathized. "No parent knows what their children are fully capable of when they are brand new. Liam will reach all the same milestones, but in his own time. We need to supply him with the tools, the motivation, love, and support he needs to succeed. He'll get there, you'll see."

Over time, my depression gradually seemed to lift as Liam grew and accomplished the same milestones that all babies do. Speaking with other parents of children with Down syndrome, hearing their stories, and watching the success of their children would also lift my spirits. I still have days when the diagnosis of Down syndrome seems to loom over me, but with our new network of support, Gary and I are learning to embrace new thoughts and ideas, and to erase the old feelings and stereotypes that we grew up with. Retarded no longer means stupid, normal has been replaced with typical. And our son is just as special as all new babies, no more and no less. We're taking on a world that offered only sad sighs and "I'm sorry" statements when they learned Liam had Down syndrome. Together, we are proving that there's no need to pity us; instead, see us and think, *What a beautiful and happy family.*

Looking back, I feel that my celebration of Liam's birth was cut short. I realize that the son I was rejoicing over just hours before the diagnosis is the same baby I hold in my arms today. But his story doesn't end here. Each time he welcomes a new day and celebrates a new achievement, it's a beginning. Whenever we cross paths with parents who challenge and change a system that does not see our children as typical, eventually making our journey smoother, it's a beginning. Meeting other children and adults who have an extra chromosome, I understand that Liam is not alone in his beginning, but part of a community of unique individuals who are continuing to prove that they are more like everyone else than different from them.

And I have discovered a beginning within myself. When I look at my son today, I no longer see Down syndrome, but an amazing and astounding little boy. Liam is beginning.

Renee lives in the Midwest with her husband, Gary. After dating for fifteen years, they finally married in 2000 (they wanted to be sure!). Their son Liam (2005) is challenging his parents to keep up with him.

40

Entertaining Angels
by Barbara Curtis

Daniel, Jonny, Maddy, Jesse, and Justin Curtis

FOURTEEN YEARS AGO the world changed for me when Tripp and I had our eighth child, Jonny. When I saw my son's sweet almond-shaped eyes, I knew life would never be the same—but that somehow it would be indescribably, immeasurably better.

On the other side of the looking glass, Jonathan and I embarked on many new adventures. In our weekly Easter Seals play group, we sang songs I'd been singing with my seven other kids for years, only now we used sign language as well. I gazed around the circle at the other mother/infant pairs, knowing I was seeing things fresh and new—not as I would have seen them before Jonny.

There was feisty, one-eyed Christopher, whose head was heavy, swollen, and asymmetrical. And bossy one-year-old Anna, who resembled a twelve-pound, wrinkled, old woman. Gabriella was blind but oh-so-curious, and Sam and Jenny, though they both had cerebral palsy, were no more alike than any two kids with brown eyes.

Their mothers' lives had been irrevocably changed by the birth of each child that had brought them here. All were in various stages of coping.

In our discussion group, Christopher's mother sobbed. Her husband was becoming more and more withdrawn. She knew the statistics: Following the birth of a disabled child, eighty percent of marriages end in divorce. But she had a more immediate problem—she couldn't bear to take her baby anywhere and see the horror in people's eyes when they saw him.

Anna's mom felt the same. She struggled with whether or not to get pregnant again. The genetic counselors were not sure whether Anna's disorder was chromosomal.

Jenny's mother dealt with guilt; she wondered who to sue. Her home birth had gone awry. Delays getting to the hospital compounded the problem, and now her daughter's future would be different from what it might have been.

For two years we met, supporting each other through our children's operations, subsequent pregnancies (resulting in three healthy babies in the group), and stresses in our marriages. We rejoiced with those who rejoiced and mourned with those who mourned.

I was blessed and broadened by these relationships—relationships forged simply because Jonny was in my life. And truly all the members of our family have been blessed and broadened. Jonny was only five or so when his big brother Matt said, "Wouldn't it be wonderful if every family had a kid with Down syndrome?"

Wouldn't it, indeed? If everyone understood their value, instead of being feared, they'd be eagerly welcomed into their fortunate families.

That's why all these years I've done my best to eliminate the terrible fear our culture instills in our hearts of having a baby who is somehow regarded as "less than" what is expected. The greatest gift Jonny gave me was that I could look around the circle and see all those children as beautiful—a small glimpse of how our Heavenly Father sees all of us in spite of our flaws and infirmities.

An email I received recently from a mother who reads my blog—a mother expecting her fourth child—made my heart sing: It read, "After reading your blog over the past three months, I am not as concerned about my baby having a disability!" And so Jonny's influence has grown, extending beyond his own family. He is a daily reminder to me of Paul's words, "Be not forgetful to entertain strangers; for thereby some have entertained angels unawares" (Hebrews 13:1b2).

I lived most of my life as a person with limited capacity. But God gave me an angel to entertain to broaden my perspective and enlarge my heart. Through Jonny, He showed me how little He cares about our intelligence and physical appearance, how much more He cares about the things we "normal" people will never be able to measure.

Looking back, I know that it must have been me God saw as disabled. But where I was blind, I now can see.

Barbara Curtis, mother of twelve and grandmother of ten (so far!), has published seven books, including The Mommy Manual *and* Lord, Please Meet Me in the Laundry Room. *She is also an award-winning columnist with more than 700 articles in fifty publications, including* Focus on the Family, Guideposts, Christian Parenting Today, *and* The Washington Times. *With six children still at home, Barbara and her husband, Tripp, continue their parenting adventure in northern Virginia. Since the birth of their ninth child, Madeleine—fifty-four weeks after Jonny—Tripp and Barbara have adopted three more boys with Down syndrome. In 2004, they received the Congressional Angel in Adoption Award.*

41

Defining Moments
by Sherrill Rechner

Trenton Rechner

November 1, 2004—7:20 a.m.

"DOES HE HAVE DOWN SYNDROME?" These are the first words out of my mouth when my husband, Ken, brings me our new little wrapped bundle. Why am I asking this? The baby doesn't look like he has Down syndrome; he looks beautiful and perfect. He can't have Down syndrome—they told me he wouldn't.

Ken is as surprised by my words as I am. "No, I don't think so," he replies. Satisfied with his response, I don't give my question another thought.

November 2, 2004—10:15 a.m.

"Mr. & Mrs. Rechner, may I speak to you for a moment?" The NICU pediatrician wants to consult with us—privately. My mind fills again with fears of Down syndrome. Am I just paranoid? *Just act casual,* I tell myself.

Impossible. Tears are already welling in my eyes as I listen to the doctor relate his suspicions. I was not paranoid after all.

November 2, 2004—3:00 p.m.

I am lying in my hospital bed, surrounded by our family members who have come to share this special event. We are blessed to have them with us. It had been a challenging pregnancy and everyone is happy the baby is here safely. They are celebrating and talking about our baby's dramatic preterm arrival that began on Halloween night—what a story for everyone to tell the rest of the family and their friends.

"What a gorgeous, healthy little boy."

"So small, but strong!"

"What beautiful names you have chosen."

"He looks like Dad."

"No, he looks like Grandpa."

This is all background noise to the buzz of panic in my head. I can't tell anyone yet—it may not be true. I don't want to upset anyone. This is a story they will not want to tell.

November 4, 2004—12:00 p.m.

"Your son has Down syndrome." Up until this moment, Ken was convinced everything was fine. But I wasn't. Head spinning, can't think. *Be strong.* I try to fight the tears. I can't. I love my baby, but I can't help but feel cheated.

My family will be so sad. Will they still love him? Will they still celebrate his birth?

I must put on a brave face—it's the only way I can hang on to the last scraps of my life as it gets pulled away from me. Only I can see and feel my tears.

November 4, 2004—2:00p.m.

I can barely say the words out loud. "Our son has Down syndrome. What are we going to do?"

Ken's simple reply gives me strength and I know that he is ready to face this challenge right alongside me: "He is our son."

November 14, 2004—8:30 p.m.

We've arrived at the children's hospital by ambulance. The cardiologist listens for a few seconds to my son's heart. By the sound of his heartbeat, she knows he has a large defect (VSD). An echocardiogram is ordered to confirm the diagnosis. He will be on oxygen until he receives open heart surgery.

He is two weeks old.

Dear God, what did I do to deserve this?

November 30, 2004—2:10 p.m.

The geneticist calls. No, I don't want to speak to her. I am furious with her, with all the doctors who caused this mess. They signed a paper saying my AFP results were normal. The perinatologist told us it was just his heart that had a problem, and that we didn't need an amnio done.

You didn't give me any options, I want to scream. *Now you can't make it better and you can't make it go away.*

No one can. I am in this alone. No one can wake me from this bad dream.

December 14, 2004—9:00 a.m.

It's nearly Christmas. Our seven-year-old daughter is excited. She doesn't understand why I am not. Our little boy is about to have open heart surgery nine days before Christmas. We will spend the holidays in a hotel across the street from the hospital.

We'll bring a small tree and presents. But it will not, cannot, be Christmas for me.

December 21, 2004—8:45a.m.

After a successful heart surgery, complications ensue. Septic shock. Our son is fighting for his life. I can't even count the number of wires, tubes, and lines covering every area of his body. He is swollen. He doesn't even look like himself. I put a picture up so the nurses and doctors can see him as he should be. He is so small. Will he be able to endure this? All seven pounds of him. Barely six weeks old.

I can't eat. I can't sleep. I can't think. Many, many prayers are being said across the country. Many more are being said from this hospital room.

I understand now.

How could I have been so self-consumed?

I don't want to live life without him.

Please, God. Please.

January 30, 2005—4:15p.m.

"My little brother has Down syndrome." Her words come out to her friends so easily. She adores her brother. Her love for him has no boundaries. She understands what Down syndrome is; her friends ask her to explain. I sit in awe listening to her describe in the simplest of terms what Down syndrome means to her. "It's no big deal."

June 30, 2005—10:15a.m.

My son is nestled comfortably in my arms. He is watching me as I watch him. I can't imagine not having him here with me. Tears come at the very thought; my heart feels like it will explode. I think back to all the events of his life so far. He will never understand the impact he has made on us. He will only feel comfort and love. He reaches for my face and the tear runs down his finger. *These are tears of love for you. I need you to know that, my dear.*

The geneticist saved his life—I realize that now. She had eased my fears about my risk factor for Down syndrome. She led me to believe an amnio wasn't necessary. She saved his life. I must let her know how these events have changed me. I may never have known this life, his life.

Thank you.

July 30, 2005—3:00 p.m.

"Mum!"

Did he just say that? I cannot believe it! He just said his first word. He is almost nine months old and he has said his first word! Yes, he has said "Mum!"

They told me not to expect words for at least another year. But "mum" was soon followed by "hi," "up," and "uh-oh!"

Relating this monumental moment to my parents, I can hear the tears on the other end of the telephone. They can imagine his future. He will talk after all, and do many more things besides.

January 27, 2006—7:00 p.m.

It is our daughter's ninth birthday. The family is here for the annual celebration. I listen as everyone talks about our son's surgery, his recovery, and how proud they are of him. It is overwhelming to hear it. Apparently this story is worth telling after all.

Again, I try hard to hold back my tears. But they are not tears of sadness.

July 15, 2006—8:15 a.m.

We watch as our son works on independent walking. He is still so small for his age. In fact, he doesn't look old enough to be almost walking. It is a scorching hot summer day, yet he waddles like a little penguin in just his diaper. The heat can't stop him. Nothing can.

He only needs our pinkie finger for support. Any day now, he will let go. The grin on his face and the squeal that escapes his lips are proof enough that he knows he has made his parents proud. I don't think I have ever seen a tear in Ken's eyes—until now.

July 20, 2006—3:15 p.m.

"Does he have Down syndrome?" It's a beautiful summer day and I am out with the kids shopping. An older woman has been watching us, and unlike many others, she doesn't hesitate to ask this question. I am caught off guard. I always feel the need to explain his diagnosis and the challenges he has and will overcome. But his life deserves more than a two-minute explanation. A simple answer will suffice this time.

"Yes, he is our miracle baby." And I smile.

Sherrill lives in Southern Alberta, Canada, with her husband, Ken. Their daughter, Tristyn (1997), is already an advocate for Down Syndrome, having written her first piece on awareness for her class. Their son, Trenton (2004), is a healthy, thriving, active little boy who did let go of that pinkie finger at twenty-one months of age. Sherrill is a fulltime municipal administrator who devotes her spare time to raising awareness of Down syndrome and providing support for other families touched by the diagnosis.

42

Slow Motion
by Stephanie Bissol

Megan Bissol

SHE HAD BEEN PLOTTING her big move for weeks. Positioning a foot this way, grabbing the cushion that way, grunting loudly, using every muscle in her body—all to no avail. But today is different, and she knows it. This time, her arm is just long enough, her tiptoes just high enough, her shoulders just strong enough for success. Reaching, grasping, pulling, sliding—and she's done it! Megan beams at me from her new throne. She has claimed her rightful position on the couch, and is now the reigning Queen of the Remote.

Her denim-colored eyes shine with accomplishment as she hits the slow motion button and watches Elmo and the other characters inch along the screen. This is power! Not only has she conquered gravity, but she also has control of the TV, just like her mom, her dad, and her big brother, Joey. She has shown her little sister that she is the boss, being first to master this task. It is a day to celebrate in the Bissol household. I go to the baby book and jot down a little note, "September 17, 2005. Megan was able to get herself up on the couch today—one year, ten months, and nine days old."

We seem to celebrate occasions like these all the time now. Just three days earlier, she stood by herself for four seconds, which was another first. Then, shortly before her second birthday, she learned to rise slowly from the floor, with just a little wobble. She held her arms out to steady herself much like an Olympic diver getting ready for her ultimate attempt. She completed her gold medal achievement and I noted it, "October 3, 2005—one year, ten months, twenty-five days old."

I know every little detail of these events, and others, because Megan has had to work a bit harder and try a bit longer than most children to accomplish them. Special dates and milestones seem to come to me easily when asked by a doctor or a friend, because Megan's progress is full of extra meaning. Her sheer determination to master new skills gives me continual cause to celebrate.

And to think, just two years ago our family was at an emotional standstill, sitting in the recovery room of the hospital, listing in our minds all the things she wasn't going to accomplish. We never spoke the words out loud but our looks, our tears, and our silence spoke volumes. Doctors and nurses were coming and going, apologizing to us, and consoling us. Social workers were coming in and out giving us pamphlets on Down syndrome and our local "mental retardation department." We kept hearing about "these kids" being delayed, as in, "They don't talk 'till much older and walking may not happen until age three to five. They are inevitably slow."

Slow. That was a hard word to swallow. My favorite thing when I was little was participating in field day at school. I loved racing the other kids, playing kickball and tug-of-war. These activities were things I was good at. I played basketball and softball through my school years, running up and down the courts and hitting balls pitched at me at 70 mph. All the kids who were slow or who couldn't hit the pitches didn't make the teams. I never wanted my own children to be too slow to make a team.

In a way, my fears came true: Megan's development in some areas has been slower than average. But I was wrong to have thought that this was something to be sad about. She has enabled us to view the world in slow motion—rather than the fast-forward many other people seem to be on—and it is wonderful.

Megan has taught me to notice and appreciate things I never paid attention to before. Like the subtle complexity of picking up a Cheerio. Did you know there was a name for this? "Pincering" is now a commonly used word in my vocabulary. Megan practiced with casino chips, first learning to grasp them, and later learning how to put them into a piggy bank. After months of work, she was able to reward herself by feeding herself a Cheerio.

Seeing these subtle accomplishments add up to a major event helps me appreciate the little things in life, the good things that I used to take for granted. When someone goes out of their way to hold open a door, or someone helps an elder carry a heavy bag to their car, I notice. I also notice the colors in the flowering dogwood tree in my front yard. I used to complain that the flowers weren't in bloom long enough; now I relish those few weeks of gorgeous flowers, taking pictures and showing my children the beauty of nature. I more fully enjoy the way my bed sheets feel after a long day, the smell of a fresh load of clean laundry, the taste of a perfect cup of coffee, the sight of my kids giggling with each other, and the touch of my husband when he comes in from a long day at the office.

Slow motion is an amazing feature. It enables us to take in the details that otherwise fly past our eyes. It helps us examine each and every tiny step which adds up to an amazing accomplishment. It shows us the beauty and grace hiding in everyday happenings. Cable and satellite companies are trying to offer this at a price so that TV audiences can savor every moment of their favorite programs.

Thanks to Megan, we get it for free.

Stephanie and her husband, Joe, live in Yardley, Pennsylvania, in a historic village. Stephanie recently left the financial industry to be a stay-at-home mom to their three children, Joey (1997), Megan (2003), and Olivia (2005). Joe currently works as a senior software architect for an insurance company. As a family, they enjoy going on vacations, playing board games, watching movies, and watching Joey play baseball and basketball.

43

When the Other Shoe Drops
by Beth Price

Jude Price

I THINK WE ARE FINALLY ready. The pulled pork and deviled eggs have been made, the fireworks have been bought, and the house is clean. It is July, 2006, and the Price family consists of a teenage boy, a preadolescent girl, and twin toddler boys, one of whom happens to have Down syndrome. As we prepare for company this weekend to celebrate the Fourth, my mind aches as I try to take in all the changes our family has experienced over the past six years.

As I mentally rewind back to another July 4th six years ago, I can't help but laugh as I remember sitting out on the front curb of our suburban, colonial-style house, watching our three young children make loops in the air with their sparklers. At ages seven, three, and two, our little gaggle was the pride and joy of our lives. Our youngest, Seth, had been put into one of those horrible toddler leashes for this occasion, as his strongest ambition in life at the time was to escape. How could we have imagined that this Fourth of July would be his last?

Three days later, he got the escape job done. During a split-second of inattention on the part of his distracted parents, Seth made his way out into the world for a few unsupervised moments. He met with disaster: a neighbor's unfenced, uncovered, unattended swimming pool. Despite the fact that we found him quickly and despite everyone's best efforts, Seth did not make it. Even as I write these words now, six years later, the pain of his loss is still fresh. I have replayed the events of that warm, summer afternoon a million times trying desperately to change the outcome. But each morning, I wake up and Seth is still gone.

My husband, Steve, and I began dreaming almost immediately about having more children. We were all too aware of the fact that we could never replace Seth, who had been so beautiful and unique in his zest for life. But having more children seemed to us a positive and hopeful step. In the face of complete devastation, our only other alternative was to curl up into a ball in a corner and rock back and forth for the rest of our lives.

Four years, several medical procedures, and several jumbo-sized bucketfuls of tears later, we learned that we were pregnant. One might expect that we were elated at this news, but our happiness was tentative. After weathering such tragedy, we couldn't shake the feeling of always waiting for the other shoe to drop. Worry plagued us at every turn. As soon as we learned I was carrying twins, we worried about vanishing twin syndrome, as one of the babies looked much smaller than the other, and we had read that this phenomenon is common. After both twins made it into the second trimester, we began to worry about preterm labor. I had already endured three c-sections and our doctor was concerned about how much more stretching my tired, old uterus could withstand. We worried about pre-eclampsia, low birth weight, and a whole host of other unpleasant things for the entire thirty-five weeks of the pregnancy.

Our boys' birth was scheduled a month early due to my impending uterine explosion. Just moments after the delivery, which is mostly a blur to me, the babies were whisked off to the special care nursery and I was wheeled into the recovery room. Shortly afterward, I was visited by my husband on one side of the bed, and the neonatologist on the other. The doctor announced rather matter-of-factly that he thought little Jude, weighing just three pounds and fifteen ounces, had Down syndrome. While Simon, the big one at five pounds, ten ounces was doing well, Jude needed a little help getting enough oxygen. After the doctor left, Steve crumpled on the bed beside me and began to cry. I didn't know whether he was crying because he was relieved that we had all survived the surgery, or because of the possible diagnosis of one of our precious newborn babies.

"Both," he would later tell me.

As for me, I was just numb. Reeling. Here was our other dropped shoe. We had known it was coming all along.

Those first few days in the hospital, I was in denial, spending hours examining Jude's tiny features searching for signs and telling myself there were none. On the fourth day, the karyotype results came back confirming in cold, hard, black-and-white what the doctor had suspected. There it was: An extra chromosome on the twenty-first pair. Trisomy 21.

My tears came, not in a gentle stream, but in a torrid outburst that frightened and surprised even me. *How could this be?* I thought. *After all we have been through?*

My first fears were for my relationship with Steve. The responsibility of parenthood is daunting under any circumstances, but would we be able to rise to the occasion of raising a child with a disability? Our marriage had already endured so much. Would this be our breaking point?

Even though we were weeks from bringing Jude home from the hospital, I was already wondering about whether he would ever be capable of leaving, of living on his own someday. Parents work hard for nearly two decades to try and instill everything they think their children will need to fly when it is time to leave the nest. But would Jude ever enjoy any independence? It bothered me to think about my husband and me never being alone again.

I was scared of what this would do to Jude's twin brother, Simon. I had been preparing to be the parent of twins since we saw two tiny hearts beating on the ultrasound, early in the first trimester. Having learned from books and even firsthand accounts of the unusual and sometimes difficult dynamic of being a twin, I was mind-boggled at the prospect of also throwing a disability into the mix. I imagined an older Simon feeling resentful and embarrassed by Jude, and immediately began inventing snappy comebacks for him to use when bullies at school ask him if he's retarded like his twin brother. Before I'd even changed either of their diapers for the first time, I was already strategizing the best way to handle future birthday parties, concerned that Simon might not always want a special-needs component to his celebration.

What would this mean to the future of our family? Though I hoped our older two children, Jake and Chloe, would love Jude unconditionally, I did not want them to feel burdened in caring for him, should anything happen to Steve or me. I couldn't relate at all; I had been an only child. I knew that having siblings would play a large part in shaping who these children would become. Having a sibling with a disability added a whole new dimension that was sure to affect them dramatically in many ways, some positive, some maybe negative.

And Jude himself—this was not the life I had hoped to give him. Would he be the sickly child that some of the literature described? Would he suffer? I flashed forward eighteen years and saw Simon excitedly packing for college and asked myself, *What will Jude look forward to?*

After we all came home, I had trouble bonding with the twins. Grieving for the "perfect" son I had pictured, I found Jude to be foreign and terrifying. He didn't look like any of our other babies. He was so tiny and fragile, connected to monitors and looking so frail. I went through the motions of caring for both babies, but I was struggling to sort through all of my emotions. Sleep deprivation, cold Midwestern winter temperatures, and postpartum depression made the continued care of my older two children a difficult task. But they still needed us, too. Homework, sports, and social lives all needed maintenance.

It wasn't long—maybe a couple of weeks—before I had my moment of clarity. One morning after a long night, while sitting in our darkened bedroom, I looked to the foot of our bed where both babies were finally sleeping soundly in their bassinets. At that moment, God tapped on my shoulder and gently, lovingly reminded me. I didn't hear his voice, but it was just as clearly imprinted on my mind as if I had. If I could put it into words, it would go something like this: "You prayed for more children. You have been given exactly that—two beautiful boys to love." And I remembered Seth. What I wouldn't give to have him here again. How I would treasure each moment, and not take even one of them for granted. Suddenly, the fog lifted enough for me to be able to take advantage of something that I had earned the hard way: Perspective. Down syndrome was no tragedy. I knew tragedy, and this was far from it.

This Fourth of July, Simon and Jude will probably be long asleep by the time it's dark enough for our own little family fireworks display. They will no doubt be worn out from a day of toddler mischief—climbing on stuff they shouldn't, pulling books off shelves, throwing food from their trays. At eighteen months, the developmental differences between them are noticeable, but do not keep them from being partners in crime. They are both sticky-fingered imps, typical little boys. And Jude, by the way, has been our healthiest baby.

It's true; a diagnosis of Down syndrome was the other dropped shoe for our family. But unlike the first shoe, which landed with a harrowing, irreparable thud, this shoe bounced deftly back upward with an enthusiasm we never expected. I'm even more convinced now that Down syndrome is not a tragedy. I wish I had known when Jude was born all that I know now about the bright future that is within reach for him. It's certain that our circumstances will present us with more than a few challenges as time goes on. But in the grand scheme of things…so what?

All kids are that way—challenging, messy, determined, curious, exhausting, frustrating, inspiring, without guarantees of any kind, and worth every bit of the effort.

All kids, whether they have forty-six or forty-seven chromosomes.

Beth and her husband, Steve, live in a rural town just south of Fort Wayne, Indiana. Steve is an ER physician; Beth is a stay-at-home mom who was previously employed as a middle school English teacher. Together they have five children: Jacob, Chloe, Simon, Jude, and Seth, who passed away in 2000.

44

Ups and Downs
by Bethany Balsis

Payton Balsis

HOURS AFTER PAYTON was born, four doctors walked into my hospital room, one after another, with somber looks on their faces. I already knew in my heart that our baby girl had Down syndrome. Deep down, I was still hoping that I was wrong, but they confirmed my worst fears. Then they quietly filed out of the room. As soon as the heavy, metal door closed behind them, my husband and I looked at each other and began sobbing. Then the questions began.

What are we going to do with a child with Down syndrome?
What kind of life capacity is she going to have?

What are we going to do financially?

Will she be able to go to daycare so that we can both continue to work?

We continued talking and crying and worrying, with all of our questions boiling down to one: *What will life be like for our daughter, and for us?*

That was the beginning of the roller coaster of emotions that we experienced over the next several weeks. It seemed that our new reality was a ride of happiness and sadness, hope and fear—a ride that we could not control.

About an hour after we met with the doctors, some of our family came to visit. Through tears, we told them of the doctors' suspicions. "I'm sorry," they said. Even though we were devastated, we did not want people feeling sorry for us. At the same time, it felt weird for people to say, "Congratulations!" I thought to myself, *Congratulations for what? Congratulations for having a baby that is in the NICU? Congratulations for having a baby that has Down syndrome? Nobody asks for their child to be born with Down syndrome, so why would anyone congratulate me for that?*

While I knew that they were simply congratulating us on the birth of our beautiful little girl, it was hard for me to swallow their comments. I felt as though they were tiptoeing around her diagnosis, which obviously had thrown everyone for a loop. I understood that these sorts of situations were hard and had I been in their shoes, I probably would not have known what to say myself. Still, nothing seemed to make me happy. And at the same time, I was ashamed at my feelings of sorrow. Why was I drowning myself in tears over her diagnosis, when Payton was in the NICU, hooked up to what seemed like hundreds of wires and monitors, fighting for life?

Later that evening, while my sister was visiting, we were doing some research online on our laptop computer. My husband ended up on the Special Olympics website.

"Payton is going to be the best bocce ball player in the Special Olympics!" he announced.

I said, "No, she is going to be the prettiest cheerleader in the Special Olympics!"

In hindsight, I realize that was our way of coping. We had quickly become determined to make Payton's life the best it could be. My sister later told me that our attitudes surrounding the situation helped her to cope. She said that as long as we were okay with everything, she was too. This made us realize that people were going to follow our lead regarding Payton's diagnosis. If our attitude was positive, others would be more likely to feel the same way, and that would make the world a better place for our daughter.

In the days that followed, I would sit and stare at my beautiful baby girl while she slept so peacefully in her isolette. Despite my hope for her future, a million worries continued to run through my head. How would other people react to her? Would she be stared at or teased? Would she have friends? My fears continued to churn in my stomach. I knew she would be okay as long as I was there to defend her, but I also knew that she would eventually have to blossom into her own being, and that scared me.

Prior to my discharge from the hospital, an unfamiliar nurse knocked on my door. She came into my room and sat next to me. There were tears rolling down her cheeks, but she had a sense of peace about her. "I've been in your shoes," she said. I looked at her intently, anxious to hear what she was going to say next. She said that years ago, her oldest son spent some time in the NICU at birth, due to a severe heart defect. *Finally,* I thought to myself, *someone that truly understands the emptiness that we felt at not being able to have our baby by our bedside to bond with.*

Smiling through her tears, the nurse went on to tell us about her friend's daughter who has Down syndrome. This girl was in love with life, she said. This girl had sleepovers with her friends, and they would run around giggling about boys. Imagining this future for our daughter brought us incredible relief. We were starting to realize that our life, and hers, could be a good one.

We spent the next several days traveling back and forth to the NICU, continuing to try to swallow what had just landed on our plate. At one point I came upon a former neighbor who knew I had been pregnant. After noticing that I was no longer pregnant, she naturally starting asking about the baby—the typical questions, like

"When was she born?" and "What did you name her?" At first I didn't mention that Payton had Down syndrome, but then I felt like I was cheating her with the answers I gave. So, in a sad sort of voice, I said, "She also has Down syndrome." Her response was one of obvious disappointment.

After we ended our conversation, I was angry with myself. Hadn't I already figured out that people were going to take my lead? I didn't feel disappointed anymore about the diagnosis, so why was I pretending to be? After that encounter, I never felt obliged to tell another soul that Payton had Down syndrome. If they already knew, then that was fine. But if they did not know, then that was fine too!

A couple weeks after we were able to bring Payton home from the hospital, some of our other family members came to visit. I was sitting at the kitchen table assembling the birth announcements that I had so proudly made, when someone said to me, "You know, your lives are never going to be the same." The tone of the statement was clearly negative. I was dumbfounded. I didn't know what to say. Had I been living in a dream world, thinking our lives wouldn't be different? I was confused, so I just nodded in agreement. Hours later, I was once again angry with myself for not defending our family. And just as before, I had feelings of confidence that Payton's life was worth living, and so was ours.

My confidence grew in the days that followed. At one point, I was talking to some other parents of children with Down syndrome about my worries for the future. Those parents told me, "Kids will be kids. They get teased for wearing glasses or for what they wear or for the things that they say. A typical child has just as high a chance of being teased as Payton does. You just never know. Try not to focus on the future." I had never thought about it that way. I felt a solid sense of peace—for a while, at least.

Payton is now seven months old. In some ways we are still on that roller coaster, although the ride does not feel as wild now. These days, we are trying to focus on doing everything we can to help Payton maximize her potential. Sometimes, the therapies and exercises and techniques can be overwhelming. Whenever I start to feel sad or scared, I find it refreshing to see my son, Mason, interact with his sister. At two years old, he is oblivious to the fact that Payton has Down syndrome. He adores her just for being herself. As he runs through the house day after day, he constantly makes quick pit stops to give Payton a kiss on the forehead and adoringly say, "Look at baby sister. Isn't she so cute?" His love is unconditional, as is mine and my husband's. And that love will ensure that we have more ups than we do downs.

Bethany and her husband, Kyle, live in Bristow, Virginia. Married in 1999, they have two children, Mason (2004), and Payton (2006). Kyle is employed as a human resource director and Bethany works as a United States probation officer. In her spare time, Bethany enjoys being with family and scrap booking.

45

Miracle Man
by Katy Servos

In loving memory of Allen D. "Bill" King

Sebastian Servos

EACH MORNING AS I walk into my son's room he is already awake, babbling his morning greetings to me in his own baby talk. No matter what side of the bed I have woken from, my mood is immediately brightened as I pick him up and receive my morning hugs. "Good morning, Sebastian. Did you sleep well?" While I dress him for the day, my eyes look over the room. It is filled with love and is a perfect place to begin and end each day. I see the stenciling his grandma placed on the wall displaying planes, trains, and cars in primary colors, and the dark, oak dresser that belonged to his other grandparents. I see the framed artwork purchased by one great-grandma and the blue curtains hand-sewn by another. There is the antique rocking chair my husband's grandmother rocked him in, and the handmade cradle that was crafted by my grandfather. Then there is the crib purchased as a collective gift by several extended family members, the changing table that my uncle built, and the woodcarving that hangs above it.

As I prepare to begin a new day with Sebastian, I reflect on the deep significance this carving holds for me as well as my son. The 10" by 13" relief carving was lovingly created on basswood by my grandfather. It is a beautiful display of a baby in the hands of God. Around it is framed Psalm 139:16, "You saw me before I was born. Every day of my life was recorded in Your book. Every moment was laid out before a single day had passed."

This verse has been my favorite ever since I was a child. I grew up in a household that was constantly changing as my father's occupation required frequent relocation. This did not set well with my aversion to change. I have always been a "control freak"—unable to cope with the unknown. My personality has reflected that of a perfectionist, bound to the details and schedules of the day. It has always been a comfort to know that even if I am troubled by change, God is in charge of my future. I know that the world is not random. While we are granted the ability to use free will, God can protect us and give us the guidance, if we only ask.

My grandfather was a major influence on my life. Rather than constantly preaching his feelings on God's love and desire for our lives, he chose to be a living example. One of the biggest lessons he taught me was faith in healing. My grandpa was diagnosed with cancer for the first time in the late 70s and was not supposed to live much longer after I was born. My mother used to sneak me into his hospital room as a baby because she knew the joy of his first grandchild would lift his spirits and bring him comfort. Grandpa won his battle with cancer, but continued to struggle with many other health issues throughout his life until he passed away in 2006. Among his many battles were various heart complications, which required several surgeries.

My struggle to deal with the unknown regarding my unborn son began when I felt obligated to have the routine Triple Test blood screening. I did not want the test for reasons of decision for my child, but rather for reason of preparedness in any situation. My OB called me with the results, informing me that I had a much higher risk of Down syndrome than most parents of my age. I was scheduled for an in-depth ultrasound to check for other markers associated with birth defects. During the exam, I was informed that my child had a large hole in his heart, mild hydrocephalus, and dilated kidneys. The doctor told me that while he suspected Down syndrome, there was also a high risk of various other genetic conditions that could be associated with death. He told me the only way to know for sure was by amniocentesis. We were informed that if the amnio did indeed predict a fatal syndrome, my child would not be afforded any lifesaving procedures should anything happen, since survival would presumably be impossible.

That was when I decided to battle the unknown. I was not willing to give in to my desire to be all-knowing if it would risk my son's best interest. No doctor, no person of any kind would tell me that they would not do anything to save my child. I told my doctors to book me in the most advanced hospital and get ready for anything. They would be prepared to give my child every chance he deserved.

Many months of prayer, speculation, trepidation, fear, and worry began on that day one week before Christmas. I realized that one of my worst fears was about to be revealed to me: The fear of birthing a child with a disability.

At that time my parents were spending a year in Rome on a missionary assignment. They faithfully called their congregation to prayer for their first grandchild. Among the congregation was a woman named Mirvana. This woman had gone through a similar situation with prenatal testing and knew full well the worries I was carrying in my heart. She had been through so much with the recent birth of her child. She was a prayer warrior—a woman with the gift of intercessory prayer. She came to my mother with visions granted by God regarding the birth of Sebastian. The visions gave details of a long, tough journey through which we would travel but overcome. *What did this mean?* I wondered. *Was this to say that my child would be born healthy and everything would be alright?*

The unknown finally began to reveal itself on May 18, 2005. My son was born by c-section after almost twenty-four hours of intense labor. Sebastian, the name I had chosen years before for its unique character. It was almost as if, like the scripture on the carving says, I knew my son before he was born! As the nurse handed Sebastian to my husband for the first time, there were no typical congratulations commonly associated with the birth of a child. Instead, my husband was greeted with, "You know he has Down syndrome, right?"

Before birth, the hydrocephalus and kidney dilation cleared up on its own. The only problems remaining were the prenatally diagnosed AV Canal heart defect and the suspected genetic diagnosis. My husband and I had been told that upon birth Sebastian would most likely be whisked off to the NICU for observation. There was even the prediction that I would not see him until days later due to health problems. Instead, I was blessed to have him with me for his first day of life. When one day old, Sebastian did land a spot in the NICU, but only for jaundice. Four days later, Sebastian's genetic makeup was confirmed. My world suddenly went into yet another ball of chaos. *No, this can't be true. The vision said he would be alright....*

I had all these views of Down syndrome based on outdated studies and people that had not been blessed with all of the opportunities available today. I spent the first several months of Sebastian's life immersed in anything I could find related to Down syndrome. I remember posting on an Internet support forum and asking if my seemingly insatiable desire for knowledge would ever slow down and stop taking over my every thought. Slowly, I learned to accept the facts of the diagnosis and dispel the outdated views and stereotypes I had once envisioned. Clearly, times have changed. There is a world of possibilities available thanks to early intervention therapies and inclusion in the school systems. I discovered that I did not have to segregate my son from his peers or shelter him from a cruel world.

Of course I knew that there might be many obstacles I would have to face, but knowledge is power. Power to battle the unknown! It became clear to me that rather than worrying about Sebastian's future, I needed to concentrate on his present. If opportunities for people with Down syndrome were able to change so positively just in the past several years, I knew his future would be even brighter.

When he was five months old, Sebastian had open heart surgery to repair his AV Canal defect. My husband, grandparents, and in-laws gathered in the hospital waiting room. My grandfather, who knew full well the recovery that Sebastian would face, was there to see him through his long day. We were all anxious to put this long-awaited day behind us.

During the surgery, Sebastian had a complication that would have been fatal ten years ago. But the surgeons were prepared for this, and all was well. We breathed a sigh of relief as we walked into his room in the intensive care unit. I was so grateful to have been prepared for the sights that awaited us thanks to a good friend in Canada who had sent us pictures of her son's same surgery. Yet again, I had not quite surrendered my need to control the situation and had needed some assistance from the photos. Thank God for her or we would've been blow away from the sights of Sebastian on all of those machines! However, nothing could completely prepare me for the sight of my own child so helpless, so reliant on everyone else to keep him safe. *Okay, God, maybe once again you are showing me I am not in control. Sebastian is in your hands now.*

Eight days later, he was home with us. A perfect, living miracle. Complete with the "zipper" down his chest that mirrored his great-grandfather's own.

Today, Sebastian is fifteen months old. We have taught him sign language since birth and he has learned those signs and a few spoken words. He continues to amaze his parents, relatives, and therapists with skills of all proportions. At this time, he shows no signs of cognitive delay and only a few months of physical delay attributed to heart surgery and recovery. Would I have ever imagined this in my outdated view of Down syndrome prior to Sebastian's birth? Absolutely not. I thank God every day for the gift I have been given in

Sebastian. I have even told Him that I would consider myself blessed to have another child with Down syndrome. Sebastian has taught me that complete control of everything is not always necessary. My fears are erased and my love is expounded beyond recognition. Ironically, my biggest fear has become my biggest joy.

The sun is just setting behind the clouds as I carry my son to his crib to sleep each night. Usually, he is still awake and wanting to play peek-a-boo with his blanket in an effort to extend his bedtime with playful smiles and giggles of delight. He always grins as I sign "I love you" and touch my finger to his nose. Obviously, God did know Sebastian before he was born. The vision was right and everything is going to be just fine. Once again, my grandfather's actions spoke louder than words when he carved the plaque for Sebastian.

I whisper, "Goodnight, my miracle man. Sleep tight."

As my mind wanders to the future, I think of all of the conversations we will have. At some point I will have to face the dreaded "coming of age" discussion. We'll have chats about girls. And that thin, white scar that becomes smaller as he grows bigger will be the topic of one very special talk we will have someday. "This, my son, is why I call you Miracle Man...."

Katy lives in Grandview, Missouri with her husband, Nathan, and their son Sebastian (2005), who is featured on the cover of this book. Katy works in the insurance industry. In her spare time, she enjoys being with her family, which includes three little lap dogs. She is also a volunteer in her local Down syndrome community.

46

Stepping Out
by Stefanie M. Miller

Luke Miller

MOST FAMILIES BEGIN to stress and worry if their twelve-month-old has yet to take a first step. My husband and I had long accepted the fact that we would experience delays in Luke's development, but we really began to question ourselves when Luke's second birthday came and went and he wasn't even pulling himself to standing position.

Gross motor skills, I believe, are the most obvious to show a delay. A shy and quiet child can hide the speech and fine motor delays, but how do you hide the fact that your three-year-old is still crawling and needs to be carried? I consider myself a strong parent overall, but Luke's early years were mentally draining just from answering all the questions and concern about the evident fact that he wasn't walking. They weren't terribly impressed with his great fine motor skills—he could self-feed with a fork by age two, he started using sign language shortly after age one, and he could work and manipulate all sorts of puzzles.

By nineteen months, we had hoped that Luke's younger sister would motivate him to want to walk. After all, she had motivated him to learn the "correct" way to crawl; he had been getting along just fine by "commando" crawling. But it didn't seem to be happening. Then, just before Luke's third birthday, Luke had become a big brother again. Now, I had three small children under the age of three—two definite non-walkers, and one that had just learned.

In my heart I felt Luke had the skills needed to walk, but lacked the confidence. I could see the fear in his eyes each time he would grip my hand to attempt it. One-year-olds fall all over the place; that is how they learn balance and coordination. Intellectually, Luke was beyond what strangers gave him credit for. He knew he could potentially get hurt. He had an understandable fear of pain, so he would rather not take the risk.

On Luke's third birthday, a longtime family friend told us they would like for Luke to be the ring bearer at their wedding, and for his sister, Grace, to be the flower girl. We were flattered and immediately accepted their offer. After they left, my first thoughts were that they must be crazy. Grace would just be turning two, and with only eight months before the wedding, I thought the only option for Luke to participate would be to have someone pull him down the aisle in a wagon.

Luke would be starting preschool in a couple of days, and I secretly hoped that being around lots of mobile children would give him the push of confidence he needed. He made progress over the next few months, learning to walk with the aid of a walker. At first he'd use it for about ten feet, then would drop down and begin crawling. Eventually, I was able to get Luke to use the walker the length of the driveway and back, and he would walk barely holding on to our fingers, but he still seemed nowhere close to taking those first steps alone.

Three months before the wedding, I gave up. This was tough. I felt that as a parent, his lack of skills was a direct reflection on me. Was it my fault that Luke was still not walking? Could I have taken him to more physical therapy sessions? Didn't I spend enough time with him? I felt awful whenever anyone asked me why he was still not walking.

On October 6, 2005, I got Luke off his school bus, as usual. Each day, Luke would hold on to my hand as we walked past each of the five houses until our own; then he would sit in our driveway. On this day, as soon as we reached the first house, Luke let go of my hand. He was walking all on his own. I was in shock. I cheered him on so much that he started laughing, and that caused trouble with balance. He started to fall halfway, but caught himself with his hands. At that point, I expected him to give up, and I was more than satisfied with the progress he had just made. But Luke had other plans. He just stood straight up again and took off walking the rest of the way home. Just a month later, it was as if he'd been walking since he turned one.

Our excitement in Luke's new skill peaked during his big moment—walking down the aisle, all by himself. He and Grace stole the show for a couple of precious minutes. I had the best "seat" in the house, standing at the end of the aisle with a package of candy, ready to tempt them if they got cold feet. Grace refused to throw her rose petals, and Luke stopped every so often to wave, but I wouldn't have changed a thing.

In a way, it seems silly to me now that I was so worried about Luke's walking. But that's how hindsight works. In my mind, I know that Luke will eventually reach each milestone; however, as a parent, it's hard to relax until it happens. It's because of Luke's disability that we have come to appreciate each and every little accomplishment that our three kids make. We have not lowered our standards, but we now realize that there are other disabilities that prevent other children from meeting the milestones that are so often taken for granted.

I once dreamed of sports trophies, great jobs, weddings, and grandchildren, and was devastated to think that Luke would not meet those expectations. But I realize now that he will have his own dreams to step toward. And that goes for all of my children: I will be proud as they reach for their dreams, not mine. I want them to be happy, appreciated, and loved. Period. My job is to support and guide them as they step out into life.

Stefanie lives in Hamilton, Ohio, with her husband, Adam, and their three children, Luke (2002), Grace (2003), and Liam (2005). Luke was given a prenatal diagnosis of Down syndrome via amniocentesis at 24 weeks gestation as well as a prenatal diagnosis of duodenal atresia. Other soft markers were seen on ultrasound such as a VSD, dilated kidneys, and hydrocephalus; however, all of these conditions resolved before birth. Luke was born when Stefanie was only 21 years old, her husband was 23. At birth, Luke was also diagnosed with esophageal atresia and the duodenal atresia diagnosis was confirmed. All needed surgeries were preformed during his NICU stay and he has not had any significant medical problems since those early months. Currently, Stefanie is back in school fulfilling her dreams to become a nurse. She is hoping that one day she can offer firsthand support to new moms when given an unwanted diagnosis.

47

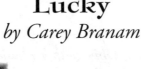

Lucky
by Carey Branam

Carey and Chelsea Branam

IT WAS FINALLY QUIET. The oxygen machines in the neighboring rooms were silent, the baby down the hall had drifted to sleep, and the nurses were busy reviewing paperwork. With only a speck of moonlight shining in the window, I lay in bed watching my precious baby girl. Her face was dry and red from the tape which held the oxygen tubes to her tiny face. She was perfectly peaceful. Then the faint sound of an ambulance arriving outside our hospital room awoke her. She began to squirm under the covers next to me, and by her soft cry I could tell she was scared. Without opening her eyes she reached her hand toward me. As soon as her little fingers touched my arm, her body relaxed again. She needed me, and I needed her. She was ten days old, and I was finally beginning to feel like the mother I so badly wanted to be for her.

Soon after Chelsea's birth our pediatrician told me she suspected Chelsea had Down syndrome. I thought the doctor must be wrong; doctors can be wrong. She ordered some tests and went home for the evening. I felt sick. I was all alone at the time; my husband had driven home to shower after a long night at the hospital. I waited for him in the nursery while the nurses took blood from my newborn baby. All I could do was stare at her. The waiting was unbearable.

I finally saw my husband entering through the security doors of the maternity ward. He was carrying an overnight bag with a clean change of clothes. His face was freshly shaven and his hair was still wet. The delicate skin under his eyes still dark from our sleepless night. But through those tired eyes I could see the fear. He knew something was wrong. As he locked his arms around me I whispered into his ear, "They think she has Down syndrome." His emotions took over. I could feel his body shake with every tear. For what seemed like an eternity, we stood there, in the middle of the nursery, holding one another.

I could feel the eyes watching us. While other parents were looking in on their perfect little babies, we were mourning the loss of ours. I would soon learn the staring had only just begun.

I spent the next forty-eight hours in the hospital. Instead of enjoying Chelsea and basking in new baby bliss, I was obsessing over the possibility that my precious daughter would be different. I had no idea how she would be different, but I imagined the worst: A chubby girl that couldn't talk well. A girl who was placed in a special classroom for retarded children throughout her life. A dependent adult who would never marry and have children of her own. And then what? Who would take care of her when we're gone? I had no idea. I had no books, no pamphlets, no computer—nothing to help me understand this disease (so I thought) called Down syndrome.

At four days old, the initial testing confirmed that Chelsea had an extra chromosome. Any hope that there was an awful mistake was gone. It was true. I was crushed. I had already planned my life, and my family. I didn't ask for this.

I sobbed as we walked through the waiting room after receiving the confirmation of the diagnosis. I could feel everyone staring at us again. They had no idea what it was like. They all had healthy children…and I hated them for that. They had no idea how lucky they were.

For the next week I became my own worst enemy, lying in bed all day looking for ways to "fix" my life. I continued to mourn for the baby girl I never had, for my family, and for myself. I was angry, but I had no one to be angry at. I tried to accept my daughter and I longed for the bond a mother has with her baby. One book said there was a high demand at adoption agencies for babies with Down syndrome. In the past, I never would have considered giving up a baby for adoption, but now it was an appealing possibility. I imagined her going far, far away with a family who would love her and give her everything she would need to grow and learn. I knew my husband would never allow it, though.

I even contemplated leaving. I constantly imagined how I could disappear and start over. The idea of packing a bag and sneaking out of the house with my toddler was tempting. But again I thought of my husband, a man who has dedicated his life to caring for and loving his family. He would be heartbroken.

On my darkest nights, when I lay in bed listening to my infant coughing as she struggled to breathe through her tiny nostrils, I would close my eyes and beg the Lord for an answer. I asked him to take away the burden of raising a child with special needs. I even gave him permission to take her back. I justified these awful thoughts by telling myself that Chelsea would be better off that way. I truly didn't want her to suffer her entire life.

It wasn't until the second week that my feelings began to change. She was ten days old when she was admitted to the hospital with a bronchial infection. Although she wasn't eating much, I was determined to breastfeed, so I stayed by her side day and night for five days as she recovered. Once on oxygen, she began to feel better quickly. She finally began to nurse. The first night I slept in a bed next to her bassinet, and brought her in bed with me when she needed to eat. By the second night, she refused the bassinet and would only sleep by my side.

Our five days in the hospital brought us together. Although it was difficult to watch my daughter lie there connected to oxygen tanks, we were lucky to have the time alone to bond as mothers and daughters normally do. As she continued to feel better, she was more awake and alert. She would clench my finger tightly in her tiny hand as she nursed, then she would peek up at me with her sparkling blue eyes. She seemed to be checking to make sure I was still there. That's when I realized that she needed me, and I needed her.

Six months have passed now and she still holds onto my finger and watches me as she eats. She smiles at me when she wakes up in the morning, and even leans in to give me kisses when I ask. She laughs at her big brother's silly faces, she rolls around the floor to get her favorite toy, and she even sits up by herself to listen to a story. One would never know just from looking at her that she has an extra chromosome. She's just a baby. I understand now that children with Down syndrome do not spend their lifetime suffering; they are just like all children. They love us, and they need our love and acceptance in return.

While Chelsea has grown tremendously in her short lifetime, it is possible that I have grown even more. My new plan is to live the life I have been given to the fullest. I still feel people staring at us when we are in public, but now I smile and think to myself, *If they only knew how lucky we are!*

Carey lives in Topeka, Kansas, with her husband, Ryan, and their two children, Logan (2003) and Chelsea (2006). Before Chelsea's birth, Carey taught a class for first and second graders new to the United States who do not speak English. When Chelsea was born, Carey made the difficult decision to put her career aside and stay home. They haven't looked back since, and Chelsea is happy, healthy, and thriving.

48

Nolan: A Little Dream
by Catherine Finn

Catherine and Nolan Finn

MY HUSBAND, SEAN, and I welcomed our first child, Nolan Sean Finn, on February 15, 2005. He truly is the light of our lives. Yet as much as I hate to admit it, I did not always feel this way. When we found out shortly after Nolan's birth that he had Down syndrome, we were shocked. Our dreams for the future seemed shattered. We thought our lives would never again be normal.

After learning about Nolan's diagnosis, I naturally turned to my family and friends for support. My family was very encouraging and listened whenever I needed them to. My friends were also there for me. At the same time, though, there were many instances where they could not relate to the special challenges that Sean, Nolan, and I were facing on a day-to-day basis. This made me feel increasingly stressed and frustrated, and my anxiety about my family not being normal grew stronger.

Thankfully, my anxiety quickly subsided when I found out about the Down syndrome bulletin board online at BabyCenter.com. The people who posted on this board reached out to me and helped me understand that my life was actually normal after all. Although all of our children are unique, we found that we had so much in common and we enjoyed sharing our experiences. For example, Nolan has had several surgeries, feeding issues, and some developmental challenges that these women's children have also experienced. Being able to communicate with them day or night has gotten me through several hard times. I can ask questions, express concerns, celebrate milestones, and share pictures. A few of us have become close friends, calling one another on the phone and meeting for play dates.

Today I have a changed view of what "normal" means. I've realized that each one of us not only has unique experiences, but also a shared set of experiences that in fact make us normal. To illustrate this belief I created a video montage of photographs of Nolan and me called "A Life Worth Living," accompanied by the song "Dreams" by The Cranberries. I shared it with friends, family, and, of course, my online friends at BabyCenter.com. How amazed I was at the response the montage received! In three months, more than 16,000 people viewed it online. Everyone who meets Nolan, either in person or online, notices what a lovable, beautiful little boy he is. More than anything else, they see him simply for who he is.

These and other experiences inspired me to continue spreading positive messages about life with a child with Down syndrome. Recently, I told my friends at BabyCenter.com about my desire for Oprah Winfrey to do a show dedicated to raising Down syndrome awareness. With their help, I am sending to Oprah a scrapbook of all of our children, along with a personal letter, my montage, another montage that includes the children of my BabyCenter friends, and a copy of this book, *Gifts*.

My dream is to allow the world to see how these children are blessings, not just to us, but to everyone. After all, Down syndrome is one of the most common genetic anomalies in the world, and I feel it is time that the public was made more aware of the large population of families living with Down syndrome. I want the world to understand that every child, whether they have a disability or not, deserves equal opportunities to grow and develop. I want to emphasize that children with Down syndrome are more similar than different when compared with other children.

My life was normal before I had Nolan, and I've come to realize that it is still normal today. The only difference is that now I have new dreams.

Catherine lives in Northern Illinois with her husband, Sean, and their son, Nolan. Catherine was a high school science teacher but now is a stay-at-home mom. Sean is a middle school science teacher. Catherine enjoys being a mother and is grateful that she can stay home with Nolan every day. Catherine was twenty-eight and Sean was thirty-one when Nolan was born. They learned of Nolan's diagnosis of Down syndrome at birth. Nolan had open heart surgery at three months old to repair his VSD and had three surgeries at twelve months old to repair one of his kidneys. Today he is a healthy and happy little boy. Catherine's montage "A Life Worth Living" can be viewed online at http:// onetruemedia.com/otm_site/view_shared?p=41811d19928d655419aea.

49

The Eighth-Grade Dance
by Nicol Hudson

Alex Sachs and his friend

AS THE SCHOOL YEAR came to a close in June 2006, I found a notice in my son Alex's backpack. It was an invitation for Alex, a seventh-grader, to attend the eighth grade farewell luau. At first I thought this must be a mistake, so I called the school. The administrator for the eighth grade told me that Alex had been personally invited by the eighth grade student body.

The dance was to be held in the courtyard of the school on a warm Friday evening. I rushed home early from work that afternoon and picked Alex up from school. I knew that, like any teen, he would be spending a lot of time preparing for the event. Excitement was in the air immediately.

When we arrived home, off he went into his room. On came his radio blaring his favorite Kenny Chesney music. Occasionally, I would peek my head through his bedroom door to see him trying on different outfits.

Finally, the door swung open and there before me was my boy—or was it a young man? Alex is a pretty handsome kid, I must say. He stands five feet, two inches tall and because he is very active, he has a slender build. Dressed in a button-down shirt, khaki shorts, and his cool dress shoes, he was off to the bathroom for a shave (No, he doesn't quite have a mustache—his shaving entails a coating of shaving cream and a practice run with a fake razor). Then, on with the hair gel and cologne, both to the extreme. Ready to go, Alex hopped into the car, wearing a smile from ear to ear.

When we arrived at the school we walked around back to the courtyard. Streamers and paper flowers hung on the trees. Kids were filing in and music was blaring from the speakers. The smell of grilling hot dogs and hamburgers filled the air. My plan was to stay with him, walk around, grab a bite to eat, be by his side the whole time. It's a mom thing, I suppose. But Alex had other plans.

As we walked up the courtyard steps, we heard voices say, "Hi, Alex." Once inside, Alex motioned for me to stand over by the wall. He said, "I'm fine," flashed me the peace sign, then walked away with that typical teenage strut. He approached one of his teachers; I could see they were holding a pretty good conversation. Then he sauntered over to the refreshments. I was holding myself back from going to rescue him. He seemed to be searching for a face he recognized. I strategically positioned myself behind various trees to keep an eye on him.

Just as I was about to grab him and say, "Okay, are you ready to go?" a group of girls came over to him. After a brief conversation they placed their arms around his shoulders and walked him over to another group of kids. The next time I saw Alex, he was dancing with about ten other kids. Boys were giving him a handshake or a high five. It was all I could do not to cry, I was so proud. This is what I have always wanted for him: Acceptance.

We stayed for about an hour or so. He posed for some pictures with his friends for the yearbook, as well as for me. When we arrived home he was beaming with pride, and he ran to tell his dad how much fun he had.

Now after returning home from a school dance, at a school where all the kids in the neighborhood attend, at a school where Alex is just another kid, I realize that I have a pretty typical teenager on my hands. This is a bit of a surprise. Fourteen years ago, when I was thirty weeks pregnant with Alex, he was diagnosed with Down syndrome. Back then, I worried that he might never walk. I worried when he would ever talk. I worried about his first day of school, when he hopped on the school bus at three years of age. I worried about his health. I worried that I was not doing enough for him day after day. But I never worried about my choice to bring him into this world, or about my ability to deal with these day-to-day concerns.

When it came time for him to transition from elementary school to middle school, I pressed for him to be included in our neighborhood school, instead of being bused to one that had a "special program." I hoped that I was doing the right thing. Alex is now mainstreamed in all his classes except reading and math, for which we have him in a small focus group. Inclusion always seemed to be a fight, but the more we fought for it, the more the school administration realized its benefits—not only for Alex, but for all the students.

Those fears of the past are gone, perhaps replaced with new ones like my worries about him having a girlfriend, driving a car, or living on his own. He is a typical teen who loves loud music, PlayStation 2, basketball, and swimming. He attends regular summer camp at the YMCA and, as I write this, is spending a week away from home at resident camp. Do I still wonder what his future holds? Sure I do, but I have learned to take things day by day, week by week, year by year. I'm learning to avoid setting my sights too high, but refusing to set them too low.

And if I ever forget that, all I have to do is look at his photos from the eighth-grade dance.

Nicol lives in Baltimore, Maryland, with her husband, Chip, and son, Alex. In 1991, during her twenty-eighth week of pregnancy, Nicol was undergoing a normal ultrasound exam when the doctor noticed a "bubble" in the baby's stomach. After an amnio was performed at thirty weeks, the results came back confirming duodenal atresia and Down syndrome. Alex was born prematurely at thirty-two weeks. Nicol and Chip both work full-time outside the home, and Alex will soon begin his last year of middle school.

50

What I Know Now
by Carla Reeves

Amelia "Mia" Reeves

DEAR CARLA,

Everyone always says, "I wish that I knew then what I know now." Wouldn't it be nice to know the future? Well, now you can.

You are sitting at your desk at work. It's just a regular day, you think. But in just a moment the doctor will call. "Mrs. Reeves, you are having a baby girl!"

Your heart will jump with excitement. Having two boys already, this is something you had always hoped to hear. But the next sentence is not. "I'm sorry to say that she has Down syndrome."

At that moment, every fiber of your being will seem to burn with pain. You will start crying and fall to your knees. Someone will help you up, take you into the office, and call Mom to come get you. When Mom walks in the door you'll just hug her and cry, all the while asking her, "Why me? What did I do to deserve this?"

You'll even say, "It's a girl, Mom, why her?"

You will go to the doctor in the afternoon and she will explain what Down syndrome is. There will be no encouraging words. She'll say there will be medical problems and mental retardation, and that you need to think about the option of abortion. At first you'll be completely stunned by her words. *Abortion?* you'll think. *Why would I do that?* You will leave the doctor's office with orders for more tests and an appointment to see a genetic specialist.

You'll go home and talk with Mom and Dad and Joel. Right away Mom and Dad say they will support you no matter what you do. Joel is going to be in shock, not saying too much those first few days. Later on, he'll come around and be there for you when you need him most. At first you're going to feel like this is all being left up to you, and that you're alone in the world with this big decision to make. You have never thought about abortion in terms of yourself before, but then again there was never a situation like this before.

You're going to sit at home for the next few days thinking about your daughter. You'll search online for some kind of hope. You'll secretly wish that you will find a place that offers some kind of experimental drug that would "cure" your baby girl. There is nothing of the sort; however, you will find a lot of websites that offer information about Down syndrome. Very little of it is encouraging.

With every passing day the idea of abortion will keep popping back into your head. You will remember the illnesses that your other children had as babies, and deep down you will question your ability to go through more hospital stays. You will question yourself as parent: *Am I good enough and strong enough to be a parent to a disabled child?* You will keep thinking to yourself, *Can I really have an abortion? Can I move past it if I do?* With every thought your heart will break more and more for the little girl you thought you were going to have. It's almost as if you had the perfect little girl and now she is gone. And to make things worse, there's another little girl in your stomach wiggling around.

You and Joel will go to see the geneticist. She will not be reassuring either. She's going to tell you that you still have time to have an abortion, and that in a few months you can try again. This theme will seem to echo around you when you talk to other people. You'll do another ultrasound that day, a more advanced one where they examine and measure every little thing possible. You won't pay attention to any of that. All you will see is your little girl on the screen sucking her thumb, kicking her feet and moving around, making it hard for the technician to complete the exam.

The doctor will come in when it is over and tell you the baby has a very large hole in her heart. And your first panicked thought will be, *Is she going to die?* You will finally realize that you are not going to let this little girl go without a fight.

On a beautiful spring morning Amelia Reeves will be born by c-section. The doctors will bring her early because they think she is going to be a whopping ten pounds if you wait until forty weeks.

She will be just gorgeous.

She will have open heart surgery at two months old to repair the hole in her heart, and you're going to spend every moment of her surgery praying that you will hold her in your arms again.

She will come out of surgery just fine. Much to the amazement of the doctors, in just two days, she will be off all medications and smiling like normal.

At age two, Amelia will have no health problems. She'll be a little delayed at reaching her milestones, but she will be reaching them. She'll love her brothers and they will love her. Sometimes you even have to fight them to get your turn holding and playing with your daughter.

You will learn that having a child with Down syndrome is an incredible experience—sometimes heartbreaking, and sometimes so wonderful you feel like your heart is going to explode.

You will have some scars from the rough times, but the good times will make them fade away until you almost can't see them.

It won't be easy, but it's not going to be as hard as you think.

Amelia's laugh is going to make you laugh; her smile is going to melt your heart. You're going to get up every morning and see her smiling in her crib, and know that everything is wonderful. You're going to beam with pride at every accomplishment. Best of all, you're going to lay Amelia down at night and rub her face and tell her what a beautiful fairy princess she is, and she is going to rub your face back, telling you that she thinks you are too.

And the most important thing I know now? You won't lose a perfect little girl. You will gain one.

With love,
Carla

Carla is a thirty-year-old mother of three children. Her youngest child was prenatally diagnosed with Trisomy 21 via amniocentesis. Carla comes from a large Hispanic family. They live in the southeast. They enjoy spending time with their family, playing on the computer, and going to theme parks and museums.

THE GIFT OF LOVE

51

The Life that Chose Me
by Monica Braat

Mikey Braat

I HAVE COME TO UNDERSTAND that there are moments in life that seem ordinary, yet become deeply rooted in us and eventually serve to shape the course of our lives.

When I was a preteen, I watched a movie with my parents one night about a mother who was fighting for her child with Down syndrome to be included in society. I had no idea what Down syndrome was, but I was touched by the story this mother told. Another night soon afterward, I snuck out of my room so that I could see another movie my parents were watching. This one was about a teenage mother who tried so hard to be a good parent, but ended up deciding that adoption was the best choice for her child. As I secretly watched from around the corner, I began crying, which gave away my hiding place. My father reassured me that the baby would be going to a better family, and that sometimes this was how families were formed.

Those moments were powerful, but eventually they got pushed into the place with all my other growing-up memories. They became vivid again years later when I held my son in my arms for the first time.

I do not know where this story really starts, as there have been a million moments in my life that have led me to this point. But one important piece to the story is what happened after I completed my education degree. My first job was far from home, and I quickly met friends who became like family to me. A few months before I knew them, their fourth child, an adopted son with Down syndrome, had passed away before he celebrated his first birthday. Over the next few years, they adopted two more children with Down syndrome. These two children touched me to a depth that I never thought possible. They defined for me what is important in life and taught me many lessons of love, acceptance, and the importance of living every minute to the fullest.

In time, both my friends and I felt the pull of our extended families and moved closer to our respective homes. A few months later, in November of 1998, these same friends phoned me to tell me how a stranger had approached them at church that week to ask if they were interested in adopting her sister's baby with Down syndrome, who would be born in a few months. My friends considered it briefly, but came to the conclusion that their family was complete. After relating this story, they asked me if I would consider adopting this child, or any child with Down syndrome. I quickly said no, feeling that I did not have what it took to be such a parent.

Although that should have closed the book, the next months became ones of much soul-searching for me. I began to long to hold a child in my arms, and the child I envisioned had Down syndrome. But I struggled with my belief that children are better off in two-parent families, with one parent home fulltime. I questioned how I could even think of taking on the responsibility of adopting a child who might be dependent on me for life. I wondered if I had the knowledge, patience, support, and financial means to give this child the life he or she deserved. I worried that I did not have the right personality to be an advocate for a disabled child. And through all the questions and concerns, the images and feelings of desire only became stronger. It was like I was doing battle with myself—explaining to a heart that knew where it was going why this logically did not make any sense. For some time, the logical side of me prevailed. I moved forward believing that there was no way I could be an adoptive parent. But a seed had been planted within me, and the battle between heart and mind raged on.

A few weeks later, I flew down to visit with my friends for Christmas. During this visit, the topic of adoption was once again brought up. At this point, all that I had been thinking about caused me to become defensive, and the conversation quickly stopped. I felt strong and in control again, as I was sure that my mind had finally, completely won out. Looking back, I can see that whole conversation as my one last fight before giving in to what had been fated since the beginning.

I returned home on New Year's Eve and didn't sleep for the next couple of days. There was a feeling of restlessness growing inside me. By the evening of January 2, 1999, I was completely exhausted, and finally slept. I woke the next morning knowing that I was about to give in to my heart.

That day, January 3rd, I made a phone call to my friends to tell them what I was about to do. On that same day, unbeknownst to me, a little boy was born by c-section in a hospital on the other side of the country. He was not breathing well and was taken quickly for treatment. The doctor looked at him and also noted that he would need to be tested for Down syndrome.

In the days that followed, I got busy with the job of finding out about the adoption process. I initiated my home study, and the next few months were crazy, as I went through all the steps that one needs to go through to adopt. By mid-June, I was waiting for the final write-up on my home study, which would put me on a waiting list. Given all that had happened to this point, I was looking specifically for a child with Down syndrome. The agency told me that my wait would probably be about a year, and I mapped my life out accordingly. But I was soon reminded once again that I wasn't really in control of this, and that the little life map that I had written in my head just wasn't going to work.

In the middle of June, a friend who I had met on an online single adoptive parents message board emailed me about a little boy that the local children's aid society was trying to place. Although I had heard of other children over the course of the long adoptive process, I seemed to know immediately that this one was "mine." And he was. Things fell quickly into place after my first contact with his social worker. By late July, I was able to fly out and meet Mikey, who was then six-and-a-half months old. He was that same little boy who had been born on that morning I had woken up with the knowledge that I would adopt a child.

It has now been just over seven years since I first picked up that little imp of a boy whose smile took up his entire face. I've often tried to describe the impact that he has had on my life, but words always fall short. He challenges me every day to remember all the things that are important in life and to live my life with those things as my guide. He has shown me a new pace to living—one in which I have time to stop and enjoy all that is around us. He has pushed me to the brink of my patience as I've waited for him to reach a milestone, and then brought me to a place that was higher than I knew was possible when he finally found success. He has taught me that perfection is not about who or what you are, but rather about what you bring to others—and that there is nothing that comes closer to perfection than making someone else smile from the bottom of their soul.

Each night before I go to bed, I still sneak in to his room and look at him, sleeping peacefully with his little hands balled up close to his face, and whisper a prayer of thanks. Some nights I watch him and think back to all the worries I had about being able to parent him or be an advocate for him or shield him from the ignorance of others. These worries have not disappeared, but they have paled in comparison to the blessings that my son has brought into my life. As

I close the door to his room each night, I know I will be able to sleep in peace knowing I am living the exact life that I was meant to live.

I am so glad that my heart won out.

Monica is a single parent living in southern Alberta, Canada, with her son, Mikey (1999). As a result of parenting Mikey, Monica has changed careers from teaching high school mathematics classes to teaching in a self-contained classroom for children who have severe to profound disabilities.

52

Tiny Hands
By Courtney Koblitz Fields

Koby Fields and Courtney Koblitz Fields

Faith is stepping out on nothing and finding something there.
—Jeff Atkinson

"TIME OF BIRTH 11:58 a.m.," shouted the sweet nurse who had been with me all morning.

They laid my new son—my first baby—on my stomach. He was barely crying. I looked down at him in amazement and relief after an intense seventeen-hour labor. *He is precious*, I thought. *Wow, he has the tiniest hands!*

But within a few minutes, they whisked him away with careful nonchalance. There was an uncomfortable silence as the nurses rushed around cleaning up, and I asked, "When will I get my baby back? They told me I could have him for an hour before they took him."

One of the nurses looked up at me and said, "Well, Mrs. Fields, he is having trouble breathing, not uncommon for babies with a double nuchal chord like your son had. We will move you across the hall and the pediatrician will be in to talk to you in a bit."

We waited for what seemed like forever. My husband, Chris, and I tried to be patient. About two hours later, I finally heard a knock at the door, and relief flooded over me. "Come in," I shouted before Chris had time to even realize that someone had knocked. In walked the pediatrician, the same pediatrician Chris had had as a baby.

"Hi, guys," he said. "Congrats."

But he wasn't smiling. Nervous, we waited for what would follow. "I need to talk to you about the baby. He is having trouble keeping his oxygen saturation levels up on room air so we have him in a vent hood, and he will have to stay there until he does well enough off of it."

"How long will that be?" I asked through tears.

"Hard to say right now, because there are some other concerns. Koby has a heart murmur; I have ordered an echocardiogram to be done first thing in the morning so we will know more then. We have strong suspicion that your son has Down syndrome. I am getting a blood test now, and we should have it back within two weeks."

Chris and I were numb. We decided to wait until morning to tell anyone what the doctor had said. We spent the remainder of the day silently, just trying to collect our thoughts.

The next morning, while the results of the echo were being read, we entered the level II nursery. There he was, even more beautiful than I had remembered, with hair slightly red and curly like his Daddy's, and with almond-shaped eyes and very petite features, like mine. He was as still as could be. Even though he was hooked up to a wall full of machines, he wasn't fazed. Holding him briefly, we noticed a card on the side of his bassinet, which informed us that he weighed six pounds, ten ounces and was nineteen inches long at birth.

We headed back to our room to wait for the test results. As we passed by the glass window of the "regular" nursery I noticed lots of babies, some wrapped in pink, some in blue. "Oh, look! A set of twins," I said to Chris. Then I noticed something else: These babies all had names on their bassinets. Isabel, Luke, Bethany, Mickala. The twins, Rylie and Cameron.

Nobody asked me if my baby had a name.

I thought of those beautiful tiny hands. They held so much promise. This child deserved to be called something more than "Baby Boy Fields." Did they think he wouldn't make it; did they think we wouldn't want him? I rushed back to the nursery, dripping tears of anger on the concrete floor. I ripped the card off of his bassinet and thrust it toward the nurse. "His name is Koby. Please write down his name."

She paused, and looked at me. "Koby it is," she obliged.

With that we headed back toward our room, feeling solemn, my tears still flowing. As we passed door after open door, I listened to the laughter of other parents as they received guests and presents and rejoiced in their new babies. The sound broke my heart. I wanted to hold my baby, and have guests and gifts. Instead, I just had this empty sick feeling and a sense of hopelessness, wondering if my baby would even live.

A few hours later the pediatrician returned, this time a little more anxious. "I talked to the doc at our children's heart hospital in Charleston. He wants to see you right away. It appears Koby has two holes in his heart, as well as a valve that isn't closing all the way." That being said, he left. And I felt that my life was over.

I was terrified that Koby might need heart surgery. *I am going to lose my son. That baby I had wanted for so long. The baby we named after my dad.*

I was terrified that Koby might have Down syndrome. *He will never leave home. We will always have to care for him. I don't know how to do that. I don't know if I can do that.*

And when our visit to the heart hospital confirmed our worst fears, I was angry. *What did we ever do to deserve this? We are good people, we follow the laws, we don't do drugs, or drink. I'm too young for this! I want it all to go away. It isn't fair!*

I thought those tiny hands would only bring us pain. I was so wrong.

Two months later we handed our precious boy over to a surgery team donning green scrubs and white coats. We expected the worst. "Please take care of him and bring him back to us safely," I pleaded. "He is all we have."

He is all we have. I had not fully realized the transformation in my feelings about Koby until I heard the love and longing in my own voice. As we sat in the eerily quiet waiting room, those words kept ringing in my ears.

Six grueling hours later I finally heard another voice. "Mrs. Fields, the doctors are ready for you now." It was the sweet gray-haired lady from the reception desk. We jumped up and followed her back to a room filled with beeping monitors and busy nurses. We looked down at our sweet boy covered with tubes and telemetry, IVs and restraints. I could barely breathe as the surgeon gave his report. The procedure was harder than he thought it would be; Koby's stay would be longer than expected.

Day in and day out, I sat at his bedside. The beeping of the monitors and the flurry of medical terms seemed like a foreign language. Even harder to handle were Koby's own communications with us. He had a tough time keeping his heart rhythm as he came off the anesthesia and the life support; his little body was so shaken up by all of the constant poking and prodding. But through it all he continued to smile his wide, gummy grin we all so loved. We knew he was in pain, but he wouldn't cry. Instead, he would look at me in the most helpless way. *Mommy, please help me!* his eyes would plead. At night I would cry myself to sleep, praying that the pain could come to me instead of my son.

But morning always came. I filled the dragging hours with all the care I could give him, singing to him and helping him play with the toys he had received as gifts. And I realized that Koby was helping me learn far more than how to read a heart monitor. He was showing me how to endure the difficult things in life, how to rise above pain and find the strength to go on.

After seven long days in the hospital, Koby was discharged. With Chris in the driver's seat for the two-hour trip, I sat in the back seat with my sleeping angel in his car seat next to me, gently stroking his tiny hands the whole way home.

Koby's influence has reached to other loved ones as well. Not long after his birth, my mother was diagnosed with breast cancer at the age of forty. She had no symptoms; we had no warning. We were devastated.

Hearing her voice on the phone one day, I knew she was deeply depressed. I packed up Koby and headed to her house. Walking in, I saw Mom curled up in her favorite chair, surrounded by all four of her dogs. Her eyes were red and puffy and barely open. She scarcely looked up when we entered the room. "Mom, I brought someone to see you," I said, holding Koby up like a prize.

She quickly sat up and took the cooing baby from my arms. "Boy, is Granny glad to see you, Buddy!" she sighed happily, and set off on a trot around the house, holding Koby close and whispering to him.

This was the first of many such encounters. When Mom lost her hair, Koby didn't care; he would reach up and rub her bald head and laugh like crazy. When Mom was so sick from chemotherapy that she could not leave the house, Koby would spend the night there with her, playing and talking till all hours. When Mom would start to complain and get down on herself, Koby was there to remind her of all he had been through in his little life and all he still faced, which drew her out of the darkness.

Mom went into remission after eight months of treatment. I give credit to God's grace and to modern medicine, and also to my son's tiny hands of comfort.

Koby's hands bring hope not just in troubled times, but to everyday life. Even simple pleasures like speaking become celebrations. "Indian!" he says, clapping for himself even before he gets the word out. "Dahdah!" he shouts, while showing the sign for *Dad*, then quickly erupts into a frenzy of applause. "Adag!" he exclaims, patting his leg in the sign for *dog*, and laughs wildly at his own success. This is something I never thought I would see or hear. And he is just as proud of each of his accomplishments as we are.

Walking through the grocery store, pushing my sweet boy all strapped into the metal cart with the rickety wheels, he flashes his contagious smile and waves to all the passersby. "Hey!" he exclaims, throwing his hand in the air.

"Keep those hands in the cart, you silly boy," I tell him, as he tries to pull the veggies from the shelves, all the while laughing and signing "eat." "Tell them bye-bye!" I prompt as we finish checking out and head for the door.

As sure as rain, he lifts his tiny hands, curling each little finger in and out. "Buh-buh!" he says, leaving everyone with a smile on their faces.

These hands are what we found when we stepped out into nothing, into fear and confusion and dread. These hands have led us to places we never could have found alone. These hands are full of goodness, light, and love. These tiny hands have touched so many lives and hearts—most of all, my own.

Courtney, Chris, and Koby live in Myrtle Beach, South Carolina. Originally from Atlanta, Courtney is a nursing student and hopes to work in pediatrics. Chris works as a manager for Puma North America. As a family, they enjoy the beach, the pool, and anything outdoors. Courtney loves family and food (and especially the two of them together) and has a collection of cow memorabilia. She hopes to someday live on a farm so she can own a real one! Chris loves video games and anything else electronic, and Koby loves the Doodlebops, eating, and signing. The family attends church at East Conway Pentecostal in Conway, South Carolina.

53

Brothers
by Dena Castellano-Farrell

Garrett, Griffin, and Braeden Farrell

IT'S NEARLY DINNERTIME. I'm sitting in the living room, savoring the smell of dinner coming from the kitchen, and smiling at my three boys. Garrett, age six, is leading his brothers in an energetic version of "Ring Around the Rosy." Braeden, age five, is putting his heart and soul into the song as he teaches his little brother Griffin, age two, the moves. Griffin is giggling so hard just watching his brothers that he can barely stand up. "Ashes, ashes, we all fall down!" The three of them collapse and the giggling escalates. When Griffin stands up unassisted, you would think he just hit a grand slam.

"Mommy! He did it!" his brothers chorus.

"Griffin stood up all by himself!"

"Way to go, Griffin!"

Of course I'm smiling; I am the luckiest woman on earth.

When Griffin was diagnosed with Down syndrome, I had so many worries about what this would mean for all three of my sons. Garrett and Braeden had just turned three and four years old. How could we manage this? I worried that we wouldn't be able to give them enough attention because we would be devoting all our time to Griffin's special needs. (I thought for some reason that Griffin would require round-the-clock care and our undivided attention.) I dreaded the seemingly inevitable neglect of their needs. I even planned ahead, teaching them at their young ages to write their first names, figuring I certainly wouldn't have time to teach them once I was consumed with Griffin's care. And as I envisioned the older boys' futures, I worried that they would somehow be burdened with their brother. I imagined they would have to take over the role of parent to a grown child someday, sharing the responsibility of caring for Griffin.

I worried that our marriage was not strong enough for this. Sure, I always felt that we were happy, but this was something we had never been through as a couple. We had gotten through challenges before, such as unexpected job changes and parenting two boys born thirteen months apart. But could we handle all three of these brothers?

I also worried about how I would handle these difficulties on a personal level. Would I feel resentful of this child who would no doubt take up most of our time? Would he depend on us for the rest of our lives? In my darkest moments, I worried that I wouldn't love him as much as his brothers because he wasn't my idea of "perfect."

Most of all, I worried about Griffin. Would he suffer? Would he be able to attend his brothers' school? Would he be teased? Would he ever be independent? I cringed at the words "group home" when reading the literature from our geneticist, and couldn't even utter the phrase without crying. I equated allowing him to live in a group home with sending him away to an institution; I couldn't begin to fathom that situation.

Well, Griffin is now two, and my heart is much more settled. No problems with loving him—I'm totally smitten! And my fears about resenting him or favoring him have been laid to rest. We spend three hours a week with Griffin's therapists; one each for speech, gross motor skills, and fine motor skills. Part of their job is to show us how to incorporate his therapies into our family life. Whether it's chasing his brothers through a tunnel, letting them "read" to him, or teaching him the fine art of dumping water in (and out of) the tub, Garrett and Braeden are the best models and motivators Griffin could have. But we don't always make Griffin our focus. His three therapists understand that Griffin is not our only child and we shouldn't take away from our other boys for his sake. So Garrett and Braeden get their turns in the spotlight, too.

Griffin does not make us worry any more than our other boys. We no longer worry about his dependence; instead, we are planning for his independence. I no longer worry about his future; instead, I wonder about it. I used to think I knew what was in store for him. Now, I realize that I honestly have no idea. He might go to college. He might get married. He might live with us if he wants to—although, considering his desire to do everything his brothers are doing, I don't think he will.

Most importantly, his brothers adore him. They see him as any other little brother, sometimes annoying, sometimes getting into their toys. Yet they fight over who gets to help change his diaper (unless it's a stinky one). If Griffin needs or wants to live with one of them someday, arguing over who gets him may just tear them apart. But, I don't think that will be the case.

I think they will be competing to see who gets to be best man at his wedding!

Dena lives on the east coast with her husband, Christopher, and their three children, Garrett (1999), Braeden (2001), and Griffin (2004). Griffin was diagnosed with Down syndrome via amniocentesis twenty weeks into the pregnancy. Dena is an adjunct instructor in the math department at a local community college.

54

Birthday Guilt
by Michelle Helferich

Kayla Helferich

I CAN'T BELIEVE THAT my little girl is almost three years old. Has it really been almost a year since her last birthday party? It seems like just a few months ago—that hot July afternoon in our backyard, with beloved friends and family members gathered together. Kayla's big gift was a sand and water table, and the kids all had a blast with the messy, hands-on play. It was a wonderful celebration. But underneath all the fun and laughter, I secretly harbored a layer of guilt. The same thing happened on Kayla's first birthday. And here I am again, preparing for another party, feeling guilty yet again.

When I was pregnant with Kayla we knew there was a possibility of her having Down syndrome, because of the results from the AFP. We declined the amnio. I was afraid of the needle, afraid of the risk of miscarriage, afraid of the results. I wasn't ready to let go of my hope that she had the typical forty-six chromosomes.

We also didn't find out the gender, even though we had a few 3D ultrasounds. My husband, Joe, and I were both hoping for a girl. When I went into labor, I remember being so anxious to find out if we had a daughter. As soon as I felt the baby's body come out I leaned forward and saw that we did indeed have a girl. At the same moment I heard my husband Joe exclaim, "We have a daughter!"

They placed her on my tummy. I looked into her face—and I knew. I just knew she had Down syndrome.

In that instant I felt completely detached. This wasn't my daughter I was holding. Who was this stranger? I felt like my heart stopped beating, like I couldn't breathe, like I was looking down on this scene and it wasn't me.

What happened to that instant bonding I've been told mothers are supposed to have with their babies? Why don't I feel that? I kept wondering. *Where is my motherly instinct and love?* It didn't seem fair—Joe was walking around beaming like the proud father he was. I had just given birth to my first child. Why wasn't I elated? I felt like something was terribly wrong with me. This is one reason for my guilt.

Another is my regret concerning how I told my mom about the diagnosis. She, my sister, and my aunt arrived at the hospital a few hours after Kayla was born. When they entered the room I quickly handed Kayla off to my mom. "They think she has Down syndrome," I said.

"What?" she said, shocked.

"What's Down syndrome?" my sister asked. My aunt whispered something to her.

I couldn't even give my mom the pleasure of five carefree minutes with her first grandchild. I had to get the words out, fast, before she noticed that Kayla looked different. I had to tell her before she could question me. But I wish I had let her get to know her granddaughter first.

On Kayla's third night, Joe slept at home instead of at the hospital. For the first time I was really alone—just me and Kayla in the hospital room. For the first time, I started sobbing. I just completely lost it. I was so worried one of the nurses would come in and see me crying; I wouldn't know what to say. What if they thought I didn't love my daughter? What if I had to talk to someone? Could I go home the following day if I was such a mess? What was I to do with this child? I didn't know anything about Down syndrome, what was our life to be like? And why, oh why, was I so sad?

A week later the pediatrician called to confirm the diagnosis through the blood test results. From the moment I saw Kayla, I never had any doubt that she had Down syndrome. But as soon as I heard Joe on the phone confirming the results I broke down and sobbed again. He came in holding Kayla and we just stood there hugging and crying. The first thing I asked him was, "Do you still love her? You're not going to leave us, are you?"

He must have thought I was crazy. "Of course I still love her, and no, I'm not going to leave either of you. Why would I? Why would you think I would want to? She's my daughter and I love her no matter what."

"What are we going to do?" I asked.

"Love her and raise her the best we can," he said.

Joe called his mother to tell her about the test results. After he hung up the phone, his mom called back almost immediately. I could hear her crying through the phone, and I could hear her words: "I just wanted to let you know I love you, I love Michelle, and I love my granddaughter. Nothing's going to change that." She didn't know it, but I really needed to hear her say that.

My mom, stepfather, and sister were out when the pediatrician had called. When they came back home I told my mom the news. "You still love her, though, don't you?" I asked anxiously.

"Oh Michelle, of course I do! She is my granddaughter!" she assured me.

When I called my dad later his response was, "So? What's the big deal?" He asked me what the diagnosis meant for Kayla and I couldn't really answer that question—I didn't know myself.

I finally realized why I was asking everyone if they still loved her. I couldn't allow myself to fall completely in love with this child until I knew that the important people in our lives were also going to love her, no matter what. Once I knew they did, I could finally open my eyes and see my daughter. My daughter—not the Down syndrome. But it still weighs heavily on my heart that I couldn't see this from the moment she was born.

I'm grateful that my feelings during those early days didn't have a negative impact on Kayla. I know I shouldn't blame myself for how I felt then. It's a normal thing to be afraid of the unknown. And I did the best I could. I took this little newborn home with me and got to know her. All she needed was what every newborn needs—her parents' love—and that's what we gave her.

Kayla has come such a long way since then. She's grown so much, learned so much. She'll be starting preschool this fall. At her party next week she'll be old enough to blow out her own birthday candles for the first time. And I know she won't have any trouble ripping open her gifts! As I make the reservations for the party to be held at Kid Zone (an indoor play area for children under five), send out the invitations to six of her little friends, and make the strawberry cupcakes, I realize that I have also come a long way since Kayla was born. I feel it's time to let go of the past and give myself a gift, too: Forgiveness.

Michelle lives in New Mexico with her husband, Joe, who is in the Air Force. They married in 2000. Kayla (2003) is their only child. Michelle resigned from her job in civil service to stay home with Kayla and she's now a consultant with Discovery Toys, Inc.

55

Kindness Received
by Francine Ferraro Rothkopf

Sofia Phoebe Daniella Rothkopf

WE FOUND OUT ABOUT Sofia's extra chromosome during pregnancy. David and I were both fine with the diagnosis (we'd both had lots of very positive interactions with people with Down syndrome), but other family and friends needed time to adjust. My mom, especially, was very upset for a few weeks. But by the time Sofia was born, everyone was just happy to see her. In fact, my mom quickly became one of her biggest supporters. It was helpful for all of us to be prepared for the diagnosis in advance.

What we weren't prepared for was the incredible outpouring of love and support we received. Two weeks before Sofia was born, some of the women from our synagogue threw us a "Baby Seder." Traditionally, Jewish women don't have baby showers, as it's considered bad luck to have gifts for the unborn child, for fear of attracting the evil eye. But a Baby Seder is a gift for the mom (and dad). This Saturday evening event is combined with *Havdalah*, the farewell service for the end of the Sabbath, and includes readings about the coming new life, special foods, songs, and "promises." I was so touched by the written promises submitted by each guest: a meal, babysitting, use of a swimming pool for a special "date" with our two sons after the baby arrived, an embroidered dress for the baby's naming ceremony, some mother's helper hours. The entire evening was profoundly moving.

I still get teary when I think about how wonderful these women have been to us. I don't think I cooked for three months after Sofia was born, because so many people brought us such delicious meals (and everyone was mindful both of our son Micah's allergies and of the issues of *Kashrut*, the Jewish dietary laws).

Sofia received a very warm welcome from many other members of our religious community. One of the older gentlemen mentioned to me, with misty eyes, that he was so proud that Sofia would be a part of our community. When we had her *Simchat Bat* (naming ceremony and celebration for a daughter), more than a hundred people came back to our house after services, and everyone felt like a loving part of the family.

The kindness we've received as a family also includes our community of friends, many of whom happen to be occupational therapists, special education teachers, or work as caregivers to people with special needs. Our early intervention coordinator has been an incredible source of information, comfort, and training for Sofia and me. I'm more mindful of how everything I do affects how my daughter learns to move and communicate. I wish that I'd had all these services for my boys!

Our relationships with school professionals have also been very positive. Micah's nursery school director informed me that "of course Sofia is coming here!" and the principal at Sam's new Jewish Day

School applied for a special needs grant with an essay titled, "How Do We Get Ready For Sofia?" Whenever I walk into either of the schools, everyone tumbles over each other trying to get some time with Sofia.

I find it deeply satisfying that so many people have embraced Sofia with open arms. This same warmth has been extended to me and to our whole family as I have become involved in the "Trisomy 21 Family," that unofficial network of connections that exists for people whose lives are touched by Down syndrome. I have learned so much about compassion and understanding from the other families we have met, in person and online, in this new world. All of these wonderful relationships have opened the way for me to be more involved with helping other people. I have been able to educate others who lack understanding about Down syndrome. I have spoken with several new or expectant moms of "chromosomally enhanced" children, and I have been glad to be able to give them comfort, support, and advice when they needed it, just like I was given help when I was in need. I only wish that every family facing a new diagnosis could be welcomed the way ours was.

Because of our experiences with Sofia, our whole family strives to reach out to others in various ways. Through the Caring Committee at our synagogue, we cook and deliver meals or visit with community members who are sick or housebound. As members of the Education and Ritual committees, we make sure the formal and informal education programs offered are accessible to children with all sorts of learning styles. We encourage our young sons to make people feel welcome and cared for at the synagogue, at school, and in the community at large, by being friendly, open and inviting. We regularly host guests for a traditional Friday evening Sabbath dinner. At our early intervention playgroup, Sofia and I have befriended several moms and kids in need of encouragement, which we try to provide. Some of our medical providers have introduced us to other families juggling similar issues (food allergies or gastric and cardiac issues, for example), and we have been able to pass along useful information and resources, as well as lend a sympathetic ear.

My family may not be able to reach out to everyone in need, but we can make a difference, one family at a time. We have been the receivers of great kindness, and we hope to return the gift by becoming better givers of kindness as well.

Francine lives west of Boston with her husband, David, sons Samuel (1999) and Micah (2001), and La Principessa Sofia Phoebe Daniella (2005). An ex-computer support and database specialist, Francine now spends most of her time driving the kids where they need to go. The Rothkopfs are very active members of Temple Israel of Natick, and involved parents at the MetroWest Jewish Day School. Francine is also the High Holiday Cantorial Soloist for Congregation Sha'arei Shalom in Ashland, and a freelance proofreader. She is pursuing her master's degree from Hebrew College, one class per semester. Her son Sam has learning disabilities, Micah has severe food allergies, and Sofia has Trisomy 21 (diagnosed by amnio). Francine notes, "Of the three, Down syndrome has so far been the easiest special need to deal with—at least there are books, support, and services readily available!"

56

The Blessing of an Imperfect Life
by *Janis Gonzales*

Cariana Gonzales

I SUPPOSE IT STARTED when I was three or four. I distinctly remember entertaining myself (in those dark ages before Cartoon Network and Nintendo) by skipping around the house with glass cleaner in one hand and dusting spray in the other, trying to be the perfect housekeeper like the high-heeled women in the TV commercials. It certainly got worse when I started kindergarten. I never expected anyone else to be perfect, but for some reason, I felt I had to be—and, not surprisingly, I could never quite measure up. Perhaps I was genetically burdened with high self-expectations, or possibly my parents and teachers accidentally gave me the impression that my entire value as a person came from getting all A's, all the time.

Although I had always planned on being a writer, at the age of twenty-two I took a detour into the world of medicine. Perfectionists are drawn to medical school like moths to a flame. Medicine feeds the perfectionist beast inside us by insisting that it is possible—indeed, it is required—to never make mistakes. After all, if my mistake could cause suffering or even death, that mistake can't be permitted in a compassionate and just society. No one wants to go to an "average" doctor—they want the best. And so, we need to be the best, or we risk losing our patients, our confidence, our colleagues' respect, even our own livelihood.

Medical students are, by and large, left alone to deal with the cognitive dissonance of knowing that we are imperfect, while at the same time feeling that once we accept the responsibility that comes with the title of Doctor, mistakes are unacceptable. When you realize that you can never meet the expectations of your profession (let alone your own), it can lead you to the point of desperation. Some people deal with it by leaving medicine altogether; others simply hide their doubts and fears behind a mask of authority, competence, and even arrogance. I couldn't bring myself to do either, so I lived in a constant state of fear that my imperfection would be discovered and exposed. Then my life was changed by the birth of my daughter, Cariana.

Cariana's diagnosis of Down syndrome shattered my dreams of leading a "perfect" life. But as I got to know her, I realized that she wasn't flawed at all; what was flawed was my definition of perfection. Cariana showed me that merely seeing an analysis of someone's chromosomes tells you next to nothing about the person herself, and that the most important questions can never be answered by a blood test. No test can tell us who our children will be, or what gifts each child might bring into the world.

In her first year of life, I scrutinized Cariana's development, read stacks of books, and spent hours searching the Internet for therapies, determined to make every minute count, to make sure no possible opportunity was wasted. Surely my daughter would be the exception to the rule, the superstar of the Down syndrome community who would meet all milestones early, defy her therapists' expectations, and leap tall buildings with a single bound. But that was my agenda; it was never Cariana's.

I had always tried to be the best at whatever I did: The best student, the best wife, the best mother. I thought if I worked hard enough, learned enough, and studied enough, I would be able to make everything turn out right. But Cariana was different; she seemed to live her life according to the Taoist principle of *wu wei*, action through nonaction—otherwise known as "going with the flow." No matter how much I worked on something with her, such as standing, walking, or reading, she would wait until the day when she suddenly decided she was ready, and then show me that she could do it perfectly, as if she had been practicing all along while the rest of us were sleeping.

Cariana was blessed with the gift of emanating love and peace. It was as if love just flowed more easily through her than it did the rest of us. And her love was completely unconditional—the kind of love that says, "You are good enough, just the way you are." For years I had felt that nothing I did was quite good enough, but Cariana and I fit perfectly together. Taking care of her was my ideal vocation—we each needed exactly what the other had to offer. Cariana was kind enough to overlook my failings and disabilities. She simply loved me, totally and deeply, exactly the same way I loved her. We basked in each other's love like two cats stretched out in a warm patch of sunlight. And I slowly began to accept that if she was perfect just the way she was, then maybe I am too.

Cariana was completely at peace with herself. She reached out to others with love and didn't fear rejection. This trait was apparent from the time she was born, but it became even more evident when she developed leukemia just before her second birthday. I couldn't stay bivouacked in that little hospital room with my stash of snacks and magazines, because Cariana was determined to connect with people, waving from her little red wagon, scooting into other patients' rooms, and holding out her arms to the doctors and nurses at every opportunity.

What I know about Buddhism and Taoism is that they both emphasize accepting impermanence—change as part of the cyclical nature of life. Rather than fighting to keep things from changing, I learned to ride the wave and be grateful for the water that supported me. I had to accept that despite all my years of training as a pediatrician, nothing I could do was going to save my own precious child. I realized I couldn't change what the future held for Cariana, but I could change the way I would live in it.

I watched how Cariana lived her life—not struggling against it but accepting it and enjoying every moment. She was a master at finding joy in every single day. Even in the last few months of her life, living every day in constant pain, she radiated happiness, love, and peace. She sparkled with joy and sprinkled it like glitter onto everyone around her.

As parents, we expect to teach our children many things, but we don't always stop to think what we can learn from them. I spent twenty-three years as a student, being thoroughly indoctrinated into a culture in which people are stratified by their ability to perform well on intelligence tests, but I could never have predicted that this amazing little girl with Down syndrome would turn out to be the best teacher I ever had.

Thanks to her, I learned that it makes no sense to judge one another. I learned to accept myself for who I am; to see strengths, not limitations; to honor each person—including myself—for their own unique gifts and innate dignity.

Now, when I miss the warm weight of her in my arms and the touch of her soft, small fingers in my hair, I think of her not just in sadness, but in gratitude. Now, I think that if what we're given doesn't match our expectations, maybe the problem is that our expectations were too low in the first place. If we could look at ourselves and one another without judgments or preconceptions, we might see that the imperfections we most fear may turn out, in the end, to be our greatest strengths.

Janis lives in Santa Fe, New Mexico, with her husband of fifteen years, David Gonzales MD; her two other children, Placi and Liesl; and their dog, Chelsea. Cariana, their third child, was diagnosed with Down syndrome soon after birth and died of AML in 2004 at two and a half years of age. Janis earned her MD from the University of Illinois and also received a Masters in Public Health from the University of New Mexico. She is board certified in pediatrics, but most of her time is spent writing and being a mom. She is the author of the memoir Lessons from a Gentle Life, and is working on a yet-unnamed novel.

57

Growing
by Sarahlynn Lester

Sarahlynn Lester and Ellie Lester-Boal

I WAS SCARED OF the baby growing inside me.

It hadn't started out that way. Paul and I had been married for two years when we decided that we were ready to start our family, and, six months later, we were delighted to learn that I was pregnant.

We had our moments, of course, of being a little startled and wondering what we were getting ourselves into, but mostly we were very excited.

We went in for the level II ultrasound with high hopes. We joked with the technician and tried to get her to explain what we were seeing on the screen. She was reassuring, explaining that all the measurements were within normal ranges.

We didn't even notice right away that she'd gotten quiet. Then she said, "I can't see everything that I want to see with the heart. I'm going to go get the doctor and see if he can get a better look."

Even after the doctor came in and began describing what he saw, we were still unconcerned. It took us a while to tune in and process what this quiet little man was saying. Surely he couldn't be serious. I mean, his name was Dr. Dicke. That's "Dicky." In obstetrics and gynecology! Slowly, we began to focus on what he was explaining to us.

Major heart defect. Most common in children with Down syndrome.

I had a regular OB appointment about an hour later, so we killed some time at Starbucks and let it all sink in. I can assure you that those rough, brown, recycled napkins are no good for mopping up tears and mucus. And when you sob at a Starbucks in a posh suburb, mostly people just look at you like they wish you'd quit being such a drama queen and let them have your primo couch seat already.

My OB hadn't had a chance to really talk to Dr. Dicke yet, so we had to go over everything with her. "Whatever you decide to do, I will not judge you," she said. "Today is the last day that you could legally terminate this pregnancy in the state of Missouri. But if you decide to go that route, come to me and I will help you arrange something in another state. I don't want you to go off and try to manage this on your own."

I thought that was the most sensitive thing I'd ever heard.

But termination? We were so far from contemplating that. It had taken us months to get pregnant. We didn't know for sure that there was anything wrong with this baby. What if there was nothing wrong and it was all a big mistake? And even if it wasn't, could we really—surely not.

I had my first prenatal yoga class scheduled for that evening after my appointments. I'd been really excited about this class, but there was no way I was going now. I skipped that class and every one that followed. Money down the drain. Inconsequential.

Early the next morning, I was supposed to leave for a business trip to Las Vegas, of all places. I called the corporate travel agency. I called the airline. I tried everything I could think of, crying so hard that the travel agent's heart must have been breaking for me, but I couldn't find a way to change my flight. I didn't sleep much that night.

The next morning, as I traveled, I was busy making notes. On my layover, I made calls to the genetics counselor and to Dr. Dicke, following up and getting more information. There was still hope. We needed to know more. I set up an appointment for a fetal echocardiogram—who knew that they could do such a thing?—and amniocentesis. I never thought that I would agree to have an amnio, given the almost one-percent chance of miscarriage. But suddenly, I just needed to know. And a quiet little part of my mind was thinking that, perhaps, a miscarriage would be the best way out of this situation.

I have never felt such pain in my entire life. Everything felt incredibly bright, and raw, and sharp. My eyes burned. My chest ached. Acid ate through the walls of my stomach. A bubble of silence followed me and surrounded me everywhere I went, like my ears had never adjusted from the flight. A few days later, Paul followed me out to Vegas and we hid in a hotel room together.

But before we could briefly escape from our new reality, it was time to tell a few people. We couldn't talk about it yet, so I typed up the notes we'd taken after talking to the doctor. Atrioventricular Septal Defect (AVSD): Big hole in the middle of the heart. Open heart surgery within the first six months of life. Chance of Down syndrome about fifty-fifty. We sent this terrible email to our families, and I printed out a copy to keep in my leather business portfolio. At work, my last hours working a convention before Paul arrived and escape began, I sat down with my boss and showed her the email. She read it and was silent. She's smart. Her husband's a doctor at Washington University. Her teenaged daughters are brilliant. Like me, she was stunned, floored, horrified at the idea of having a child with a developmental disability.

Once the sharing began, there was no hiding from it. I kept disappearing from our booth to cry. I'd slip away from a customer and stand behind the curtains in the back of the booth, sobbing.

Everyone could hear me, of course, and everyone was incredibly sensitive about it, but no one knew what to do. I don't cry. I don't share much of my personal life at work. I'm not even a big hugger. Seeing someone like me break down had to be uncomfortable for everyone. I know that it was uncomfortable for me.

I was so glad when Paul arrived in Las Vegas. Paul is...Paul. He's twelve inches taller than I am, and even when I was pregnant he outweighed me by a fair margin. He's comfortable. And comforting. Plus, even though we don't gamble and aren't big drinkers—and I was pregnant—what better place to escape from reality than Vegas? We visited unbelievable buildings and saw incredible shows. We went for long walks in the sweltering heat and sat in a freezing cold theater to see a movie in the middle of the afternoon. We lay in bed and talked about everything that was in our heads, even the ugly, secret, painful stuff. As we did our odd little Vulcan mind-meld, we realized that our thoughts were exactly aligned. These are the sorts of things that could tear a marriage apart, but we'd never felt so close to each other.

It was perfection. And it was the worst weekend of our lives.

Shortly after we got back to St. Louis, it was time for my amnio. My mom drove 300 miles to come along for support. I was so glad to have her there, and so was Paul.

I don't buy that "weaker sex" stuff at the best of times, but any woman who's been through amniocentesis deserves a medal for bravery. With me completely unsedated and with no local anesthetic whatsoever, good old Dr. Dicke (whom we liked very much and trusted implicitly) inserted a needle the length of a brand-new number-two pencil into my distended abdomen with only the ultrasound to guide him.

Our expected one became very active whenever I had an ultrasound. Paul rested his hand on my stomach.

"Be still, little one. Lie very still," he said.

And she did. The baby floated quietly down to my back and lay there, hardly moving except for the rapid beating of her heart, while we stared at the monitor and watched that surprisingly bright and sharp needle enter my womb so close, so very terribly close to the back of her head. He took more fluid than I expected him to take.

Leave enough for the baby! I thought frantically.

Very soon, it was all over. I gingerly got up and let Mom and Paul take me home. Paul went back to work, and I sat quietly on the couch, working on my laptop and napping while my mom brought me lots of water to drink and generally was perfectly unobtrusive and supportive.

I did not miscarry.

I got the phone call from my OB giving me the "positive" test result on my way home from work. I pulled off the side of the road and parked so that I could take notes. Then I went home, sat in the rocking chair in the spare bedroom, lights off, and waited for my husband to get home.

Telling Paul was one of the hardest things I've ever had to do. And then we had to call our parents and sisters. Everyone was crying. I was doing a great job of being strong for all of them, though their disappointment and sadness broke my heart. But no reaction would have satisfied me, I think. It was still too raw.

Paul's mom said, "We love all kinds of babies," and this made me furious for no good reason. She was right, of course, but I wasn't ready to see it. Suddenly, I felt like maybe I didn't love my baby. Suddenly, I didn't know my baby. I couldn't picture my baby; imagine her life, our life together.

I was scared of the baby growing inside me.

I was afraid that I would be unable to bond with her after she was born. I'd wrap my arms around myself and say, "Oh, baby; oh, baby," as I rocked from side to side. I didn't realize at the time how close I already felt to my child. I didn't realize how confident I already was that Paul and I could do this, could love and raise this unknown, surprising child, could provide the best possible home for her.

The second half of my pregnancy was certainly hard, with only bitter news and no baby to hold. But as soon as Ellie was born, I realized that bonding would not be a problem. Immediately, I was smitten. And because I had done my mourning already, bonding was instantaneous and strong.

For months, I'd wake at my daughter's slightest noise, smiling and happy to get to watch her breathe in the quiet dark of night, glowing with love.

Sarahlynn lives in suburban St. Louis, Missouri, with her husband, Paul, their daughter, Eleanor (2003), and a snoring pug. The family is expecting their second child in early 2007. Eleanor was diagnosed with Trisomy 21 and a heart defect during the second trimester of her mother's pregnancy. This essay is excerpted from a longer piece Sarahlynn has written about that pregnancy and the first year of her daughter's life.

58

Through the Eyes of Love
by Tammy Bonser

J. Robert, Tammy, Dale, and William Bonser

The Lord does not look at the things man looks at. Man looks at the outward appearance, but the Lord looks at the heart (spirit).

—1 Samuel 16:7b

DECORATING FOR DALE'S arrival was a lot of fun. My in-laws bought us a beautiful crib and a matching changing table. We got a baby blue rug and paint, and I picked a Peter Rabbit theme for the bedding. I was more than happy to give up my "quiet room" for the baby's bedroom. For years, all of my doctors had been saying I probably wouldn't get pregnant because of my health issues, which included hydrocephalus and epilepsy. Having proved them wrong, every day felt wonderful—even with morning sickness.

With every month prior to Dale's birth, I prayed for him, talked to him, took him to movies. At one tense point during *Jurassic Park III*, Dale and I both jumped together! In the eyes of others he was not yet real, not alive. But for my husband, Bob, and me, he was. At bedtime, Bob and I would lie on our bed with our hands on my stomach, feeling Dale's kicks. *There's going to be a new kid in town,* he seemed to be telling us. He was my miracle.

His having Down syndrome didn't change that.

When Dale was born he had obvious signs of Down syndrome. The doctors had been expecting a blue, sick baby, but he had a great pink color and a lusty cry. They gathered around and examined his muscle tone, finding it lacking. They listened to his heart and warned me about its condition. When they looked at him, they saw a medical case with many problems.

But when I looked at him, I saw perfection. His eyes were an amazing shade of blue, like his Daddy's. The large palms of his hands and his mop of dark hair also reminded me of Bob. When he was an hour old he gave me a little smirk that made me laugh—an easy, knowing laugh, as if I had been enjoying his funny faces for years. I welcomed the medical assistance but never left his side. I think a lot of nurses were thrilled to see me cuddling with what they thought was an imperfect child.

That night my mother-in-law created a poem about Dale. "If all you see is the outside of me, then you're not seeing me at all," she wrote from Dale's perspective. Those words filled me with hope and motivated me to keep looking, as the poem invited, "through the eyes of love."

When Dale was three days old, he needed his first intestinal surgery. The doctors saw a fragile child who would likely need to use a respirator and a feeding tube for a very long time. When Dale was weaned from the respirator a week after surgery, they continued to see him as very ill, because of his oxygen saturation levels. One doctor looked right at me and had the gall to say, "This child isn't going to amount to anything; he has Down syndrome."

I was livid. Needless to say, that was the last time she saw me or Dale—I made sure of that immediately. Dale had enough challenges to overcome. He didn't need to be around people who looked at him and saw a lost cause. To me, he was a little person with strength and vibrancy.

I knew I needed to fight for Dale, like he was fighting for his own life. I wouldn't leave the room at any time when the doctors were putting in IVs, doing x-rays, or even reviewing his chart. When they did their morning rounds I would update them on his status, including oxygen saturation levels, heart rate, and feedings. I even explained multiple times to the team of physicians that his saturations would not be normal until he had his heart surgery, and they finally adjusted their expectations.

When Dale was discharged, others saw a struggling child with a feeding tube up his nose. The doctors thought he would require the tube for years. Because of his heart condition, they thought he would not thrive while breastfeeding, due to low oxygen intake. But Dale and I had an agreement—*I'm eating from you, mama.* A few weeks after being home, Dale took out the feeding tube because he wasn't using it. The doctors were amazed.

Therapists came to help all of us learn how to manage Dale's condition. Years later, his physical therapist told me that when she first started working with Dale, she thought he would never walk. She and the occupational therapist actually had a friendly bet on what the outcome would be. They saw a little boy with low muscle tone and many impediments to development. But I saw a little boy showing great endurance and promise. We faithfully did the exercises the therapists taught us, and wonderful things began to happen. Milestones were slow in coming, but they came. The therapists were so proud of every small thing we accomplished together. I wish they could have seen Dale the first time he walked on his own.

It touches me that Dale has helped not only me and my family, but also his doctors, nurses, and therapists see with new eyes. I know that some people may not see Dale the way I see him, the way God sees him. But many do. And many others are learning to do so because he is here.

If all you see is the outside of me,
Then you're not seeing me at all.
Come look deep inside of me.
Look through the eyes of love.
See the gift of life in me,
Perfect from the Father above.

—*Bonnie Bonser*

⤴

Tammy, Bob, Dale, and little brother, William, live in York, Pennsylvania. Tammy's first pregnancy was monitored very carefully because of her diagnosis of epilepsy and hydrocephalus. After Dale was born, Tammy's medical problems disappeared. The Bonsers enjoy playing inside or out as a family, and are big fans of NASCAR. Dale was named after the family's hero, the late Dale Earnhardt.

59

Crecer Con Amor
by Charo Boggian

Zoe and Charo Boggian

WHEN ZOE WAS BORN, I knew right away by the look of his eyes that he had Down syndrome. The nurse showed him to me for a second, but I didn't have the chance to kiss him or take him into my arms before she rushed him away to intensive care. He was there for the first ten days of his life due to pulmonary hypertension, three holes in his heart, and low oxygen saturation.

When the chromosome analysis confirmed that Zoe had Down syndrome, it was very difficult for me to accept. Before his birth, I had imagined my baby in many ways. I imagined his little eyes, his little mouth, and his tiny feet, but I never imagined him this way. I had entered the hospital with many dreams and expectations. Now, I was going home with a baby who was very sick and had an extra chromosome, which would make him different from others for the rest of his life. At the time, it felt as if destiny had given me a blow that was not just unexpected, but difficult to overcome. *Why did you give me a son like this?* I asked God. *Why my first son?*

I felt like a completely different person than who I was before. The things that used to make me happy now meant nothing. The things that seemed like problems before now meant nothing. There was no consolation for me.

I was so upset that I did not know how to tell the news to my family and friends in Argentina. It took me a week to even be able to talk with them. Thankfully, they took the news very well. They all sent letters in support of me and Zoe. My father's letter is the one that moved me the most. He wrote, "A son is a son always. It does not matter how he is. A parent loves his or her children no matter what. You must accept your son as I accepted you, exactly how you were, without wanting to change anything about you."

With these words my father taught me about unconditional love, a love that conquers all. From that moment, I stopped seeing Down syndrome and I began to see the beautiful soul of my son.

Not long afterward I had to bring Zoe back to the hospital because he began to have difficulty breathing. A social worker there asked me if I wanted to meet a mom that spoke Spanish and also had a son with Down syndrome. I accepted, and Nellie came to visit me. She spoke with me of many things, and I felt that for the first time someone understood my fears, my doubts, my frustration, and my worry about the future of my son. She gave me her support, and little by little I began to feel even more accepting of Zoe. I began to educate myself about his condition and I started to attend different conferences to get information.

I realized there was no support group for Hispanic parents, and I decided it would be very helpful to create one. So, I gave contact information to the hospital staff, nurses, and therapists, and I began meeting with Hispanic families that had children with Down syndrome. I called the group *Crecor Con Amor* (Growing Up With Love) because love is the most important thing that we, as parents, can give to our children.

There were many challenges that Zoe and I faced together during his early years—he required a feeding tube for two and a half years, as well as oxygen supplementation. He had a strong desire to live and he fought as a brave one. At times, I still cry when I remember those moments, but I'm crying less and less now. The most important thing is that my son is now a healthy boy.

Zoe is five years old. Next month he will begin kindergarten. With the aid of the therapists and teachers, he is doing very well. He can count to ten, and he knows one hundred signs, including colors. He understands English and Spanish, loves to learn new things, plays baseball and soccer, and as a good Argentine, he takes *mate* (a native tea). To me, he is the most beautiful child in the world and I would not change him for anything. Our history has been full, and difficult, but today I'm proud to say that we did it. Together, we are growing up with love.

I wrote the following thoughts after the geneticist reported to me that Zoe would have mental retardation. I dedicate this to Zoe, whom I love and respect deeply.

Mi hijo
Tiene retraso mental, ellos dicen
Pero digo,
retraso mental
tiene los que hacen bombas, y las tiran
los que, anestesiados por dinero,
dejan morir a millones de niños en Africa,
en India, en todos los lugares del mundo
Los que, cegado por el poder,
destruyen el medio ambiente
extinguen los animales
Envenenan los ríos y los mares.con quimicos.
Retraso mental

tiene aquellos que, por ignorancia
discriminan a las personas diferentes.
Los que no respetan, ni aceptan a al pró ximo tal y como es.
Esos tienen retraso mental y espiritual.
Mi hijo es el ser mas puro y valiente que he conocido.
Y probablemente lo que tenga es una manera diferente de ver
y vivir la Vida;
Una mejor manera de vivir.
Una forma más sencilla,
sin agresión,
sin egoísmo,
sin maldad,
sin mentiras,
Una forma mas elevada,
llena de felicidad
más cercana al Amor.
Una forma que esos,
sin retraso mental, no entienden.

My son
has mental retardation, they say.
But I say
mental retardation
have the ones that use bombs, that throw them
the ones that, anesthetized by money,
leave to die millions of children in Africa,
in India, in all the places of the world
the ones that, blinded by power,
destroy the environment
extinguish the animals
poison the rivers and seas.
mental retardation
have the ones that, through ignorances,
discriminate
the ones that do not respect, neither accept others
just as they are.

My son
has mental retardation, they say,
yet pure and brave he is;
a better way of living he has.
A form more simple
without aggression
without selfishness
without wickedness
without lies
A high form
full of happiness
closer to love
A form that those others
do not understand.

Charo is from Argentina and lives in Tucson, Arizona, with her son,
Zoe. She has a paralegal degree and is completing her BA in criminal
justice. Charo wants to become a lawyer so that she can defend and pro-
mote the rights of people with disabilities. She is the founder of Crecer
Con Amor, a support group for Hispanic parents of children with
Down syndrome, and has coordinated the group for six years.
The group's website is www.crecerconamor.com.

60

Quality of Life
by Renee Parker

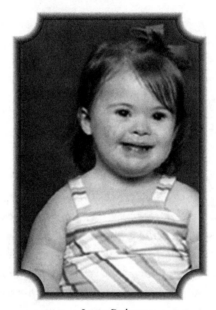

Lacey Parker

I SIT ON THE COUCH and watch as Lacey Paige pulls her sister Kassidy's hair and tries to snitch the remote from her other sister, Haley. They're in the living room watching "Blue's Clues," each on their own pillow, with Lacey trying to take all the covers for herself. The older girls can't stay mad for long. "Lacey!" they groan, then all three break out in giggles. *A normal life*, I sigh with contentment. Two years ago when Lacey was born, I didn't think that life would ever feel normal again.

The moment Lacey was laid on my chest, the doctor turned to me and said, "I think Lacey has Down syndrome." Those words seemed to cast a spell on everyone in the room. None of the nurses or the doctor would look at me; none of my questions were answered. My husband, Chris, and I were crushed. I didn't want to see anyone or talk to anyone. Then the cardiologist told us that Lacey had a large heart defect (VSD) and would need open heart surgery by six months of age. All I could do was cry.

They must be wrong, I kept repeating to myself. *I'm only twenty-seven. They did all the tests, the ultrasound exam—nothing ever showed up. And I have two healthy daughters!*

The information about Down syndrome that we were later given was discouraging, to say the least. All we kept hearing was, "She will not do this or that; she'll have delays here; don't expect a lot." I saw nothing but darkness and pain in our future. What quality of life would Lacey be able to have? And what about me, what about the rest of the family?

Things went from bad to worse. Released from the hospital after three days, we returned ten days later due to problems with Lacey's feeding and digestion, which stemmed from her congestive heart failure. She suffered from bowel issues and significant weight loss. Multiple tests at an advanced medical center followed. Lacey was given a nasal-gastric (NG) tube and placed on high-calorie formula so that she could be adequately nourished. Once we were home, we had to manage the feeding tube and the worries. I felt like I was in the middle of a bad dream.

Three months later I woke up to see this smiling baby looking at me from the bassinet beside our bed. For the first time I saw Lacey Paige Parker, not Down syndrome. She was the tiniest, sweetest, most perfect creature. She had dark brown hair and the most enchanting brown eyes. Her skin was tinged with blue because of her low oxygen saturation, but that did not color my view of her. I saw her daddy's smile in her own. And I knew that I was hooked.

Quality of life is learning to see the beauty that dwells within each of us.

A few months later we arrived at Dallas Children's Medical Center for Lacey's open heart surgery. Prior to the procedure, I sat in a tiny room holding Lacey, receiving the family visitors who were only permitted to come in two at a time. But I couldn't focus my attention on anyone. People came and went, and all I felt was a numbing in my heart as I feared I would never hold Lacey like that again.

Then the doctors came for her. "Please," I begged them. "Please let me carry her to the door of the operating room." They agreed. But I knew my minutes were numbered.

"We need her now," they told me when we reached the last set of doors. But I couldn't let go.

"Honey, they're going to help her," Chris reminded me gently. After several long minutes, I finally let them take her from me. As soon as she left my arms I collapsed to the floor, sobbing my heart out.

Hours later, I saw a miracle. They wheeled her up next to us and for the first time she was pink. Baby pink. The blue tinge to her skin was gone. Her little body radiated a sense of triumph—the same triumph that I felt in the deepest part of me.

Quality of life is understanding that joy grows out of pain.

Lacey's first trip out into the world took place on a rainy Saturday morning. My mom and I decided to take the girls to Target. As we loaded everyone into the car, I was nervous. How would people react to Lacey? What would they say? Would they stare? Would I have to respond to any rude comments? I was full of fear as I pushed the shopping cart with Lacey's car seat attached. But it seemed that every time we turned a corner, someone would approach us and admire Lacey. "How beautiful she is," they said. "She looks so much like her sisters." All I could do was smile, say thank you, and shed a few tears.

A similar thing happened the first time I took Lacey with me to pick up the older girls from school. I pulled in to the pickup zone and waved to them. Within a minute, a crowd of their friends gathered around the car door, hoping to catch a glimpse of Lacey. They all wanted to hug and kiss her. This kind of reaction to Lacey has become a pattern for us, no matter where we are.

Quality of life is enjoying the goodness of everyday people.

When Lacey was seven months old we bought her a miniature Shitzu. The girls named it Pudgy. Pudgy is the cutest thing—she looks like one of the Furby dolls. Being the runt of the litter, she is very small. Her fur is white with spots of brown all over, and she has a bark that pierces your ears, although Lacey never seems to mind. From the time Lacey could get around she would chase Pudgy everywhere, wanting to cuddle and play with her. We are always having to tell Lacey "no" because she loves to pull Pudgy's tail and ears. In the morning, Lacey loves to grab Pudgy, watch cartoons, and feed Pudgy and herself strawberry yogurt-covered Cheerios. Thank goodness she loves Lacey just as much as Lacey loves her.

Lacey has a large vocabulary now, but "Pudgy" was the third word she learned—which, of course, made the grandparents wonder whom she loved more. When the two of them are snuggling, I often hear tender sounds coming from across the room: "Awww, Pudge!" I can imagine Lacey when she's older, walking through our green pastures to see the cows with Pudgy beside her. I'll bet Pudgy will be waiting at the foot of her bed every morning, and waiting by the door when she comes home from school.

Quality of life is having a special friend.

When I was pregnant with Lacey I dreamed about how close she and her sisters would be. I imagined them giggling under the covers together, trying on each other's clothes, sticking up for each other. My deepest wish was for them to always take care of each other. But when Lacey was born I worried that the older girls might be embarrassed to have a sister who is different. Or that they might resent the special care Lacey might need. Would my dream ever become reality?

Every day, I see the answer. I see it in Haley's face when she reads to Lacey or plays blocks with her (even though Lacey's idea of playing blocks is knocking down the tower Haley has built). I see it in Kassidy's eyes when she "teaches" Lacey how to do gymnastics tricks (like turning flips and standing on her head), and when she's showing Lacey how to open the kitchen cabinet where the treats are hidden.

I hear the answer in the laughter that comes from the older girls' bedroom, where Lacey is standing like a queen on their polka-dotted beanbag chair, demanding to be a part of their game. Or the squeals coming from the den, where the girls are playing slapjack (with Lacey shrieking happily every time someone slaps the deck).

And I hear the answer, too, in the words of my older girls as they introduce Lacey to others: "This is our sister Lacey. She has Down syndrome, but we aren't down about anything."

Quality of life is being part of a family.

Renee and her husband, Chris, live in Louisiana. They were married in 1996, and have three daughters. Renee is a stay-at-home mom who loves to take care of Haley Alyse (1997), Kassidy Ann (1999), and Lacey Paige (2004). Chris works as a supervisor for a local oil company. As a family, they enjoy having get-togethers, riding four-wheelers, fishing, hunting, going out to eat, and watching sporting events. They love to watch their two older children play softball and practice karate. They live on a family-owned dairy farm, so they are surrounded by cows and nature. Despite Lacey's many problems at the beginning of her life, she is now a thriving, healthy toddler.

61

The Luckiest People in the World
by Jane Leahy-Smith

Melea, Miranda, Jane, Adrian, Eric, and Colin Smith

WE GET A LOT OF INTERESTING reactions to our family. Some people pity us. Some go on about "how brave" or "how patient" we are. We hear "you must be so strong" all the time, along with a long list of other comments (and sometimes they are not so nice). Our story is very different—we chose this road after many childless years, and our road just keeps expanding and growing all of the time.

The story begins with my husband, Eric, and me meeting in college in 1985, a beautiful outdoor fall wedding in 1994, and the desire to immediately start a family on my part. But as luck would have it, that wasn't going to happen in the typical manner. We tried for several years, went to many doctors, spent a lot of money, and never received the privilege of becoming parents in the usual way.

In the spring of 2000, I started to look into adoption. My husband had already decided that parenting wasn't going to happen for us, and felt that was okay—but not me. I wanted a child. Any child who needed love, who needed us. Private adoption and agency adoption were, and still can be, extremely expensive. I also knew it was highly unlikely that we would get an infant through the Department of Family Services (DFS), and I was scared to undergo the rigorous application process anyway. So we chose to go with a wonderful home study agency, the Gladney agency. We were delighted to discover that this agency had a special needs program, and the ability to place younger children, including infants. (I knew Eric would need to start with a little one to really get into parenting.) We never realized how much our lives would change because of the decision of which agency to use.

So we filled out many papers for our home study and the adoption agency, wrote biographies, collected reference letters (from many people who thought we were nuts), and started our series of home visits. It was exhausting. However, the hardest thing for me was the form (seven pages long) detailing every single thing that could ever be wrong with a child. My job was to indicate which of these conditions I would be willing to accept, and rank my selections accordingly. This form made me cry. It made both of us search our souls and wonder if we really should try this. There are many situations out there that are much more scary to me than Down syndrome.

My first moments of thinking about parenting a child with Down syndrome are encased in memories of the people we have known with Down syndrome: A beautiful young adolescent named Summer, my friend's older brother named Michael, and a young man who lived near my grade school named Tommy. Each of these people has different skills and abilities and made us realize that being a parent of a child with Down syndrome would be challenging, yet was something we could do.

We sent our paperwork in—and the waiting began. It took almost nine months from the start of the process until we received our first call. It was funny how it happened: Eric and I were out for dinner, and I leaned over to him and said, "You know, we will be parents soon—I just feel it."

I got the eye roll from Eric. "If this is meant to happen, it will," he said. At that point I think he was half-hoping that it would not. He was really worried that I would be disappointed again, after all we had been through. Adoption is not an easy process.

I still remember so vividly the big day: December 15, 2001. Our social worker called to say they were having a meeting that afternoon with the birth mother of a little Hispanic boy with Down syndrome. Would we be interested in being presented to his mother? I jumped at the chance. This was what we wanted. Eric had just left for a business trip to British Columbia, so for six hours I waited on pins and needles with no one to tell. (Okay, so I called his hotel and left an urgent message for him to call me as soon as he got there. And I called his boss. And his mother. And everyone else I knew.)

At 4:00 p.m., the agency called and said the birth mother had decided to place her child, and that she had chosen Eric and me to parent him. I was elated. I received more information about our little three-week-old bundle of joy, along with a promise that they would call me the next day with more information. Problem: I had the most important news and was still unable to share it with Eric. He finally called me—and I think he jumped up and down in the middle of his business meeting. We couldn't wait for the process to start so that we could bring our son home! That was one sleepless night—I read everything and more about Down syndrome on the Internet. Then I had to wait two long days to get emailed photos of our little guy.

The next six weeks of waiting were the longest of my entire adult life. I cried and tried to wait patiently—not the easiest thing for a mother who has waited almost seven years for a child. The Gladney agency was finally able to place our little boy into our arms on January 24, 2001. I bawled and hugged our new son, Colin Miguel. Eric actually cried, too. I knew that he and I were now a family—never again to be just a couple. It really was the happiest moment of our lives.

Almost six years later, as I am preparing to send my son to his first day of kindergarten, I sit here and try to remember our life without him. Was there was a time before therapists, social workers, case managers, and service coordinators? Did I ever carry a purse and not a diaper bag? Was there really a point at which I did not know what an IEP, IFSP, MR, DMH, and all those other acronyms stand for? Or didn't feel that we knew enough to be specialists in common health problems associated with Down syndrome? And really, why should I try to remember my life way back when? We were not a family then, nor were we very happy people. We just existed.

Since adopting Colin, we have been given the privilege of adopting two more children through the Gladney agency. Two beautiful daughters have been placed into our family and have brought us such joy and excitement: Melea Isabel in March of 2002, and Miranda Olivia in February of 2005. We also were finally blessed with a surprise biological little girl who burst into our lives on July 4, 2003: Adrian Elliott. She challenges us each day and loves her siblings with fierceness and devotion I have never seen in other little ones her age. Our newest addition will be joining our family in late August of 2006: Eliza Marisol. This will be our first time adopting an older child. I imagine this will present our family with many challenges, but also many new joyous moments. Although Eliza is being adopted through DFS, the Gladney agency was instrumental in having her placed in our home. It amazes me how what seemed like a little choice six years ago—which agency to choose—has made such a radical change in our lives.

I recognize that our story differs from so many other parents', in more ways than one. We never experienced many of the difficult emotions that most parents of children with Down syndrome struggle with. Adopting Colin was the most wonderful and special moment of our married life. Eric and I did recognize that this joyous moment for our newly created family was the saddest moment for someone else's. That is probably the hardest thing that I live with every day. I can look at my son (and now three other adopted children with Down syndrome) and see and only feel joy about them and their births, while knowing in my heart this was the saddest day for many others we may never meet or get a chance to know.

Will we adopt again? We are asked that so many times (at least once a day, it seems). I do not know. Likewise, I do not know if we will be blessed again and become the parents of another biological child either. I do know this—you can only get five car seats in a Suburban, so we are trading ours in for a twelve or fifteen-passenger van. (I have to have room for grandma. And a lot of diaper bags, a friend or two, and maybe another car seat....)

When we respond to those many comments we receive from others, we insist that we are not special or brave or saintly or pitiful or even charitable. We are just "the Smith family of Wildwood, Missouri." We have four—soon to be five—children. When our fifth child arrives, four of those five will have Down syndrome. We take dance classes and play T-ball. We go to the movies, the theater, the zoo, on trips, and to museums. We enjoy shopping (though the store has to have big carts in the parking lot), have a lot of fun, and do about fifteen loads of laundry a week. Most importantly, we feel we are the luckiest people in the world.

Jane is thirty-nine years old and is currently a stay-at-home mother. She used to be a lot of things, including a high school physics, chemistry, and mathematics teacher for eleven years, a theater director for high school and community theater groups for fifteen years (with some overlap between the two). She has a BS and MS in Secondary Education, and feels like she has been through medical school since adopting her children.

62

Live Long, Laugh Often,
Love Much
by Andi Matthews

Andi and Riley Matthews

THANKSGIVING, 2001. I was in the fourth month of my first pregnancy. My husband and I spent our time with family showing off our baby boy's ultrasound pictures, discussing names, and thinking of nursery ideas. I had undergone an amnio because of suspicions regarding my AFP test. I was slightly nervous about receiving the results, but I was certain everything was going to be fine. I even went shopping with a friend and bought the baby a little San Francisco Giants outfit, complete with tiny socks.

I was so excited to be a mom. I dreamed of volunteering in my kid's classroom, of driving him to soccer, of cheering him on at sports events, of reading stories together, taking walks together, and leaving sappy "mom" notes in lunches. I envisioned starting college funds, preparing for his wedding, having grandkids. I wanted the whole, wonderful parenting package. I recorded all my excited feelings in a special journal. It was yellow and white, and on the cover were the words, *Live Long, Laugh Often, Love Much.* That saying represented everything I wanted for my child in this life; it was the perfect journal for documenting this pregnancy.

Four days later I heard a voice on the telephone say, "I'm so sorry, but this baby has Down syndrome."

What happened next is a blur. I know we sat together and cried a lot. When my husband went to lie down, I called my parents and somehow managed to tell them what had happened. I cried and cried on the phone to my mom. She offered to come over and hug me, but I said she didn't have to do that. I called one of my sisters and cried and cried to her. Then I went to bed where I cried and cried some more, getting no sleep. I left the house the next morning at 5:30 a.m. to go write sub plans at school. I was in no condition to teach kindergarten.

I was driving home that morning when I found myself pulling up to my parents' house. I parked in their driveway at 7:30 a.m. and called them from my car. "Hi, Mom. Is that offer for a hug still good? I'm sitting in your driveway."

"Of course, honey," she said. "I'll be right out." A minute later, there she was in her comfy bathrobe, smelling of familiar face cream and hugging me like she'd never let go.

We went inside and sat at the kitchen counter. I couldn't stop crying. I talked about all the things I wanted for our baby that now would never be. I asked, "Why us?" I talked about always knowing I was meant for something special but didn't want this to be it. My dad came into the kitchen and hugged me and cried with me too. We talked about all the health problems that may come along with

Down syndrome. I wondered if I'd ever go back to work. How would we pay our brand new mortgage? How would we pay for these medical and educational bills? How could we watch our child live his life as a disabled child? This couldn't be happening to us.

My parents were wonderfully supportive. They offered to help with some of the medical bills. They offered to start doing research on Down syndrome for me. They said they'd be there for us no matter what. I went home feeling lucky to have such great parents.

Later that morning, my husband called the genetic counselor for us and spoke with her for awhile. He learned that this was the random kind of Down syndrome and that neither of us have a genetic predisposition towards the condition. He learned that it was not caused by anything we had done, or not done. And he learned about our "options": since we were twenty-two weeks into the pregnancy, we could choose to terminate with a dilation and evacuation (D&E) or through induced labor. Thus began the most awful struggle of our lives.

Mired in grief, the options were tempting—we could make this all go away by agreeing to terminate. We could try to get pregnant again in six months and have another chance at having a baby. Here was the way out.

The next morning we met with the genetic counselor for three hours. She listened to us cry and even shed some tears herself. She presented a lot of information in a very professional way, but was also very empathetic and understanding of all that we were feeling. Just to be safe, we decided to make an appointment for the following Tuesday to start the D&E procedure. She explained that I would come in on Tuesday to have laminaria sticks inserted into my cervix to start the dilation process. I would come back on Wednesday for another insertion of the sticks. By Thursday morning my cervix would be dilated enough for the procedure to take place. The baby and I would be put out and the doctor would use a suctioning machine to remove my pregnancy. I would wake up and the baby would be gone.

"Could we have a chance to hold the baby?" I asked. "Or could we have his remains cremated?"

"I'm sorry," she said. "There will be no remains intact."

We went home with two books in hand. One book was all about babies with Down syndrome and how to care for them. The other book was written by couples who had made the choice to terminate their pregnancies after receiving poor prenatal diagnoses. We put the Down syndrome baby book aside and started reading the other book. For the next three days, I sat in my house crying and reading and writing in my journal. My husband and I talked for hours on end and cried together and separately. We raged at the injustice of our situation. We mourned the loss of our healthy baby boy who we had never even met. We mourned the loss of our happiness, of our innocence. We struggled to justify this decision to terminate our much-wanted pregnancy.

I found myself wishing that his heart would just stop on its own. I felt as if we had been given a Godlike decision to make, but we weren't God. We did not know how severe the baby's condition would be. We did not know what was best for him, for us, for our marriage. It wasn't fair that we were in this position. I prayed for God to be merciful and to take this baby as his angel and to let us off the hook.

Knowing this was not likely to happen, we decided that termination was the best option. I wrote letters to our baby boy explaining why his dad and I had made the choice to send him to heaven: We didn't want him to be subjected to constant surgeries and medical procedures. We wanted a chance to have other children. We didn't want to saddle these younger siblings with the responsibility to care for their disabled brother if something should ever happen to us. We knew he'd be happier in heaven. We loved him dearly and that's why we made this painful decision to spare him a life on earth filled with prejudice, injustice, and pain.

I felt strong in our decision during the day. I was able to feel like I was being a good mother. A good mother sacrifices for her child, right? Because she loves him, right? Here I was sacrificing my need to be a mother for the sake of my son. Here I was ending a pregnancy I wanted so badly, giving up baby showers, nursery dreams, maternity clothes, maternity leave, the attention of pregnancy all so my boy would not suffer.

At night, it was a different story. I dreamt of people I loved dying. I dreamt that I pulled the baby's chromosomes out and fixed them. I would wake up crying and thinking I just couldn't do this to our baby, but I would push those thoughts away quickly.

I packed every single pregnancy related item I had, from his Giants outfit down to the stretch mark cream I'd been using, into a big box and put it into the garage. I wore only sweats and big shirts. I couldn't look at my pregnant body. The baby's kicks, once bringing me such joy, now were tortuous to feel. I slept on my back and stopped taking prenatal vitamins. I lost my appetite and didn't exercise. I even ate a bite of Caesar salad, raw egg and all. I was distancing myself from this pregnancy with a vengeance.

After sitting in the house for four days, my husband decided we needed a change of scenery. We checked into a nice hotel about thirty miles away and continued crying and discussing. We knew there was no right answer to this dilemma. Whatever we did would be the right thing, as long as we were in agreement and it came from our hearts. Somehow, this knowledge did not help a bit.

It was Monday morning and I was scheduled to begin the termination procedure in twenty-four hours. I still wasn't feeling calm or peaceful or even remotely sure of our decision to terminate. We checked out of the hotel and went to see a family therapist. She sat us down on her couch and we cried and talked to her for an hour. She said it was okay to be scared of this commitment to this child. She gave me a mantra to repeat that went like this: "I do my best for who I am today." She made me realize that I was different now, and that my old self had these standards that this new self was not living up to. That's why I felt so guilty, she said. We left her office knowing we would call to confirm my appointment for the procedure the next day.

When we returned home, I called the genetic counselor to say we had decided to terminate. "I know that must have been a difficult decision," she said. She then went on to say that the policy for this procedure had changed. "I'm sorry, but we can't start dilating your cervix until Wednesday."

"No!" I screamed. I could not wait another thirty-six hours to start this process. Every minute already felt like hours. "Please, isn't there any way I could start tomorrow?"

"I'm sorry, but this is how we do the procedure now," she said. I would start the dilation on Wednesday, continue it into Thursday, and then have the evacuation sometime on Friday.

My husband left to go into the office for a few hours. I sat on the couch crying. I planned a little memorial service in my mind where we could plant a tree for our baby in our yard and maybe read the letters we'd written him. I knew he'd understand and forgive us. I repeated my mantra, "I do my best for who I am today" over and over in my head while I began to do some laundry. I knew I would be bed bound for a few days following the procedure, so I wanted to get a head start on some chores.

Two hours later, as I was putting the clean clothes away, I started crying again. But then the crying turned into sobbing, which then turned into wailing. Before I knew it, I was in the throes of the rawest emotions I have ever felt in my life. I screamed and cried, unable to catch my breath, "I can't kill my baby! I can't kill my baby!" I threw things. I fell on the floor. I lashed out at anything that was nearby. The screams and cries kept coming from inside me and I had no control over them. I felt as if I was truly going insane. I began kicking at the walls of my bedroom and finally kicked a huge hole in my beautiful bedroom wall.

That was my breaking point. I ran for the phone and called my husband's cell number. "I can't kill our baby. I'm so sorry, but I can't kill our baby. I can't do it! I can't kill him!" I repeated, in between cries of anguish.

He told me to calm down and to try to breathe. "It's okay, we don't have to hurt our baby," he said. "I just came to the same decision myself and was about to call you and tell you. I can't do it either."

I immediately fell on to our bed and thanked him. He stayed on the phone with me until he was convinced that I was over the worst of my fit. I hung up and immediately fell fast asleep. That night, we both had the best sleep we'd had in a week. We felt tremendous relief.

I called our genetic counselor that morning and told her our newest decision. She said she wanted to make an appointment for us to see a pediatric cardiologist and to have a fetal ECG done on the baby's heart. We knew that almost half of babies with Down syndrome are born with congenital heart defects that often require surgery. If the ECG showed a horrible defect, maybe we would change our minds and continue with the procedure the next morning. She said she'd keep the appointment for the D&E just in case we decided to do it after learning about the heart.

We went to the hospital once again and waited for the ultrasound tech to perform the ECG. When she did, we were able to see our baby again. He looked so cute. We even saw him yawning and moving his arms and legs. We watched his heart pump blood in and out and were amazed at all that was going on inside of me.

When the cardiologist came in, he looked serious. "This baby does have a heart defect. I'm so sorry," he said. He went on to explain that the baby has a hole in between the four chambers of his heart. It was called an AV canal defect, and it was fairly common in babies with Down syndrome. The baby would require surgery at about six months of age, and would need to be hospitalized for about seven days. But the surgery was considered routine at this hospital and had a very high survival rate.

I went home feeling even more conflicted. I didn't want our baby to have heart surgery. I didn't want to see him in the hospital at only six months old. I didn't want his little body being operated on. With this new information, I was beginning to think that I should begin the process of termination the next morning. My husband took me home and left me alone, saying that he didn't want to influence my decision. He said I should sit and think and he'd call in a few hours to see how I was doing.

I sat by myself for a few hours. I realized that while heart surgery is far from what anyone wants for their child, this surgery sounded fairly common. I knew that he'd be in the best hands. I knew he'd probably only need one surgery and that would be it. I knew in my heart that this heart defect was not enough to justify termination, but I was still so scared. If we didn't go through with the termination, we would never have the chance again. We had lived through seven agonizing days of indecision, pain, discussion, tears, and anger. I still had fourteen hours to truly decide.

My husband called. I told him how I was feeling. I told him how I wished his heart looked worse because, while I didn't want to be the one saying to end our baby's life, I was so scared of having him. He told me, "I don't think it's enough to justify termination. I think we need to have him." I cried at his words, but I was crying out of relief as well as fear. I knew in my heart that I agreed. I did need to have him.

It was seven days after we had received the news of his diagnosis. We had made our final decision.

I called our genetic counselor, and told her the latest update and how we felt about it. She complimented us on coming to a decision. She praised us for being so honest and thorough in our deliberations and then she offered to start setting up a network of support that we would need after the birth. "I'll call you when I'm at that point," I told her. "Right now we just need to adjust to what this means." She said she understood and that she'd wait for my call.

It is now four days later. I spent the first two days feeling happy and relieved that we did not terminate our baby's life. I bought him another little outfit and told a few friends, my staff, and my kindergarten class that our baby has Down syndrome. I read the book about babies with Down syndrome and started accepting how our lives have changed.

But I do not feel this strong all of the time. In fact, I wonder if I had gone through with the termination, if I would feel relieved today. Knowing myself, I am guessing that the grief and guilt of ending his life would be eating me up right now. The words "no remains intact" would haunt me. I would wonder where his remains were. I would visualize what the procedure did to our baby. I would wonder what he looked like. Did he have his dad's thick hair? Did he have my nose? I would be tormented with feelings of guilt.

I have sixteen weeks left in my pregnancy. I am now taking one day at a time. I cry a lot when I think of what our future may be like, but I also look forward to meeting our son. I want to hold and hug him. I want to smell his baby smell. I know that I love my baby. I also know how sad I am that he has a heart issue and how scared I am for us to shoulder the commitment of caring for this child forever. I am plagued with feelings of love, sadness, fear, and anger, all at the same time.

I think back to all my hopes for my baby's future. What kind of life will he have? I am afraid to hope that he is only mildly retarded. I'm afraid to hope that he won't need many surgeries, that his vision and hearing will be ok, that he'll be able to develop the muscles necessary to walk. I'm afraid to hope that he'll be accepted by his peers, learn to read, develop some hobbies. If I let myself hope, then I set myself up to be let down again. But if I don't hope for the best, haven't I given up on our child after all?

Live long. Laugh often. Love much. I owe him this hope.

Postscript:

Riley is now one year old. We were so scared of what life with Riley would be like, and now the scariest thing I can imagine is what my life would be like without him.

Looking back at the time following the amnio, I realize I didn't know my baby. All I knew was this diagnosis. I knew what the doctors said my son and my life with him would be. I knew about all the elevated risks for disease and complications. I knew about my preconceived notions of what the words "mentally retarded" meant. I knew that I was scared and very sad. What I didn't know was my son.

I understand where my head was when I wrote what I wrote. A piece of me feels so ashamed to have had those feelings. I look at my gorgeous son today and feel so sad that I once considered not letting him show me who he was. That pains me to the core. I wish I had been stronger when I received the amnio results. I wish I could have refused the "procedure" right from the get-go. I wish I had never even considered it. But I cannot change how I reacted. I need to embrace that process as being part of my journey in this life. I learned so much about myself going through those days of torment. It also intensified how I feel about my son. Going through that pain and heartache and agony has brought me closer to him.

Looking back, I also realize that my decisions weren't really being made with Riley in mind. I was primarily thinking about myself. I couldn't imagine how it would feel to see my own son teased. To see him in the hospital. To see him possibly not be able to achieve his dreams. I realize I was trying to protect myself from the pain I envisioned.

Little did I know how much life, laughter, and love this child would bring to me and to the world.

Andi is an elementary school teacher. She lives in California with her husband, Todd, and their two children. Her oldest son, Riley, was born in 2002. The weeks following the diagnosis were very trying in many ways for the whole family, but the day that Riley was born was one filled with happiness and joy as they finally got to meet their son face to face. Two years later, Riley became a big brother to a very spunky and spirited sister named Emily. The two are good friends and they keep their parents on their toes at all times.

63

First Words

By Jennifer Graf Groneberg

Jennifer Graf Groneberg, Avery and Bennett Groneberg

ON THE FIFTH DAY of our son Avery's life, I learned the two words of his story that separated him from his twin brother, Bennett, from his older brother, Carter, from his father, Tom, and from me.

Our pediatrician was in the NICU in the afternoon. I remember thinking how odd it was, seeing her then. She always made her rounds in the mornings, the opposite of most other doctors. "She does things in her own way," one of the nurses explained to me. And here she was, watching me hold the babies. It finally dawned on me: She was waiting to see me. It was a setup.

When I'd returned Avery to his isolette, had tucked Bennett back into his purple and white knit cap and handed him to his nurse to be weighed, she came over. "I have the results of the genetic karyotype," she said. I barely remembered her ordering it. She'd had some concerns about Avery, little things, like a crease in the palm of his left hand, and the placement of his ears in relationship to his eyes. I knew, then, that whatever she had to tell me would not be good.

She sat down next to me, reached out and touched my forearm, then showed me the results of the FISH test. In front of me was a photocopy of pairs of squiggly lines representing chromosomes. One from the father, one from the mother, a map of genetic destiny. At the twenty-first pair of chromosomes, Avery had one extra.

"Down syndrome," she explained.

Down syndrome is the most common genetic condition, happening once in every 730 births. Down syndrome occurs among people of all races and all economic levels and affects more than 350,000 American families. I didn't know these statistics at the time of Avery's diagnosis—all I knew was that the hopes and dreams we had for him were lost, and I didn't know what, if anything, would replace them. One well-meaning nurse told me, "You'll get used to it. You'll get a thick skin." I didn't want thick skin. I wanted my dreams back, I wanted my baby back, the one I had felt twist and kick inside me, the one I had joked would be a soccer player.

When Tom and I spoke about it later, alone in our bedroom, I could see the summer light coming through the blinds so clearly, so sharply. Here was a man I had known and loved for fourteen years, but I didn't know what these words would mean to him, the first two words of Avery's life, words that had redefined him in my eyes, words that might redefine us. Our little family might be ending, imploding, and I thought I might be set adrift, alone. I could hear sounds coming out of my mouth, my voice hoarse and choked and unrecognizable to me even as I watched the dust settle around us, the light shift imperceptibly toward the west. Sundown. I'd never seen a look of such anguish on his face before. His fear, his love, twisted together in sadness. The comforter cover glowed a color from my childhood. Burnt Sienna. Tom reached out to me, and we held each other. We stayed like this for a long time, holding on to each other in the fading summer light. It's funny the things you remember. I was wondering if Avery would ever be able to color; if he would ever be able to even say the word "crayon."

All the possible children a woman will bear are present inside her even before she is born. They are created while she is still just a tiny form twisting and floating in utero. For a short while, three generations—mother, daughter, and child—live as one, each a link, one to another, in the long, twisted chain of my son's DNA. If you stretch it end to end, it would reach to the moon and back. A son I had wished for, yearned for, prayed for, and yet when he arrived, I was wholly unprepared.

When I think of that time now, I think of hands. Hands working for us, some belonging to people I'd known for years, like my parents, or Tom's, or my friends Phyllis and Sarah, Emily, Carrie. Others were strangers to me—nurses whose names I could barely keep straight, social workers, doctors, neighbors I knew just by sight. Hands folded in prayer, hands lifting baby clothes fresh out of the dryer and folding them into boxes for us, hands dialing phone numbers as our news spread, as others called and offered help. A woman whose name I will never know helped me find my car when I was sobbing so hard I couldn't see straight; another offered the phone number of her sister, who had a child with Down syndrome. Hands holding mine, hands helping me up when I could not help myself. One to another, slowly. Wherever I went, it seemed I was never alone. I felt cradled, loved; led by so many that it became one, one love, one light, leading me home.

When Avery was first diagnosed, we were told many things, mostly about how hard our life would be, how difficult. There might be heart defects, or thyroid problems; growth issues and developmental delays. He was presented to us as a set of complications. What they left out was Avery. No one told me how beautiful he would be. No one told me how sensitive he would be. No one told me he would hug me with his whole body, wrapping arms and impossibly nimble legs around me at once, such a strong embrace. No one factored in love.

Avery is three. He has a shy smile and a gentle personality. Hair the color of wheat, eyes blue like a river, like his brothers', like mine. He will eat pears with gleeful abandon, but when I hold up a green bean, he turns his head away in disdain. He plays the piano, making up his songs with heartfelt seriousness. At our house, people take their shoes off and leave them in a line by the door. When no one is looking, he puts things into the empty shoes, like parting gifts—a toy car, a tiny horse, a pilfered spoon. Despite the stubbed toes, the lost cutlery, the startled guests, it's hard for me to be mad at him. He is the child that I wanted, that I did not know I wanted. He is my son.

Last night I was tucking the little boys in bed, Bennett in the bottom bunk, Avery in a twin mattress on the floor next to him. Sometimes Bennett climbs down and joins Avery and I find them curled into each other, a tangle of arms and legs in a nest of blankets.

I made sure Avery had his little puppy, Bennett his stuffed monkey. I gave each boy his blanket. Each a kiss, then "I love you" to Bennett, "I love you" to Avery. I turned toward the door, making my way by the light of the glowing turtle on the dresser, when I heard a soft voice that I didn't recognize.

"ahluvyou."

I swung around and there was Avery, smiling at me.

Until now, there had been no actual words, no "mama" or "dada." I had come to think of him as my quiet boy, though I would sometimes catch him saying his sounds in the stillness of the early morning, his blanket over his head so no one could see. He was saving them up until he was ready, saving them up for me.

Before the tiniest of smiles, before the blink of an eyelash, before the first sweet breath, there was a heartbeat, echoing a twin heart, one to another, together, in the watery bed my body created beneath my ribcage, just below my heart. We started as three points of a triangle, close as could be, and though we have widened, we are a triangle still, connected no longer by blood and muscle and tissue but by one simple word: Love.

My hurt has softened into a small, quiet wish—for the world to see Avery without the almond-shaped eyes, the looseness of joints, the wide grin—to see him instead as he is inside, a pure spirit, a brave soul. It is my wish for Avery, and it is my wish for us all. Words have the power to separate us from each other. Words like disabled. Handicapped. Retarded. There are other choices we could use: Acceptance. Encouragement. Love. The power is ours. We can build our lives with words that devastate, or words that heal, giving hope and support as real as the hands that lifted me up. The choice is ours.

Choose love.

Jennifer lives and writes at the end of a twisty gravel road in northwest Montana with her husband of fifteen years and their three young children. Currently, she is working on a book called Roadmap to Holland (New American Library, 2008), about mothering Avery, a fraternal twin born with Down syndrome. You can read more about Jennifer and her family at www.jennifergrafgroneberg.com.

For More Information

The *Gifts* website at giftsds.segullah.org offers the following resources:

- More information about Martha Sears and her son Stephen

- Information about the *Gifts* Outreach program

- Links to dozens of sites pertaining to Down syndrome, including international, national, state, and local organizations and support groups

- Submission guidelines for the companion volume to *Gifts*, which will include stories about individuals with Down syndrome written by family members, friends, and professionals

About the Editor

Kathryn Lynard Soper is a mother of seven children. She is president of Segullah Group, a nonprofit producer of personal writings, and editor of Segullah, *a literary journal by and for LDS (Mormon) women. She is currently writing a memoir about her first year with Thomas. She lives with her husband, Reed, and their children in the mountain west. You can learn more about Kathryn at www.kathrynlynardsoper.com.*